JOHN MILLS AND
BRITISH

For James, who made it possible.

JOHN MILLS AND BRITISH CINEMA

Masculinity, Identity and Nation

Gill Plain

EDINBURGH UNIVERSITY PRESS

© Gill Plain, 2006

Edinburgh University Press Ltd
22 George Square, Edinburgh

Typeset in 11/13 pt Monotype Bembo
by Servis Filmsetting Ltd, Manchester, and
printed and bound in Great Britain by
Antony Rowe Ltd, Chippenham, Wilts

A CIP record for this book is available from the British Library

ISBN-10 0 7486 2107 5 (hardback)
ISBN-13 978 0 7486 2107 1
ISBN-10 0 7486 2108 3 (paperback)
ISBN-13 978 0 7486 2108 8

Contents

Acknowledgements

The completion of this book was greatly assisted by the AHRB research leave scheme. The time provided by a semester's leave was invaluable for the writing process, but it also had the effect of enabling me to develop the project beyond its original conception. The book took a little longer to finish than was anticipated, but I believe it is the better for this. I am also indebted to the Carnegie Trust for the Universities of Scotland for their generous contribution toward the cost of travel between St Andrews and London.

Jeffrey Richards, who has done so much to further debate on British cinema and national identity, has supported this project from its earliest days. I owe him an enormous debt of gratitude for his ongoing belief in it, and hope that he enjoys the end product as much as I have benefited from reading his work. I would also like to thank Philippa Brewster for her encouragement.

The British Film Institute has been a wonderful resource and a very happy place to visit. I am enormously indebted to the librarians and technicians who patiently helped and guided me (and indeed showed great fortitude in the face of my extremely inexpert handling of their film stock). From the stills department to the information service, I found friendly and knowledgeable people who made the research process that little bit easier. I'm also grateful to John Herron at Canal+ and Jill Little at London Features International for making it possible for me to use such a wide range of images. Illustrating books is an expensive process, and without the research funds made available by the University of St Andrews, it would not have been possible to include so many stills. I am very grateful for this support. There is a significant logistical problem with studying British cinema: getting hold of the films! My thanks, then, to Martin Hunt and the many other people who helped me view hard to access material.

Early drafts of Chapters 2, 3 and 4 were aired at conferences in Leeds, Birmingham and Stockholm, and at seminars in Manchester and St Andrews, and I much appreciate the helpful suggestions and advice I received. I'm also greatly indebted to the many people who have read some or all of this book. Christine Geraghty, David Martin-Jones, Susan Sellers, Keith Williams and Ben Winsworth provided valuable feedback, while Gordon McMullan not only read a chapter, but fed and housed me during my many visits to the BFI. He is a good cook as well as a good friend. Other people also provided the sustaining combination of moral and practical support. Helen Boden, who looked after me on my trips to Edinburgh, provided valuable thinking space, and a fresh critical eye. Berthold Schoene, who understands the use of the hyphen far better than I ever will, not only believed in this book, but also made sure that it was ready to face the world. His enthusiasm, advice and ideas have been an enormous help to me over the years, and I owe him a very big thank-you.

It has been a pleasure to work with Edinburgh University Press again. Jackie Jones offered advice and support when 'Acting English' was in its infancy, while the wonderfully efficient Sarah Edwards has overseen its final stages. I am very grateful to them for their consideration, and the care they take to produce beautiful books. I would also like to thank my friends at the University of St Andrews. Colleagues whose research interests couldn't be further from mine have nonetheless shown remarkable interest in my labours, making the process of writing a little less lonely and introspective. I am especially indebted to Andrew Murphy, whose unswerving belief that everything would work out just fine was deeply reassuring. I'm also very grateful to Jane Sommerville, Sandra McDevitt, Frances Mullan and Jill Gamble, all of whom have helped to make this book finally come together.

Although I didn't realise it at the time, the seeds of writing about Mills, masculinity and nation were sown between 1989 and 1992. My thanks are due to Ben Winsworth for convincing me that time spent dunking biscuits in tea in front of afternoon movies was an entirely legitimate form of research. Ben, like all my friends and family, has lived with this project for a long time. Writing books is an antisocial activity, and many thanks are due to my mother, Prim Plain, and my partner, James McKinna, for bearing with both a surfeit of British cinema, and the stresses that have accompanied it.

My biggest debt, however, is to Sir John Mills himself, and I'm sorry that he died before this book could act as a thank-you for the pleasure that his films have given me.

Gill Plain
University of St Andrews, 2005

Illustrations

1

Introduction:
Acting English

[A] good deal of the meaning of the fiction film is borne by its actors and their performances. (John O. Thompson 1978: 55)

Johnnie seems to me – the voice, the accent, the look, the hair – is [sic] quintessentially English. You wouldn't think he was anything else.
(Sir Anthony Havelock-Allen, 'A Very British War Movie', Channel 4, 28 August 1999)

A little of what it means to be British perished yesterday with the death of actor Sir John Mills.

   Many of his best-loved roles highlighted the very best of our nation's character – our steadfastness, our doggedness, our genuine kindness and modesty.

   He kept working right to the end and not just the cinema but our national life is the poorer for his passing. (Leader column, *Sunday Mirror*, 24 April 2005)

When Sir John Mills died on 23 April 2005, the obituary writers had no doubts about his cultural significance. He was the 'archetypal Englishman', 'quintessentially English', 'the most English of actors' and 'the definitive, stoical Everyman for a nation at war'.[1] With an appropriately theatrical sense of occasion, the English Everyman died on St George's Day, and without exception, the media memorialised him as an embodiment of 'national' virtues. The *Daily Telegraph* commented on his 'talent for demonstrating the qualities of English decency', and described him as 'the epitome of the most admirable kind of Englishman – restrained, determined, honourable, good-humoured and capable of suffering on a heroic scale under fire' (25 April 2005). Tim Pulleine in the *Guardian* observed that 'a quality of everyday realism seemed to cling to his best performances, without detracting from his stylistic range' (25 April 2005), while Shane Danielson saw him as the embodiment of a 'particular type of Britishness, a fundamental decency and reserve' which was manifest in his many perform-ances as 'quiet, mild-mannered men who, when pressed, [reveal] unsuspected reserves of stubbornness, courage and indomitability' (*Sunday Herald*, 24 April 2005). To Philip French in the *Observer*, he was simply 'a part of the history of our times and culture as mediated by movies' (24 April 2005).

The association of Mills and the nation was not, however, confined to the realm of screen performance. While Shane Danielson's thoughtful retrospec-tive observed that conveying the quiet qualities of 'Britishness' on the screen was in itself a significant achievement, it was noticeable that for many of the obituaries, Mills the actor was as much a representative of the nation as were the heroes he portrayed on screen. The actor, like his dominant screen persona, was perceived as embodying a set of valuable 'national' characteristics. Mills was a gentleman, a sportsman, a family man and a loyal friend, whose love of home and England kept him away from the 'lure of Hollywood' (*Observer*, 24 April 2005). In life, as in art, he was possessed of the proverbial 'stiff upper lip', and he bore the illnesses of his later years with a stoicism and good humour that would not have disgraced the screen. The tabloid press in particular focused on Mills's commitment to his marriage and his family, constructing his life story through the lens of romance. Ironically for an actor who seldom had the opportunity to play romantic leads on screen, his love for his wife Mary came close to overshadowing the narrative of his career. Nearly all the papers, for example, referred to the couple's renewal of their wedding vows in cele-bration of their diamond anniversary, while Laura Collins in the *Mail on Sunday* began her article with the headline 'John Mills loved his wife so much that every wedding anniversary he put on the suit he wore for his honeymoon' (24 April 2005).[2] Patrick Newley in the *Sunday Express* had similar priorities, working under the headline 'family man, film legend', and the *Scotsman* agreed, claiming that 'Mills gathered up many honours . . . but his greatest joy was his family' (25 April 2005).

Played out in the twin stories of Mills's life and work it is possible to detect a nostalgia for a mode of national identity long since departed. Described by the *Sunday Mirror* as 'the actor who portrayed the British as they would most like to see themselves' (24 April 2005), Mills's representation of the national character embraced a catalogue of virtues now perceived to be lost. Politeness, kindness, family loyalty, friendship, integrity; the hallmarks of a semi-mythical model of Englishness superseded in the postwar years. Evident in the response to his death is a desire to reactivate this lost national self, and to celebrate once again an 'unproblematic' concept of nationhood. The suggestion, proffered by the *Sunday Express*, that Mills's home be bought for the nation, is Churchillian in conception, and conveys a quasi-royal status upon the actor.[3] The metonymic associations are rich. To perceive Mills as royal is to reinstate the popular monarchy of wartime Britain, and to evoke the sentimental force of the people's war. Mills, the actor, achieves in life the ultimate illusion of stardom. He was the people and he was their symbol, and his death provided a brief excuse for the popular press to relive once again the nation's 'finest hour'.[4] The weight of national signification embodied by the actor finds its most redolent expression, however, in the epitaph provided by Lord Attenborough, one of Mills's oldest and closest friends. Commenting on Mills's death, Attenborough observed that he was 'almost unequalled as a world British movie star'. The paradox embodied in this phrase is enormously suggestive. It does not imply a movie star who happened to be British, rather it evokes an actor who actively conveyed Britishness to an international audience. It further suggests that Britishness, in the form of Mills, can survive undiluted in a wider cultural environment, and it imagines the nation as a brand – Britishness – that is recognisable across the world. Specifically, it imagines Mills as being so permeated with emblematic nationhood that it runs through him like the letters in a stick of rock: irrespective of how international his reputation became, he himself did not become international. Rather he continued to be seen as the epitome of a particular mode of 'English' Britishness.

The blurring of the boundary between English and British draws attention to a problem that underlies any attempt to discuss national character and identity. Although Mills both is, and is acting, 'English', he does so as part of a British film industry – a nationwide creative and economic enterprise comprising personnel from throughout the British Isles. Nonetheless, this industry is predominantly based in London and the Home Counties, and the privileged mode of 'national' heroism it promotes is clearly built of characteristics traditionally associated with the English rather than, for example, the Welsh or the Scots. Yet Englishness itself is far from homogeneous, and part of Mills's appeal was his ability to represent a more mutable Englishness of class and regional diversity. This book thus examines the screen construction of a complex and inconsistent Englishness, an Englishness which is at times just that, and at times representative of a wider British or imperial identity. Later in this introduction I will explore the subjective, but nonetheless powerful, terms through which this identity has traditionally been defined, but first it is necessary to map out the parameters of this book's enquiry.

Long before the remarkable outburst of national sentiment that greeted his death, it had become something of a critical commonplace to describe Mills as a national 'Everyman':

In a film career spanning more than fifty years John Mills was to incarnate decent Englishness – restrained, good-humoured, determined, honourable, self-deprecating . . . (Richards 1997: 130–1)

By the end of the war Mills had emerged as the new Everyman, a masculine ideal of stoicism, steadiness and modest hopes for the future.
(Spicer 2001: 27)

But although it is agreed that Mills was somehow Englishness incarnate, the
question remains as to how it was possible for an actor to embody a national
identity. Inextricably linked with the question of nation is the subject of masculinity. Gender and national identity cannot be easily separated. Mills's performance of Englishness is always implicated in a performance of masculinity,
and national identity itself is a gendered construct: historically 'woman' could,
and frequently did, embody the nation, but she cannot be said to have a
national identity comparable to that of a man. In part this dichotomy emerges
from political structures which denied women full citizenship, but it also
emerges from a long established metaphorical association of woman and nation
in such powerful symbols as 'Britannia' and 'Marianne'. Nation as landscape
and territory is gendered female, while national identity and by extension
patriotism, are male.[5] Therefore, to examine the changing constructions of
English masculinity is always also to interrogate historically shifting perceptions
of a wider national persona. But, these conceptions of 'Englishness' do not
exist in a vacuum, and their specificity is dependent upon relationships with a
range of national 'others', in particular America. In Chapter 3, I will discuss
how Mills was defensively deployed as an assertion of English values in the face
of the wartime American invasion, while Chapter 2, by contrast, will depict a
relationship that was closer to emulation.

John Mills and British Cinema, then, is concerned with unpicking and
analysing the relationship between screen representation, the concept of the
nation and the changing prescriptions of masculinity that characterised the
period 1930 to 1970. It is also about the work of the actor within the film text,
and it undertakes its examination of nation and masculinity through an exploration of performance. In the chapters that follow I provide detailed readings of
a wide range of Mills's films in order to consider the diverse and sometimes
contradictory meanings he came to embody. Yet, in contrast to the unchallenged acknowledgement of his 'nationalness', Mills's status as an actor or star
is rather less certain. David Thomson's much revered dictionary of film, for
example, damns him with faint praise: 'The Mills family has so crowded us out
with insipid, tennis-club talent it is easy to forget that Mills is a reasonable actor'
(1975/2003: 599). Geoffrey Macnab, by contrast, draws attention to his
ambivalent relation to stardom. Mills, he suggests, occupies an 'intriguing,

anomalous' position, poised between the 'unassuming behaviour of the character actor and the self-promoting antics of the star' (2000: 101). Implicit in
these uncertainties is the categorisation of Mills as a filmic equivalent of the
literary middlebrow, a middle-class populist representing neither high art nor
the counter-cultural exuberance of the 'authentic' working class. His iconic
status also seems to have worked against the appreciation of his ability: even
the effusive obituaries were more inclined to praise his Englishness than his
acting.[6] It is somehow singularly appropriate that an actor who specialised in
modest and self-deprecating performances should be classified as 'talented
rather than mesmerising' (*Daily Telegraph*, 25 April 2005), and it can plausibly
be suggested that Mills's repeated performance of middle-of-the-road 'ordinariness' in the end comes to define the perception of his acting ability. Much
the same can be argued in relation to his stardom: the archetypal British hero,
built on reserve and understatement, could only have an ambivalent relationship to such a concept. This perhaps accounts for the actor's exclusion from
Bruce Babington's enjoyable collection *British Stars and Stardom* (2001). As I
hope this book will show, Mills was both more than a modest talent and a fascinating subject for star studies, but it is not my intention to establish a hypo-
thetical hierarchy of twentieth-century British acting. Rather *John Mills and
British Cinema* seeks to examine the actor as a crucial dimension of the film
text and explore the remarkable range of meanings Mills's screen persona came
to encode across an exceptionally long film career.

Yet the question might still be asked: why John Mills? Several factors determined my decision, not least of which were the length of his career and the
number of films he made. Mills first appeared on screen in 1932, and can be
found in leading roles from 1935 until the 1960s. During this time he made
nearly eighty films that in total comprise a mini-history of the genres that
dominated British cinema. In the early 1930s he appeared as a version of the
'principal boy' of musical comedy, singing alongside Jessie Matthews and giving
smart-alec support to Will Hay. As the thirties progressed he was developing into
the prototype of the British action hero, before the advent of war caused a break
in his career. Returning to acting in the wartime 'Golden Age' of British cinema,
his roles and performances exemplified the understated naturalistic style generated by the vogue for documentary realism. As films became darker in the 1950s,
so did his acting, becoming tormented or tough, depending on the quality of
the script. As the masculinity validated by the 1940s and demobilised by the
1950s was superseded by new models and concerns in the 1960s, it was to Mills
that British cinema turned for its portrayals of frustration, incompetence and
impotence. To be an Everyman across such a range requires a remarkably accom-
modating screen persona, capable of the flexible representation of cultural norms
that were themselves in the process of undergoing considerable change.

In terms of his selection for this book, it is also significant that, once established as a star, Mills chose to remain in England. Consequently, nearly all,
rather than simply the early part, of his career is contained within the structures of British cinema. Across four decades and at least five genres Mills's name
recurs with awesome regularity, and his seeming omnipresence enables this
book to contribute a fresh perspective to the history of British cinema.
However, as debates emerging from the recent interest in concepts of national
cinemas have shown, it is far from easy to establish what actually constituted a
British film, let alone a definitively national cinema (Richards 1984: 245–56;
Higson 1997: 4–9). This is not a problem confined to Britain. As Mette Hjort
and Scott MacKenzie's thoughtful collection *Cinema and Nation* (2000) suggests, the stability of the nation as an organising category within film studies
has been increasingly destabilised by debates both within and beyond the dis-
cipline. What constitutes a national cinema depends upon which factors of
production, construction and consumption are ultimately prioritised. Should
the primary criteria be economic or aesthetic? Does nationality reside in the
funding of a film, the constitution of its labour force, its target audience or its
thematic concerns? And which comes first, the characteristics or their cinematic representation? Andrew Higson argues that the concept of a national
cinema demands the assumption that a body of films can and does share a
coherent identity and a stable set of meanings. What this means at the level of
representation is that there must be a set of codes that will signify Britishness
not just to one audience, but to many. Agreed national characteristics are
required, but to form an effective shorthand, there must also be a process of
selection and exclusion that will inevitably result in 'the interests and traditions
of a specific social group [being] represented as in the collective national interest' (1997: 7). But 'national' and 'popular' are far from synonymous, and in the
1930s, while critics and cultural commentators argued over what might be
termed appropriately British within a medium still regarded with suspicion by
a large percentage of the cultural elite, the public's preferences provided a
painful illustration of the extent to which the question was becoming redundant. Before the decade began, 'Hollywood' had emerged as a transnational
concept that circumscribed the parameters against which any national cinema
would be judged. As Higson bluntly concludes: 'If Hollywood constitutes the
international standard, then in a sense a distinctive national film production is
by definition non-standard and marginal' (1997: 8).

British cinema in the 1930s, as throughout the century, existed in the
shadow of a Hollywood that had its own very distinctive ideas about what
Englishness or Britishness might look like on screen.[7] But although the category of the national film is an unstable one, by far the majority of Mills's films
of this period can be defined as indigenous: dependent upon British money,

studios, locations, audiences and personnel. Mills's representation of nation thus took place within a recognisably national context that facilitated the expression of the subtle gradations and extensive variations that comprise English masculinity. Although he was not the only actor to be associated with British or English national identity in the mid-century period, he was nonetheless the only performer to have remained synonymous with key aspects of the nation across a period of some forty years. The following sections will consider how this representational status was achieved.

THE ACTOR, STARDOM AND EMBODIMENT

> The basic definition of a star is that of a performer in a particular medium whose figure enters into subsidiary forms of circulation, and then feeds back into future performances. (Ellis 1992: 91)

Although considerable attention has been paid to the concept, construction and ideological function of Hollywood 'stars', the same cannot be said for their British equivalents. In part this is due to the very different structure of the British film industry, which has had no studio system comparable to that of America, and in consequence no coherent policy of star production; a difference which leads Geoffrey Macnab to observe that John Ellis's influential definition of stardom cannot straightforwardly be adapted to the model of British cinema (2000: 99). Macnab is one of a number of critics who have recently attempted to establish an alternative paradigm for star studies, but it remains the case that in the study of British cinema, the dimension of the film text represented by the actor and his or her performance has been generally overlooked. The absence of Hollywood-style 'stars', however, does not imply an absence of immediately recognisable and popular screen actors, and British cinema between the 1930s and the 1960s produced an ample sufficiency of such figures, from Robert Donat to Anna Neagle to Dirk Bogarde. Yet Ellis's emphasis on the relationship between the performer and 'subsidiary forms of circulation' remains resonant and indeed seems singularly appropriate for understanding how Mills came to be such a peculiarly national actor.[8] As Jeffrey Richards observes of British cinema in the 1930s: '[S]tars had to fulfil a need and to represent an ideal. They had to accomplish the difficult task of being both ordinary for the purposes of identification and extraordinary for the purposes of admiration' (1984: 156).[9] In Mills's case, however, we might see stardom as residing in the projection of an extraordinary ordinariness. When he rose to prominence, national cinema production was emphasising the heroic virtues of the group, rather than the individual, and it was Mills's ability to be a distinctive part of that group that facilitated his success. He achieved a particularly British mode of stardom when the nation as a mass was being encouraged to admire itself, and when cinema was seeking recognisable representatives of the everyday and the familiar. And, having achieved this status, by 1945 Mills was effectively typecast as the modern English hero: white, male, middle-class and largely asexual.[10]

But while the type 'performed' by Mills can be recognised and defined, it is harder to analyse the construction of that persona in terms of acting and embodiment. Lovell and Krämer warn that:

> Both in theatre and cinema, acting is an elusive art. A performance is made out of a large number of actions, gestures, facial and vocal expressions. It's made all the more elusive when the dominant acting convention is a naturalistic one . . . Many analyses of film acting are in fact discussions of a fictional character (whose creation is the work of a writer) rather than analyses of how that character is embodied (the work of an actor). (Lovell and Krämer 1999: 5)

Although both character and performance will be of relevance to my analysis, distinguishing between the two remains a difficult and ultimately imprecise art.[11] Furthermore, the screen performance is also mediated by technology and the contributions of the entire film unit. What are the roles of director, designer, editor, camera, lighting, co-stars, costume and make-up? Film is a collaborative medium, and the historical reconstruction of the production process represents a challenge that this book does not attempt to confront. Yet a full consideration of the actor's performance can supplement other readings of the industry and its processes, contributing incrementally to our understanding of the film product. And to this end, this book is most concerned with the diverse significations that circulate around the body of the performer.

Is it possible to determine the boundary between actor, persona and performance? Does the film text depend upon performance or on the direct presentation of a fundamental corporeality? Barry King, writing in *Screen*, argues that:

> The actor is a re-presenter of signs in that he or she activates or deactivates via impersonation those aspects of the general cultural markers that he or she bears as a private individual for character portrayal . . . the actor as a member of the host culture – with a given hair colour, body shape, repertoire of gestures, registers of speech, accent, dialect and so on – always pre-signifies meaning. (King 1985: 37)

King concludes succinctly, but perhaps too glibly, that 'only actors that look the part get the part' (1985: 37). While in some respects King's throwaway remark is self-evident, reminding us of the social and cultural limits circumscribing representation, the statement can equally well be inverted: 'Only actors who get the part, look the part.' The example provided by *Hobson's Choice* (1954) gives an indication of the actor's formative role in the construction of character. Mills was called in at the last moment to replace the ailing, and physically very different, Robert Donat, who had been director David Lean's first choice for the part of Willie Mossop. Mills's acclaimed performance draws attention to the complexities of analysing film production and reception in that, while it necessitated a radical alteration of the director's vision (Mills did not 'look the part'), the actor was accepted by audiences and critics as exemplary. The relationship between actor and role is symbiotic – once embodied, it is extremely difficult to imagine another actor filling the part.[12] James Naremore argues that the actor 'is already a character in some sense, a "subject" formed by various codes in the culture, whose stature, accent, physical abilities, and performing habits imply a range of meanings and influence the way she or he will be cast' (1990: 158). The actor's value lies in the extent to which he or she can be imagined as the character, and in this context the corporeality of the performer is integral to the construction of the role. But an actor is not only a combination of physical characteristics that are read in certain culturally conditioned ways; he or she is also a cumulative cultural product made up of the sum of previous performances. Representations depend upon representations, and all film actors carry with them a perfectly preserved celluloid past which can be exploited in the present – as Graham McCann illustrates in his biography of Cary Grant:

> Alfred Hitchcock, the director of *Suspicion*, had wanted Grant for the role precisely because of . . . audience expectations. He knew that audiences on seeing Johnnie Aysgarth would know he was Cary Grant, so that however bleak the situation might become, they would not believe that a character played by Grant could really turn out to be a murderer. Hitchcock, therefore, planned to execute an audacious double-bluff, revealing Grant's character to *be* as bad, as cold, as evil as he had seemed to be, thereby administering a shock far beyond anything that the plot itself could have been expected to deliver. (McCann 1997: 140)

By as early as 1941 Mills was capable of arousing similar audience expectations but, as with Cary Grant, the potential for subversive casting was seldom exploited by directors.[13] Yet as Chapters 5 and 6 will reveal, the repetition of norms through typecasting is inevitably an unstable process. Mills's performance of archetypal English masculinity could not and did not mean the same to audiences in 1960 as it had done in 1955, 1950, 1945 or 1940. In the gaps and inconsistencies opened up by Mills's repeated representation of the masculine role, it is possible to trace the action of conflicting ideological imperatives, and ultimately to discover resistance to norms once imaged as definitive and unchanging. Ultimately, as the final chapters of the book seek to demonstrate, Mills's performances disrupted, displaced and deconstructed the very norms that the actor was assumed to embody. This of course raises the question, what was 'written' on the body of Mills, and how could one body come to have such an intimate relationship to the national ideal?

MASCULINITY AND NATION

> If masculinity has had a role in imagining the nation, then so too has the nation played its part in constituting preferred forms of masculinity. (Dawson 1994: 1)

Any analysis of film performance must pay attention not only to the skills of acting (body language, gesture, facial expression, tone of voice), but also to the pre-existing, more-or-less mutable corporeality of the actor (height, bulk, colouring, facial features and the characteristic gestures of 'self-performance'). And in these terms it is clear that over the first thirty years of Mills's career, his body undergoes remarkably little change. He never noticeably gains weight or loses hair, and the youthful nature of his face is attested to by his performance in David Lean's *Great Expectations* (1946). At the age of 37, Mills plausibly portrays the exuberant 21-year-old Pip. It is, then, possible to argue that from at least 1935 to 1960, directors and producers in casting Mills were choosing a singularly stable model of masculinity that conveyed, in its preternatural youthfulness, such qualities as innocence, honesty, sincerity and trustworthiness. He was, suggested Peter Noble, very much the boy next door:

> John Mills, perhaps more than any other actor in British films, is able to portray the average young man-in-the-street on the screen. He has a real, sympathetic quality, an authenticity which makes him down-to-earth, ordinary and likeable. When one critic said of his performance that he was 'everybody's son, everybody's young man,' he pointed to a truth which is a further indication of why Mills is among the most popular of English actors. He is as British as actors like Spencer Tracy and James Cagney are American, his acting is natural and unforced, his attractive personality possesses the appeal of seeming to combine all that is best in our national character. (Noble 1947)

This profile comes from 1947, the height of Mills's popularity. He was the top male box office 'star' in Britain, but the terms used by Noble work hard to avoid any association with stardom. Mills is average, ordinary, down-to-earth, and his ability to be national is rooted in a concept of the 'natural', suggesting that Englishness is inherent and abiding rather than something that needs, or finds, explicit expression.[14]

Chapter 2 will consider the question of Mills's national embodiment in far greater detail, exploring his corporeality through an examination of the surprisingly frequent comparisons that were drawn between the young English actor and the American icon, James Cagney. Yet what this comparison ultimately reveals, and what emerges from early photographs of Mills, is not the presence but the absence of distinguishing features. In the 1930s, Mills's face was still, bland and inexpressive. His large eyes, long lashes and smooth cheeks gave him an androgynous, even feminine appearance – not untypical of English screen actors of the period – while his bustling, energetic body spoke of youth and boyhood rather than adult masculinity. The defining blandness of his features, however, can itself be read as national, part of a tradition that reads Englishness as an *absence* of tangible characteristics. John Barrell, in an essay on the Englishness of English art, cites William Hazlitt's contention that if excellence in painting lies in the representation of characteristic expression, then:

> English painting was . . . bound to be deficient, because the national character was too phlegmatic to allow the passions that freedom of expression which they exhibited in the mobile features of the excitable Italians. The English might not be deficient in depth of character, but were certainly so in the surface, the outward visible marks of character . . . (Barrell 1990: 155)

Englishness, then, only comes into focus in comparison with other more clearly defined national bodies. Or, rather, Englishness presents itself as a neutral 'norm' against which other nations appear excessive and irregulated. Either way, to create an English Everyman the first precondition must be an 'underwritten' body and face, a corporeality that will permit the performance of understatement.

The identification of Englishness as an absence of 'the outward visible marks of character' undoubtedly renders it a difficult national identity to 'perform' – indeed, its nature was such that performance would render it invalid. Yet the concept is crucial to understanding Englishness. Krishan Kumar, for example, wittily describes English nationalism as 'the dog that did not bark', a signifying absence within the 'currents of nationalism flowing through Europe' in the nineteenth century (2003: 175, 176). In part, argues Kumar, the absence of a distinct English national identity within the wider entity of Britain is a direct product of empire, as manifest both at home and overseas:

> The English too were conscious that Britain and the empire were their creations. But rather than assertive, this made them cautious about

> insisting on their national identity. When you are in charge, or think you
> are in charge, you do not go about beating the drum. But then that leaves
> a certain difficulty about expressing your own national identity. (Kumar
> 2003: 179)

Ironically, the authority inherent in Englishness renders its expression
diffident and evasive, and in this paradox we can see the roots of the many
other paradoxes that structure 'common sense' assumptions regarding the
national character.[15] The English are trustworthy, decent, dutiful, respectable,
restrained, private, modest, self-effacing, self-contained, self-sufficient, cold,
brisk, fair, inarticulate and humorous. Alternatively they are enthusiastic,
eccentric, lovers of home, countryside and animals, individuals, amateurs
and conformists. They are tolerant, xenophobic, pragmatic and sentimental.
The contradictions are evident, but their comfortable co-existence is seldom
challenged, not least because self-analysis is considered a singularly un-English
trait:

> When an Englishman begins to think about the character of England, he
> cannot but feel, with some alarm, that he is falling into a trick of self-
> consciousness and indulging in introspection . . . but perhaps there is also
> a point in self-portraiture. Self-portraiture means self-consciousness;
> but there are, after all, two kinds of self-consciousness. There is the self-
> consciousness of egoism, preening itself before the mirror: there is also
> the self-consciousness of what might be called stock-taking, anxious to
> cast up a balance between assets and liabilities, and to put the account for
> the future on a better and sounder basis. (Barker 1976: 550)

Barker's quotation and the imagery it employs draws attention to another
crucial dimension of English identity: class. The prudent financial planning of
Barker's Englishman speaks of his resoundingly middle-class origins. This is the
class that saw itself as central to the nation. It was responsible, dutiful and sen-
sible, and it was more than happy to be regarded as the norm to which others
should aspire:

> Moderate in all things, avoiding a 'scene', trimming extremes, sidling
> carefully between its own passions, the nation came to be seen, and to
> see itself, as a temperate people well in control. No newspaper was more
> virulent in its jingoism than the *Daily Mail*, yet that newspaper also saw
> itself as modern enough to speak on behalf of all the moderate, good-to-
> middlin' folks with their ideal homes, their kodak cameras, their sweet
> peas and village signs . . . Middle-class Englishness did not confine itself
> to one aspect of Englishness. It laid claim to the national average, which
> is to say, it laid claim to the whole. (Colls 2002: 80–1)[16]

In the textbook Englishness of the twentieth century, the dominant mode of national being was middle-class and male. It was not until the Second World War that the alternative voices of class, region and gender were included within the spectrum of nationhood, and it was not until the 1960s that the authoritative accent of received pronunciation lost its hegemonic position. But the fact that these changes did take place indicates the flexibility that would be required of any actor aspiring to Everyman status. In terms of both class and character, then, the construct of the English Everyman is close to impossible, demanding that one persona somehow embody the contradictions of a nation of home-loving imperialists, uniformed eccentrics, restrained enthusiasts and tolerant xenophobes. In a country as class-conscious as Britain, that same persona must also be able to move through the subtle gradations dividing the working classes from the lower-, middle-, and upper-middle classes. John Mills gets closer than any other actor of his generation to achieving this mutability, and there are a number of reasons that account for his improbable success.

Mills's screen contemporaries included Robert Donat, Leslie Howard, Michael Redgrave, Stewart Granger, James Mason, Kenneth More, Jack Hawkins, Alec Guinness, Jack Warner, Trevor Howard and Dirk Bogarde. Why, amongst these variously taller, stronger, craggier, more gentlemanly, more Byronic, more sensual and more commanding male figures was it Mills who took on the burden of national representation? As I suggested earlier, he made an awful lot of films, he nearly always played leading men, and he did not leave Britain for Hollywood, but – perhaps most importantly for his Everyman status – he played across the class barrier. To take just two years from his career as an example, between 1940 and 1942 he moved from playing a working-class Tommy in *Old Bill and Son* (1940), to a smooth, almost arrogant, middle-class airman in *Cottage to Let* (1941), to a pillar of the establishment in *The Young Mr Pitt* (1942) – he played Wilberforce to Robert Donat's Pitt – and back to the working classes for a breakthrough role as Shorty Blake in Noël Coward's *In Which We Serve* (1942). Only the aristocracy is missing, and this omission highlights the anomalous position of aristocratic masculinities as much as the limits of Mills's versatility.[17] Mills's mutability, then, was an unusual attainment for the period, and was probably facilitated by his small stature. The combination of physical slightness, an eminently trustworthy face and an understated naturalistic performance style made him an ideal choice for rendering potentially threatening figures safe. His working classes are loyal, not dangerous: no one could mistake Shorty Blake's humour for insubordination. His figures of authority, on the other hand, are low-key and democratic, almost to the point of vulnerability. And this element of vulnerability is important. The masculinity represented by Mills is not that of class and racial superiority, rather it is that of the underdog, and as such it provides a somewhat feminised ideal for audience identification. Obviously in the 1940s it also resonated with propagandist depictions of Britain that conveniently overlooked the Empire in favour of the plucky little island standing alone against the great dictators; but even when the moment of historical crisis passed, Mills's heroes continued to encode a resistance to dominant masculine norms. Everyman cannot be Superman, and in some respects it is precisely Mills's failure to conform to the phallic masculine ideal that enables his Everyman status.

I suggested earlier that the dominant masculinity of mid-twentieth century Britain was a white middle-class Englishness paradoxically rendered self-effacing by the unchallenged scale of its authority. In discussing Mills's class mutability, however, I have also indicated his ability to represent a range of sub-ordinate masculinities that are nonetheless, equally English. Masculinity, like national identity, must thus be seen as plural and unstable. R. W. Connell offers a succinct definition:

> [M]asculinities are configurations of practice structured by gender rela-
> tions. They are inherently historical; and their making and remaking is a
> political process affecting the balance of interests in society and the direc-
> tion of social change. (Connell 1995: 44)

The observation and analysis of this political process has, however, been obscured by masculinity's status as the unexamined norm. Historically, woman has been the subject of study, with men and masculinity understood as a neutral standpoint from which to examine the 'other' of femininity. Given the evasive-ness of masculinity in general, then, what further difficulties will surround the subject of an English masculinity characterised by a horror of introspection?

The particular character of dominant early twentieth-century English mas-culinities has its roots in the Victorian era and the public school system. The nineteenth century, argues Jeffrey Richards, was dominated by 'the fusion of two powerful creeds': evangelical Protestantism and chivalry (1997: 11–12). The result was a society shaped by the thoroughly compatible ideologies of proactive, reforming 'muscular' Christianity, and the dutiful, modest virtues of the gentleman. Yet the selfless missionary qualities promoted by Victorian culture were underpinned by what Connell describes as the 'bureaucratic insti-tutionalisation of violence' (1995: 193) that gathered pace over the course of the nineteenth century. In the era of industrialisation and empire, the devel-opment of standing armies was accompanied by the growth of schools designed to inculcate evangelical values and confirm the superiority of the Englishman. From public schools to Sunday schools the same masculine code was spread with missionary zeal across the middle and into the 'respectable' working classes, and what was promoted in schools and societies was practised in the arena of sport. Robert Colls observes that, throughout the nineteenth century, 'sport had been associated with manliness', but it was the development of mass state schooling that facilitated the growth and popularity of group sporting activities. By the end of the century, those sports perceived to be 'national' were team games inculcating an ethos of 'responsible manhood':

> Especially, there was cricket. No mere game, this was the identity of England in flannels. Declared the national game by the rather 'upper' *Badminton Magazine* in 1888, revised as such in 1893, and fully authorized in 1920, cricket was 'national' because all the classes played it, though rarely in the same team. Cricket was the first sport to have national rules, and its new institutions were thought important to English manliness . . . cricket was one of those coded gestures which made men Englishmen. (Colls 2002: 122)

Cricket in particular and sport in general were thus the means through which the English communicated with each other across the barriers of class, region and education. Within their own classes, however, they relied upon the conversational style that Anthony Easthope terms banter:

> Outwardly banter is aggressive, a form in which the masculine ego asserts itself. Inwardly, however, banter depends upon a close, intimate and personal understanding of the person who is the butt of the attack. It thus works as a way of affirming the bond between men while appearing to deny it. (Easthope 1992: 88)

There is, says Easthope, a 'double bluff' in operation here. The comic appearance of the banter exchange distracts attention from its serious purpose of reinforcing the masculine ego (p. 92). These humorous exchanges stand in place of actual dialogue and disclosure, and are thus integral to the maintenance of patriarchal structures and the deflection of homosexual desire. Banter, then, is essential to the operation of homosocial communities – from public schools to the military to the public house – and it is the mode of discourse that negotiates and polices the boundaries constituting acceptable masculinities.

The codes of English masculinity described above were crucial to the formation of Mills as actor and icon. However, their status as hegemonic (that is, invested with cultural authority) was not as stable as might be assumed.[18] Robert Colls argues that at some point in the 1940s Englishness began to change, and the nation's constitutive belief in progress was gradually replaced by a concept of decline (2002: 143–4). Specifically, the transition emerges post-1945. By the end of the war, Britain's status as a world power had undergone a radical transformation. The nation was victorious, but bankrupt, caught between a hegemonic imperial past and the probability of a subordinate future, sidelined by the emerging Cold War conflict between the new empires of America and the

Soviet Union. Britain's own empire was agitating for change, and Indian independence was just the beginning of a remarkably rapid decolonisation process. Not surprisingly, these political changes had social and cultural implications, and the English hero that emerged in the aftermath of war was substantially different from the gentlemanly figure who went into the conflict. Andrew Spicer has identified Mills as the exemplary figure of postwar English masculinity, a figure who could, crucially, 'be associated with gradual change': 'It was not a radical new image of masculinity, but a renegotiation of the debonair ideal, a democratised version of the same values' (2001: 27). But the evidence suggests that what Mills came to embody post-1945 can at best be seen as transitional. Mills's modern Englishness, a hybrid of the cricket-team ethos and an evolving classlessness, was soon under pressure. The product of war, the new democratic male ideal had nowhere to go in the 'domestic' decade of the 1950s, and the tensions of gender, age and generation that emerged in this period were precursors of the revolutionary changes in national self-perception that would characterise the 1960s (Richards 1997: 18). Somewhere between Colls's decline and Richards's revolution, Mills's Englishness became a residual and outmoded construct.

It is thus the argument of this book that, over the period 1930 to 1970, the cinematic representation of English masculinities reveals long-cherished types subject to reinscription and change. Yet there were continuities too, and one thing that remains a constant in these representations is the reliance upon banter. It is the communicative tip that disguises the iceberg of English inarticulacy. Throughout this book my attempts to analyse and define (however provisionally) English masculinities keep returning to this central feature. But it is not simply an inability to speak that defines the English man, rather it is a more specific *emotional* inarticulacy. The Englishman can be fluent, if necessary, in practical matters, but he should never be fluent in the emotions – to be so would be to make him glib, untrustworthy, other. Why should this be? What is wrong with being able to express feelings, desires or needs? The answer is evident in the cultural connotations of emotion: it is the realm of the other, of women, or excitable foreigners.[19] To be emotional is thus to be associated with the feminine, and a dreadful prospect for a masculinity that aims, argues Easthope, 'to be one substance all the way through' (1992: 166). For Easthope, this is the central plank of the masculine myth: the belief in consistency, fixity and purity. The masculine myth takes no account of the contingency of gender, it does not recognise that the male subject will be characterised by any number of traits culturally associated with the feminine. Rather it renames the qualities that threaten it, turning passivity into endurance, feminine intuition into gut-instinct. Easthope's analysis is supported by the work of Thomas Byers, whose innovative account of masculine 'pomophobia' similarly draws attention to hegemonic masculinity's fear of the changeable, the multiple and the unfixed. Byers distinguishes between the solid, production-based masculinity of classical capitalism, and the 'lax', credit-based, consumer-oriented individual of late capitalism (1995: 12–13). Traditional masculinities, faced with the profound 'destabilisations' of the postmodern world (Byers lists, amongst others, theory, feminism, homosexuality, new technologies and the collapse of grand narratives) calcify, retrench or struggle to graft aspects of the new onto old and unwilling roots.

Not surprisingly, then, the archetypal Englishman distrusts fluency and the 'easy' expression of emotion. The very concept of fluency itself becomes suggestive of deceit. To be good with words is to distract attention from things, from what simply is ('a man of few words' is usually praise). Masculinity should be self-evident not self-absorbed, seen rather than spoken. Easthope concludes with a statement of the power of the masculine myth:

> Clearly men do not passively live out the masculine myth imposed by the stories and images of the dominant culture. But neither can they live completely outside the myth, since it pervades the culture. Its coercive power is active everywhere – not just on screens, hoardings and paper, but inside our own heads. (Easthope 1992: 167)

Over the course of the twentieth century no medium has been more important than film in both perpetuating and resisting this power. Within the space of the film text the myths of masculinity are negotiated and reimagined. It is the space in which the boundaries of masculine legitimacy are tested, the space within which marginal or subordinate possibilities find at least temporary expression. Alison Light prefaces her discussion of interwar women's writing with a resounding assertion of the value of textual study, and what she argues for the novel is equally applicable to film:

> All novels [or films], whether they mean to or not, give us a medley of different voices, languages and positions, and none can sustain a single 'argument' with the reader . . . because novels [and films] not only speak from their cultural moment but take issue with it, imagining new versions of its problems, exposing, albeit by accident as well as design, its confusions, conflicts and irrepressible desires, the study of fiction is an especially inviting and demanding way into the past. (Light 1991: 2)

The films of John Mills likewise invite us into the confusions, conflicts and desires of twentieth-century Englishness and its masculinities.

A 'Boy's Own' Story

This, perhaps, is the moment to explain how I happen to be called John Mills. In the Belton days, during my 'show-off, get tough' period,

> I decided that Lewis was soppy, even cissy. Ernest didn't conjure up the right image, and Watts was frankly a joke . . . I had to find a name that was short, tough, and couldn't be held up to ridicule. I plumped for Jack, and Jack it was until many years later when, at my sister's suggestion, I changed it to John. She said that . . . John Mills would in her opinion look much better in lights one day. I think she was right. (Mills 2001: 15)

Lewis Ernest Watts Mills was born in Norfolk on 22 February 1908. He spent his early years in the village of Belton near Great Yarmouth where his father was headmaster of the local school. His autobiography describes a somewhat uncomfortable household comprising an overworked but much-loved mother, a restless and dissatisfied father and a bevy of maiden aunts. His much older sister Annette had long since left home and, as the headmaster's son, he found it difficult to make friends at school. The family were somewhat peripatetic, and Mills was considerably happier when he became a pupil at the St John Leeman School in Beccles, Suffolk. It was here that he made his first stage appearance, playing Puck in the school's production of *A Midsummer Night's Dream*. Describing the surge of emotion he experienced on this childhood début, Mills writes, 'I had started an affair that [would] last as long as I live' (2001: 17). His happiness was short-lived, however, as shortly afterwards he was dispatched to the 'sheer unadulterated hell' of Norwich High School for Boys (p. 18). As a boarder at the school, Mills was subject to night after night of bullying: '[T]he gang decided I was too pretty, looked like a girl, and christened me "Madge"' (p. 19). Relief came eventually through self-help: lessons in 'ju-jitsu' from his sister's dancing partner, Robert Sielle.

Annette Mills was an enormous influence on her younger brother. A professional dancer (and later the companion of Muffin the Mule), he 'idolised' her, and longed to emulate her life on the stage and in the city. The circumstances of the family's increasing financial difficulties, however, meant an end to his now thriving school life and to the prospect of university. Leaving school at 16, Mills became a commuter, taking a position as a junior clerk at an Ipswich corn-merchants. Before long he had fallen in love and was contemplating settling down. At this point, Annette intervened, offering introductions to people in London in the hope that her brother would take the gamble of trying to make it on the London stage. In 1926, aged 18, and with savings of £25 from his corn-trading career, Mills did just that, moving to live with his father in South London.[20] Annette was as good as her word, with the result that Mills attempted to combine the dancing lessons that would be crucial to forging a career, with the economic necessity of earning a living selling toilet paper for Sanitas. Needless to say, as a travelling salesman, he was not a great success. Unemployed and running out of money, he eventually got his first break in the chorus of *The Five O'Clock Girl* at the London Hippodrome.

This brief summary takes Mills to the verge of the 1930s, and each of the following chapters will provide a contextualising survey of his career progression. My information comes from *Up in the Clouds, Gentlemen Please* (2001) an enormously engaging account of Mills's life and career that is also profoundly revealing in terms of the construction and maintenance of the actor's persona. Mills's autobiography constructs its narrative in immensely 'English' terms, and a brief examination of the text's strategies indicates the extent to which Mills's self-creation contributed to the possibilities and limits of his screen persona. *Up in the Clouds* is a story of the plucky underdog's triumph against the odds, told – appropriately – with the minimum of introspection and the maximum of modesty and good humour. It is luck rather than talent that gets the credit for Mills's successes (pp. 57, 78, 148, 167), and humour that effaces the possibility of pain or humiliation (p. 19). Masculinity is imbibed in childhood through the pages of *The Gem* magazine and school bullying becomes a 'boy's own' story. The account of the bullying given by Mills is framed as a moral tale in the traditions of the English masculine ideal. The small, unregarded figure of the hero is tormented by older, bigger boys. In desperation he contemplates running away, or even suicide, but is offered redemption through the figure of an older man, a mentor who guides him onto the path of manliness, convincing him of the virtue of going back and facing his fears, of not 'chickening out'. Crucially, this figure also provides the skills through which to fight back against the bigger opponent, leading – after a dramatic confrontation – to a triumph over adversity. The fight against the bully is then placed in the wider context of the school and its values. The bully is expelled, the hero thanked, and the school community restored to health. Justice has been done (pp. 23–4).

Behind the confidently self-effacing storytelling of the autobiography it is possible, however, to glimpse the anxieties and struggles of the lower-middle class boy whose face was 'too pretty' and whose size was too small. Not surprisingly the name Lewis Ernest Watts Mills was rejected at an early age in favour of something that 'couldn't be held up to ridicule' (p. 15), and after the bullying incident, the potentially disturbing events of Mills's life, from blood poisoning to divorce and war, are glossed over with impeccable lightness. However, the cultural forces that shaped Mills the man are nowhere more evident than in the story he tells of auditioning for what would be the first big break of his career. Mills was given the chance to audition for a touring performance of R. C. Sherriff's *Journey's End*, then the *cause célèbre* of the West End stage. Having seen the play many times, he prepared to read for the part of the eager young hero Raleigh. On arrival, however, he was horrified to be asked to read instead the part of Hibbert, the coward: 'With a sinking heart I found the place and started . . . I plunged in and did the best I could with it. But I knew it wasn't good' (p. 78). Mills's shock at being asked to perform the coward when he is convinced that he is ideal for the heroic role is heartfelt and unquestioned. And it seems that even at this early stage his self-presentation was such that he exuded heroic potential. In one of the autobiography's most striking examples of 'luck', Mills was saved by the entrance of R. C. Sherriff himself, who pronounced him 'the perfect Raleigh' (p. 79). Mills got the part and with it began his association with the performance of heroism in all-male dramatic environments.

Yet implicit in this anecdote is Mills's inability, or refusal, to play the coward, and from this we can examine the limits of his screen persona. In his influential article, 'Screen Acting and the Commutation Test' (1978), John O. Thompson suggests that it might be possible to interrogate the assumptions underpinning categories of the normal and self-evident through the process of commutation: the imagined exchange of one signifier or actor for another. Thompson illustrates his point with an example of what he terms 'ungrammatical' casting, placing the actor John Wayne in the 'inappropriate role' of a doctor (pp. 67–8). It is likewise possible to ask: in what context is John Mills simply unimaginable? Although Mills predominantly played the hero, the possibilities of this 'type' are wider than might at first be imagined. For example, it is always possible to invert the hero and the villain. Both roles involve agency and a degree of self-belief. Heroes can also be inadvertent: they can be fools and rogues and innocents abroad. All of these possibilities are plausibly compatible with Mills's corporeality and their fit is borne out by the success of his screen peformances. There are, however, a few roles that seem to fall outside both the screen and self-construction of Mills, and in so doing reinforce our understanding of the actor's constitution. Mills's career as a leading man contains no aristocrats, no spivs, no playboys and definitely no cowards. While it is possible to imagine Mills trading roles with Alec Guinness for *Tunes of Glory*,[21] it is almost impossible to imagine him trading places with Richard Attenborough in either *In Which We Serve* or *Morning Departure*. Attenborough's screen persona arguably represents the mirror image of Mills. Another small actor of youthful appearance, his physique and face for some reason led him to be cast not as the plucky hero but as his antithesis, in a career embracing cowards, spivs, psychopaths and mass-murderers.[22] Commutation, if nothing else, encourages us to query the ideological assumptions that underpin our understanding of visual signifiers. The process that concretised Mills as a hero and Attenborough as a coward was incremental, arbitrary and contingent. The following chapters attempt to trace this process and to examine its implications for the cultural constructions of masculinity and nation, and its role in the history of British cinema.

The exercise of commutation also draws attention to choices and, inevitably, I have had to make difficult ones in deciding which of Mills's many films would be the subject of detailed attention in the chapters that follow. In the 1930s the choice was relatively straightforward, my decision determined by the relatively few films in which Mills enjoyed a substantial leading role. For the 1940s and 1950s, however, the process was altogether more difficult. In order to illustrate the range of Mills's wartime cross-class performances, some seminal films of the period have received only cursory attention. In Chapter 3, for example, *In Which We Serve* (1942) was ultimately rejected in favour of *Waterloo Road* (1945) on the grounds that Mills enjoys a much larger role in the less well-known film, and this enables him to flesh out and develop his portrait of working-class masculinity. His character, Jim Colter, also has a degree of agency never available to Shorty Blake – but, nonetheless, Shorty might be seen as a crucial building block for a performance fully realised in the later film. A similar criterion of exclusion applies to *This Happy Breed* (1944). Mills's part is not substantial, and the film has already enjoyed considerable critical attention elsewhere.[23] Perhaps the most surprising omissions, however, are found in Chapter 5, which does not select as case studies either *The Colditz Story* (1955) or *Dunkirk* (1958). *The Colditz Story* played a vital role in resuscitating Mills's box-office appeal when his career was at a low ebb, but as a performance it adds little to our understanding of Mills's screen persona. Like the later *Dunkirk*, *The Colditz Story* replicates modes of performance established in wartime and extensively discussed in Chapter 3. In the 1950s, Mills's soldier heroes were popular and successful, and he did little to change a winning formula. It seemed more important, therefore, to examine in detail those films of the period which challenged Mills's comfortable repetition of norms. In films such as *Town on Trial* (1957) and *Ice Cold in Alex* (1958) the reassuring nostalgic virility of Mills's performances is infiltrated and undermined by neurosis, resentment and anger. In the 1960s the belated ageing of Mills's face finally displaced him from leading man status, and the difficulties of selection were again reduced. Yet the decade was one of quality rather than quantity. In *Tunes of Glory* (1961) and *The Family Way* (1966) Mills gave two of his finest screen performances; these are examined in detail, but there was not room to explore his much smaller, but nonetheless impressive, performance in *Oh! What a Lovely War* (1969). In Richard Attenborough's directorial début, Mills's impersonation of Field Marshal Haig presents a magnificent parody of muscular Christianity that triumphantly unites his skills as a dancer with his ability to embody military masculinities.

This book begins with chronology and ends with genre. Chapters 2–6 trace the development of Mills's career from doomed youth to the impotence of age. Chapter 7, by contrast, looks back at the subversive current of comedy that

co-existed with his dominant heroic persona, and concludes with an examination of *Ryan's Daughter* (1970), the film for which Mills won his only Oscar.
Each chapter stands alone, but there is a cumulative argument that seeks to
understand the massive transitions in self, society and cinema that characterised
the mid-century period. Above all, I argue for the importance of the actor as
a key component of the film text. Reading performance is crucial to reading
cinema, as the much-underrated British director Roy Ward Baker suggests in
his description of film production:

> What you are trying to do is to tell a story to an audience through the
> medium of actors, because they are the only contact that you have
> between yourself and the audience. (Baker 1961)

The actor, he argues, is 'the mode of expression', and film permits the ever-
changing language of the body to be fixed as representation. Yet the actor, as a
unit of meaning, is never pure, but always already contaminated by the social and
part of an infinite chain of signification. The meaning of Mills is always context-
dependent: his body will acquire different resonances depending on whether he
is juxtaposed against Stewart Granger or Richard Attenborough. Nonetheless,
just as habitual usage determines our capacity to understand language, so the
palimpsest of past performance can come to shape an actor, enabling him or
her – for better or worse – not simply to tell one story, but to provide an ongoing
narrative of nationhood and subjectivity. *John Mills and British Cinema*, then, is
not a biography of the English Everyman. Rather it is an attempt to understand
the personification of the nation and the construction of a masculinity that, for
a brief historical moment, managed to be all things to all men.

NOTES

1. *Sunday Express*, 24 April 2005; *Scotsman*, 25 April 2005; *The Times*, 25 April 2005;
   Financial Times, 25 April 2005.
2. The renewal of vows took place in January 2001. Mills described it as an opportunity to do things properly after the couple's hasty wartime wedding.
3. 'Perhaps now, after Sir John's death at the grand old age of 97 – the house where
   he died should be saved for the nation as a national monument' (*Sunday Express*,
   24 April 2005).
4. It is not inappropriate to connect Mills's continued popular appeal to that of
   Queen Elizabeth the Queen Mother, who was also regarded with great fondness
   as a residual representative of the war generation.
5. This distinction permeates British culture. Krishan Kumar, describing literature as
   'the first deity of the English nation', argues that at the end of the nineteenth
   century a central role was played by an overwhelmingly masculine canon in the
   formation of a distinctive English identity (2003: 220). Alison Light suggests that

this 'careless masculinity' was so pervasive that it created a literary history in which male authors 'are taken to represent the nation as well as those who are disaffiliated from it' (1991: 6).

6. Barry Norman, quoted in the *Sunday Express*, suggested that Mills was versatile rather than outstanding, but such doubts were not shared by all. Philip French called him 'one of the great actors of the twentieth-century' (*Observer*, 24 April 2005), while David Smith and Anushka Asthana, writing in the same paper, suggested that 'he became almost the only [British] actor in the 20th century who was a genuine leading man.'

7. See Mark Glancy's *When Hollywood Loved Britain* (1999) for a full account of American representations of Britain during the Second World War.

8. Mills's relationship to a more specific form of film stardom is discussed in Chapter 4, but it should be noted from the outset that the actor's relationship to filmmaking and its associated models of stardom was complicated by an ongoing commitment to stage performance (Mills 2001: 199).

9. A point also made by Dyer (1998: 35, 43) and Ellis (1992: 91).

10. It is a notable feature of Mills's career that by far the majority of his roles were homosocial in conception. Heterosexual desire was usually confined to the margins of the narrative, and his characters's on-screen emotional attachments were limited to the male group.

11. An extensive discussion of the process of reading performance and the relationship between character and star is provided by Dyer's seminal study, *Stars* (1998).

12. Difficult, but potentially productive, as John O. Thomson argues in his seminal essay 'Screen Acting and the Commutation Test' (1978). Commutation, the exchange of one actor-as-signifier for another, undermines the 'natural' assumptions that underpin representation and can offer insights into the construction of gender, class and racial norms. It also tells us something about the limits of an actor's screen persona, as I discuss later in this chapter.

13. *Cottage to Let* (Anthony Asquith 1941), a notable exception to this rule, is discussed in Chapter 3.

14. Noble's comments also indicate that the association of Mills with the nation is not simply a product of hindsight – it was strongly perceived and articulated throughout his film career.

15. These ideas and attitudes have been the subject of considerable debate across the course of the past century. See, for example, Barker 1927 and 1947; Orwell 1941; Gorer 1955; Commager 1974; Paxman 1999; Colls 2002; Kumar 2003. An excellent summary of the debate and its definitions is provided by Richards (1997: 1–28).

16. This metonymic relationship is also evident in the dominant geographical representation of the nation in which a gentle, rural vision of the 'south country' comes to stand for all of England and Britain (Kumar 2003: 210).

17. The masculinity of the aristocracy has historically been associated with pleasure, not duty, whereas Mills's masculinity is one of duty, of earning privilege rather than being born to it. For a succinct discussion of the playboy and the puritan as types of masculinity, see Edley and Wetherell (1995: 136–9).

18. Connell observes that hegemonic masculinity, the masculinity of patriarchal authority, 'is not a fixed character type, always and everywhere the same . . . It is, rather, the masculinity that occupies the hegemonic position in a given pattern of gender relations, a position always contestable' (1995: 76).

19. For a succinct account of phallic masculinity's rigid distinction between the 'feminine' body and the 'masculine' rational mind, see Frosh (1994: 103–4).

20. Mills's parents had separated some time previously. It is difficult to be precise with dates in Mills's early life, as the narrative of *Up in the Clouds* is timeless in character – based upon memory and anecdote rather than careful reconstruction of history and context.

21. A possibility suggested by Mills and confirmed by Piers Paul Read's recent autobiography of Guinness (2003: 326).

22. For cowards see *In Which We Serve* (1942) and *Morning Departure* (1950), for spivs and psychopaths see *Brighton Rock* (1947) and for mass murderers see *10 Rillington Place* (1971). There were, of course, exceptions to these patterns of casting – Attenborough also played comedy, and specialised in 'little' men making a stand. As an actor he, like Mills, was comfortably able to cross classes, but it is easier to categorise him as a character actor than a leading man.

23. See Andrew Higson's exemplary reading in *Waving the Flag: Constructing a National Cinema in Britain* (1995).

Part I

2

A British Cagney?
Cinema and self-definition in the 1930s

The reproduction of nation-states depends upon a dialectic of collective remembering and forgetting, and of imagination and of unimaginative repetition. (Billig 1995: 10)

I rather assumed that the chief function of the cinema in this country was to accomplish what I am sure will never be accomplished, or even attempted, in any other way – the annexation of this country by the United States of America. (Mr R. W. Sorenson, House of Commons Debates, 1937. Quoted in Richards 1984: 63)

Some day some Hollywood director will discover Johnny Mills and exploit a fact we have consistently over-looked – that for fifteen years we have been harbouring a British Cagney. (C. A. Lejeune, *Observer*, 1942, quoted in Tanitch 1993: 54)

Comparing John Mills and James Cagney was a surprisingly common pursuit of the 1930s and 1940s. Although the grounds for this comparison are perhaps not immediately obvious, there are a number of unexpected similarities connecting the two men. Both actors began on the stage: Cagney in vaudeville, and Mills in the chorus of *The Five O'Clock Girl* at the London Hippodrome. They could sing and they could dance, but both men were short, and so were denied easy access to leading-man status.[1] Cagney, obviously the more significant film star of the 1930s, enjoyed massive success, but was continually frustrated by typecasting that confined him to wayward roles as more or less redeemable gangsters. Mills, by contrast, struggled to find vehicles that allowed him an adult presence on the screen, and seemed for much of the decade to exist in a limbo between boy and man – the perpetual screen son. The actors began their film careers within two years of each other, but Cagney's early success made him available as a model to which Mills could aspire, and there is little doubt that he was influenced both by Cagney and the performative style he typified. It was, however, on the stage that this influence paid its greatest dividends. In his account of his award-winning performance as Lenny in the first British stage production of Steinbeck's *Of Mice and Men*, Mills records that he based his characterisation on what he had learnt from watching Cagney in *Angels with Dirty Faces*, and from working with another American tough-guy actor, Wallace Ford (2001: 209-10). The London critics approved of his imitation, leading the *Sunday Graphic* of 28 May 1939 to record that the play was: 'Superbly acted by all, particularly by John Mills in a Cagney role that would make James touch his cap and say, if the word was in his vocabulary, "maestro"' (Mills 2001: 212).[2]

The comparison with Cagney is, however, more than simply a matter of one actor's influence upon another. It also serves as a means of illustrating the contrasts between British and American modes of masculinity and of examining the comparative condition of the two national cinemas. In this context, there is a certain irony in the fact that Mills's greatest success in a 'Cagney' role came not on film but on stage. In spite of regular work and critical praise in the first half of the decade, by the late 1930s Mills's film career was at a standstill. British cinema had entered one of the periodic crises that dogged it throughout the century, and the industry scarcely had the resources to produce its own films, let alone develop its home-grown acting talent. The decade had begun promisingly enough with Alexander Korda's *The Private Life of Henry VIII* (1933) which, unusually for a British film, triumphed not only at home but in America. The film was critically acclaimed, broke box-office records and won an Oscar for its star, Charles Laughton, but such successes were both rare and double-edged. *Henry VIII* dangled the Holy Grail of the American market in front of the filmmakers of Britain, initiating a financially damaging quest to replicate this triumph. From this point onwards, at least a portion of British filmmakers believed that the prestige film was the only way in which Britain could conquer the American market (Richards 1984: 251–2). Sarah Street, however, argues that Korda's success had less to do with the film's prestige status than with an astute marketing campaign by United Artists, who variously pitched the film as a highbrow history, a middlebrow democratic critique of British institutions and an irreverent comic vehicle for the talents of Laughton (Street 2000: 55–9). But whether it is Korda or Laughton who deserves the credit for *Henry VIII*'s success, it remained the case that only 'comparatively small-scale films could be made and exhibited profitably in Britain' at this time (McKibbin 1998: 438). The problem was the lack of a level playing field: British films needed the American market far more than the Americans needed

Britain. Hollywood had the infrastructure to produce more films for less money, and it could recoup its costs in the domestic market before heading off to profit overseas (Landy 1991: 23). Nonetheless, the rhetoric of British filmmaking remained relentlessly optimistic throughout the decade. In a *Picturegoer* article of January 1936, boldly headlined 'Everybody wants British Films', Julius Hagen claimed that 'a vastly improved and greatly increased programme of films' had resulted in picturegoers becoming 'British film minded'; but the mundane reality was one of financial struggle, uncertain direction, and the recognition that domestic films could not match the appeal of the Hollywood product (Richards 1984: 24–33).[3] Going to the cinema attained new heights of popularity in the 1930s, but most people did not go to see British films, and barely five years after the success of *Henry VIII* the British industry was back in the doldrums. Jeffrey Richards describes a cycle of boom and bust, beginning with the glut of new production companies that emerged in the wake of the 1927 Cinematograph Films Act, and ending in what *Sight and Sound* described as:

> Pretentiousness posing as quality, ill-advised attempts to reproduce in this country types of films native to other countries, the obsession for producing international films, inefficient production methods, and extravagance . . . (*Sight and Sound* 5 (20), Winter 1936–7. Quoted in Richards 1984: 41)[4]

The verdict of *Sight and Sound* is echoed by the memoirs of Michael Balcon, head of production at Gaumont British for most of the decade:

> As we expanded, and production costs rose, Gaumont British began to look for markets overseas, which involved a further development with which I was concerned – the policy of importing known American stars to play in our films, thus making them more attractive and marketable abroad. The policy did not achieve the object we had in mind. Too often the stars were chosen more for the value of their names than their suitability for the roles, and they did not fit easily into films which were largely British in conception. (Balcon 1969: 61)

The policy, in Balcon's words, was 'mistaken' (1969: 88), but it – along with the economic crisis and decline in production of the latter half of the decade – did not make life easy for aspiring British actors and prototype leading men. With the industry in recession, Mills found worthwhile parts increasingly hard to find.

It is important to note that Mills was not a 'star' in this period, although he might, at one stage, have been described as a star in the making. His film career began with a promising supporting role in the Jessie Matthews vehicle *The Midshipmaid* (1932), but it was his performance in Walter Forde's big-budget naval drama *Forever England* (1935) that finally put his name 'above the title' (Mills 2001: 185). The part of Ordinary Seaman Albert Brown was a substantial heroic role and the reviews, for both Mills and the film, were good; but in spite of being offered a two-year contract with Gaumont British in the wake of this success, no concerted attempt was made to maximise his potential.[5] Mills's career in this period, then, is a series of stops and starts in which he veers from minor supporting roles to headline performances. In part the uncertainty of his screen trajectory can be attributed to ongoing stage commitments. By the mid-1930s Mills had an impressive track record in the West End, appearing in such musical successes as *Jill Darling* (1934) and the long-running farce *Aren't Men Beasts* (1936). His earliest career breaks had been in the theatre, and he learnt on the job, touring the Far East during 1929 to 1930 with a well-regarded company called The Quaints. It was for this tour that Mills was cast as Raleigh in *Journey's End*, but in order to play this, the part of his dreams, Mills was also obliged to take the lead in a musical, *Mr Cinders*, and a range of roles across the rest of the programme, which ran the gamut from farce to *Hamlet*. It was with The Quaints that Mills first came to the notice of Noël Coward, a serendipitous encounter that led to his casting in the monumental stage production of *Cavalcade*.

The diversity of talents developed in this theatrical apprenticeship served Mills well for the equally diverse demands that would be made of him on the screen. As Marcia Landy has illustrated, British cinema production in the 1930s embraced a broad spectrum of genres, and perhaps the most remarkable aspect of Mills's early screen career is that he was present in them all. In the *The Midshipmaid* he was required to sing alongside Jessie Matthews, beginning the film in naval whites and ending it in one of Matthews's cast-off frocks, while *Britannia of Billingsgate* (1933) called for a rather less camp performance as an aspiring dirt-track racer. By 1934 he was specialising in sons, providing support for the Northern variety comedian Leslie Fuller in *A Political Party* and *Doctor's Orders*, and in the same year he also appeared as Will Hay's 'son' in *Those Were the Days*. In *Royal Cavalcade* (1935), the film made to commemorate the silver jubilee of George V, Mills represented doomed youth, playing the public-schoolboy soldier whose lucky penny doesn't help him much in the trenches of the First World War. *Car of Dreams* (1935) was a rather creaky musical, in which Mills played the romantic lead, while his success in *Forever England* saw him cast in Robert Stevenson's *Tudor Rose* (1936) and Raoul Walsh's *OHMS* (1937). These were bigger budget pictures, with superior production values, but Mills was back to supporting roles. In *Tudor Rose* he was doomed youth in costume, playing the unfortunate Guildford Dudley, beheaded for his marriage to Lady Jane Grey; while in *OHMS* he got a taste of the tough guy, playing best friend and romantic rival to the Hollywood actor Wallace Ford. *Forever*

England also led to starring roles in *First Offence* (1936) and *The Green Cockatoo* (1937), two films which worked to construct Mills as a prototypical English action hero, and it is in these films, along with the seminal *Forever England*, that the seeds of his later screen persona can be most clearly defined.

Yet although elements of these films can be regarded as formative, by the end of the decade both Mills and the British cinema had entered a crisis of self-definition. In spite of his West End successes, Mills was keen to establish himself as a serious dramatic actor, and in the absence of cinema roles, he was happy to accept a drastically reduced salary to appear as Puck in Tyrone Guthrie's 1938 Old Vic production of *A Midsummer Night's Dream*. It was not a case of preferring one medium over the other – Mills claims he enjoyed making films and was 'fascinated by the new medium' of cinema (2001: 171) – rather it was the imperative of survival. His film career was going nowhere, and was unlikely to develop when the few good leading roles available for British actors in British films were generally reserved for Robert Donat, described by Jeffrey Richards as 'British cinema's one undisputed romantic leading man in the 1930s' (1984: 225).[6] British cinema, meanwhile, was embroiled in its own identity crisis. As Andrew Higson records, the fear of 'Americanisation' had been 'a major source of consternation within debates about the possibility of a viable British national cinema since at least the early 1920s' (1995: 19) and British filmmakers were caught halfway between the absorption and the rejection of American influence. At the same time as the industry sought to preserve and develop a specifically British mode of filmmaking, the influence of Hollywood was impossible to ignore – as was its popularity with cinema-goers – which perhaps explains why however much Mills admired Robert Donat as an actor and mentor, it was Cagney who represented the screen ideal to which he aspired.[7] Film producers were left on the horns of a dilemma. How best to respond to a critical demand for something recognisably British in the face of an audience demand for something wholeheartedly American? All too often the result was an uncertain and unsuccessful hybrid. This incompatibility is particularly in evidence in films that attempt to develop genres more usually associated with Hollywood, such as *The Green Cockatoo* (1937). This British version of gangster *noir* emerges as a deeply uncomfortable conjunction of styles, presenting the bemused viewer with the spectacle of Mills singing and dancing his way through a sub-culture of wise-cracking cockney tough-guys.

American Dreams: *The Green Cockatoo*

The Green Cockatoo could have been designed as a textbook illustration of British cinema's inability to replicate the Hollywood product. In spite of an original story by Graham Greene and a reasonably effective dramatic soundtrack, the film is fundamentally static and uneven in tone. A major problem is the sets, which are deeply theatrical, and would have appeared all the more so to audiences familiar with the more confident exteriors and large-scale bustle of a Cagney vehicle. London, in *The Green Cockatoo*, is a city inhabited only by the principal performers, and one slightly dubious extra who briefly leans against a lampost in an establishing shot of the seedy, eponymous nightclub. Although the opening section of the film provides a montage of familiar London images, these, along with the crowd scenes shot at a greyhound track, stand out as notable exceptions within the otherwise studio-bound dimensions of the film. A positive product of these visuals is a pervasive sense of claustrophobia, but any attempt to create a sustained sense of threat is undermined by a script that is at best mediocre and at worst actually painful. Mills plays Jim Connor, a nightclub singer who runs the Green Cockatoo and evinces a fundamental distrust of the 'p'lice' – perhaps on account of the criminal tendencies of his brother, Dave (Robert Newton). Dave's role is not a substantial one. After double-crossing the Terrell gang over a dog race, he is stabbed in revenge and survives only long enough to drag country-girl love interest Eileen (Rene Ray) into the narrative. When Dave breathes his last, the naïve, middle-class Eileen is mistaken for the killer and runs from the police into the arms of Jim.

Improbably, Eileen's attempt to escape the police acts as the cue for a song. In a scene that illustrates the remarkable persistence of music hall and variety influences in British cinema, the screen action halts for a set-piece routine. Paradoxically, although the song functions as an integral part of the narrative, it is filmed in a manner that celebrates its extradiegetic qualities. Jim is trying to persuade a policeman that Eileen is his new singing partner, rather than a fugitive from the law, but Mills's performance of 'Smokey Joe' could almost belong in a different film. The scene is shot in a medium close-up of Mills singing straight to camera, accompanied by occasional reverse shots revealing the policeman's appreciation of his voice, and Eileen's nervous face. The artificiality of the performance is further highlighted by Mills's intonation. In a marked contrast to the somewhat unstable cockney–American hybrid he adopts for the film's dialogue, he sings his song in impeccable received pronunciation. This lapse is indicative of a number of the problems suffered by the film. The attempt to graft American vernacular language onto a British milieu cannot help but jar, and the script is so littered with 'kids', 'dames' and 'classy joints' that it would be hard for any actor to keep a straight face. Then there is the problem of tone. This scene aims at comedy, with Mills making wisecracks about Ray's hopeless singing, but shortly before, the film had struggled to project sincerity, with Mills and Newton bonding as only screen brothers can. Later the echoes of the music hall return, as Mills is required to play straight man to Frank Atkinson's melancholic butler, Protheroe. In between these encounters there are chases and a relatively violent knife fight, building up to a final encounter in which Mills punches out the villains. While an element of edgy comedy is often integral to hardboiled narratives, here the elements do not gel. Comedy and violence are segregated, compartmentalised in different scenes and operating in seemingly unrelated registers. In terms of Mills's development as a performer, the film illuminates both strengths and weaknesses. In a key scene towards the end of the film, Jim Connor learns of the death of his brother. For the duration of a relatively long take, the camera lingers on Mills's face, which reacts subtly to the words he is hearing, absorbing the information in an understated manner that successfully conveys the character's shock. His body language is impressively still and it is not difficult to believe in this portrayal of contained emotion. Where Mills is altogether less effective is in the scenes where he is obliged to get verbally tough with the gangsters, and this 'failure' returns me to the 'relationship' with Cagney's screen persona.

Irrespective of the cultural difference dividing the two actors, there is an obvious limit to Mills's corporeal capacity to imitate the 'Cagney' ideal, and while this limit makes him less than wholly convincing in *The Green Cockatoo*, it was fundamental to his later success in the 1940s. The similarity between the two actors lies in their bodies. As trained dancers they were both particularly agile performers, using hand movements and gestures with care and precision. In his account of Cagney's screen persona, James Naremore cites voice and speed as the actor's primary distinguishing characteristics. Observing that his very untheatrical voice and his capacity for dynamic movement made him a revolutionary and authentically cinematic leading man, Naremore concludes that 'Cagney was one of the first actors to show Hollywood how to give movies a truly big-city energy and tempo' (1988: 159).

The differences, however, lie in their faces, which encode a series of sharply contrasting characteristics. Cagney was, in Naremore's terms, 'the most graceful of the pug-ugly Warner's gangsters', a paradox intensified by make-up that created a troublingly androgynous impression (p. 60). Naremore compares the impact of Cagney's face with the leering extravagance of Malcolm McDowell in *A Clockwork Orange*, and his description of the actor in *The Public Enemy* exactly captures this disturbing quality:

> Cagney stands under a street lamp and grins back at us; the eyes are heavy-lidded, shaded with thick lashes and tilted up at the corners with Satanic points; the mouth is dainty, the cheeks dimpled and cherubic; the aggressive, phallic stare and the knowing smile are perverse, mocking the illusion of innocence, charming the audience as they threaten it. (p. 160)

Cagney's face, then, is a mass of contradictions. He talks, through his teeth, from only one side of his incongruous rosebud mouth. His pugnacious, jutting chin threatens even as his snub nose suggests boyish appeal. In the 1930s, Mills's face simply could not match the dynamism of Cagney's contradictory features [Fig. 2.1]. Like Cagney, he has remarkable eyes: technicolour would later reveal them to be blue, but in the monochrome 1930s they are dark reflective pools, almond shaped, with scarcely noticeable lids and long, soft lashes. Protected more by lashes than by lids, they suggest openness, sincerity and vulnerability. These trustworthy eyes are set in a face without dimples and creases. Although the lines of his eyebrows and nose are strong and elegant, Mills also has the smooth cheeks and unblemished complexion of the girl-next-door. On stage, his body language might have carried the day for toughness, but certainly at this early point in his career, the proximity of the camera could not but discover the femininity of his face [Fig. 2.2]. It is this almost bland, unthreatening feminine appeal that made Mills so useful in the early part of the decade performing as a 'principal boy' in the pantomimes of Leslie Fuller and in the romantic comedy of *The Midshipmaid*.[8] It is also this, however, that undermines him as both tough-guy and lover in *The Green Cockatoo* [Fig. 2.3]. The film ends in a train, carrying Mills and Ray back to middle-class safety, and as it draws to a halt, the two actors finally kiss. Standing stiffly together, with eyes shut, their chaste and conventional representation of desire evokes the kisses of childhood, and *The Green Cockatoo* ends not with passion, but with the babes in the wood.

A final problem that beset the British gangster movie was that of censorship. The British Board of Film Censors, like the Hayes Office in America, provided extensive guidance as to what was unacceptable viewing for the British public. Having listed some of the many prohibitions at length, Marcia Landy concludes that, 'it is important to see that any reading of British films must take into account not only the subjects selected for representation, but also the absence of many subjects' (1991: 27). Alongside such traditional danger areas as the representation of sex, prostitution, suicide, incest, abhorrent native customs and scenes ridiculing the monarchy, Landy lists a more subtle prohibition, namely the representation of 'doubtful characters exalted into heroes' (p. 26). A similar prohibition was in operation in America where the Production Code insisted that screen criminals should be punished – and the usual solution adopted by filmmakers was the death of the morally ambivalent hero. *The Green Cockatoo*, however, seems to have taken to heart the uncertainty encoded in the word 'doubtful' and not knowing where the boundaries might lie, plays safe through the deployment of an ersatz gangland hero who is morally uncontaminated by his surroundings. This is not a case of an innocent man drawn into an unfamiliar and compromising milieu. Jim Connor is adept at surviving in the London of night clubs, dog tracks, betting scams and stabbings, yet rather paradoxically, the narrative insists that he is not part of this world. Only the criminality of his brother brings him into proximity with crime, and his rather old-fashioned

Fig. 2.1 Toughness incarnate: James Cagney in *Angels with Dirty Faces* (1938). Warner Bros/First National/The Kobal Collection

Fig. 2.2 A beautiful boy: *Britannia of Billingsgate* (1933).
British Film Institute/London Features International

mode of heroism deprives the film of the tension for which it strives. As
Douglas Kellner argues in his account of Hollywood film and society:

> The gangsters are fantasy characters who act out secret audience desires
> to get ahead no matter what, although it is still not clear if their repeated

Fig. 2.3 Acting tough: Mills and Rene Ray in *The Green Cockatoo* (1937). British Film Institute/London Features International

punishment (mandated by the Production Code) actually helped prevent crime through dramatizing what would happen if one broke the rules of the game and stepped outside the law, or promoted crime through making the gangsters – often played by popular figures like James Cagney or Humphrey Bogart – extremely dynamic, attractive, and vital figures. (Hill and Gibson 1998: 357–8)

The fundamentally unthreatening nature of *The Green Cockatoo* that emerges from its clear-cut boundaries and lack of ambiguity, is finally confirmed by the 'boys-own' conclusion of the narrative. A happy ending is provided, but it does not see Jim and Eileen united in London. Rather the lovers return to the countryside from which Eileen emerged, and to which the incorruptible Jim ideologically belongs. Together they escape to a roses-round-the-door model of Englishness that has been ridiculed throughout the film, but in the end is revealed as ideal and morally superior to the contaminated city. Even as the film wants to embrace an Americanness of threat and excitement, it pulls back from any endorsement of this desire, restoring instead a more familiar, hegemonic

England, recuperating 'good' Jim Connor into the bourgeois landscape where, deep down, he has always belonged.

'A Fit Country for Heroes'? Genre and Ambiguous Masculinity in the 1930s[9]

As the example of *The Green Cockatoo* suggests, not only did the British cinema lack direction, losing its way in unsuccessful imitation of American genres, it also faced problems in the construction of its heroes. On the one hand, heroic complexity was rendered problematic by the constraints of censorship, while on the other hand, the dominant genre of British popular cinema – comedy – did not really depend upon heroes at all. A high proportion of British films of the 1930s were comic vehicles for established variety artists that dispensed with the model of the fictional hero and did not even attempt the pretence of narrative cohesion. The films typically presented a series of more or less unmediated set-piece performances by the stars, loosely connected by flimsy plot devices such as mistaken identity or romantic misunderstanding. Exploiting the popularity of musical comedy and variety stars was, according to Andy Medhurst, a fairly immediate response to the arrival of sound pictures. In a succinct survey of the relationship between the music hall and British cinema, Medhurst examines *Elstree Calling* (1930) as a typical example of this technologically-induced hybrid genre. Films of this type, he argues, not only lack narrative structure, but also, in their approach to the medium, reveal a degree of discomfort with the developing codes of mainstream cinema. Performers such as Will Fyffe and Lily Morris ignore the conventions of internal coherence and play 'quite deliberately to some putative off-screen music hall audience' (Medhurst 1986: 174). This is a tension that retains the capacity to resurface throughout the decade. Drawing simply upon the canon of Mills's films, it is possible to identify repeated attempts to disrupt illusion and reinscribe the contract between audience and screen.

Those Were the Days (1934), the first film made by comic actor Will Hay, provides both an illustration of the prevalence of music hall structures, and an example of British cinema's fondness for stage adaptations, in this case Sir Arthur Pinero's *The Magistrate*. Mills plays Bobby, the step-son of Will Hay's magistrate Mr Poskett. The story calls for Mills, then aged 26, to play a 21-year-old pretending to be 15. As a drawing-room farce the film works well enough, and Mills is convincingly cocky as the old/young son who leads his naïve and respectable father astray. Where the film reveals its divided loyalties is in its location shots at the music hall. Transgression, for Hay's middle-class, middle-aged magistrate, is a late night visit to this den of iniquity, where the working classes heckle from the stalls and the wealthier clientele take boxes and private rooms above. Each time the action of the drama demands a visit to this space, the camera is drawn inexorably to the stage, where it lingers, providing the cinema audience not just with glimpses of the stage show, but with full scale musical numbers – most notably Lily Morris performing 'My Old Man Said Follow The Van'. Considerable screen time is also given to comic Harry Bevan, and the illusion of cinema is finally comprehensively disrupted by a minstrel performer who, in a direct address to the camera from the stage, invites both the intra-diegetic and extra-diegetic audiences to sing along with the chorus. The nostalgic desire to reconstruct an interactive relationship between performer and audience that is encoded in this rupture of narrative convention is equally present in the work of comedians catering to a known constituency of spectators. Leslie Fuller concludes *Doctor's Orders* (1934) with a close-up to camera in which he speaks as both his character, a quack doctor, and as a comic touting for business: 'If you're ever feeling blue come and see me!'.[10] The films of Fuller and Hay, like those of George Formby, undoubtedly had considerable box-office appeal. But while these performers can be described as stars, they are about as far removed from dramatic conventions of heroism as it is possible to be. Indeed, British cinema of the period seemed to have remarkably little time for strong male roles, and this absence can only partly be attributed to the constraints of genre.

British cinema's lack of ostentatious virility in the 1930s was a product of continuity rather than change. The phenomenon had first emerged in the 1920s, and was most clearly illustrated in the rise to stardom of Ivor Novello. According to Lawrence Napper and Michael Williams, Novello epitomised a very particular form of British interwar male celebrity: exotic, sophisticated and epicene, his screen persona combined 'an unthreatening version of masculine charm for a female audience' with 'the unarticulated suspicion of . . . real-life transgression' (Babington 2001: 46). Audience enthusiasm for ambiguous masculinities continued unabated into the star culture of the 1930s, manifesting itself in such leading men as Henry Kendall, and finding perhaps its ultimate exemplar in Noël Coward. Napper and Williams attempt to account for the prevalence of effeminacy by quoting Herbert Wilcox, who suggested, in 1934, that a lack of interest in manliness might well be a legacy of the First World War (2001: 46). The impact of the war on conceptions of masculinity in Britain has been widely examined, most notably in work on shellshock and male hysteria (Showalter 1987), but it is the work of Alison Light that gives substance to the cultural dimension of Wilcox's claim. In her analysis of popular middle-brow fiction, Light attributes the interwar popularity of such 'superficial' occupations as crossword puzzles and the reading of detective stories to a culture of convalescence. Arguing that the whodunit was a form of 'popular modernism', she observes that this is a world in which 'nothing is sacred' and the tastes of a post-traumatic culture have shifted from melodrama to farce (1991: 67–8). Central to this transition was the rejection of much, if not all, that had traditionally been embodied by British heroic figures:

> The crime story was the one place where the reader might reasonably expect violence, but what had formerly been enjoyed as one of the most aggressive of literatures, became distinctly pacific in its retreat from old-fashioned notions of the heroic. The universe of these novels, secular, largely amoral and anti-sentimental, marked a shift in the self-perception of the respectable reading public away from the notions of mastery and destiny which had so governed the idea of English character and with such disastrous consequences. Naturally the dominance of women writers in the interwar years and their reworking of what had formerly been a largely masculine genre must give us pause, but both male and female writers in the period found a kind of modernity in making fun of heroes. (Light 1991: 69–70)

The avoidance of bloodshed and the preference for making fun of heroes that Light identifies in fiction is equally to be found in film. Alongside comedy, crime flourished as a popular cinema genre, giving rise to such products as Bernhard Vorhaus's *The Ghost Camera* (1933), a quota quickie starring Henry Kendall and giving brief exposure to Mills as a man wrongly accused of murder. The film is a visual equivalent of the cosy interwar detective story. The corpses are bloodless, the supporting cast stereotyped, and Kendall's amateur sleuth seems to be constructed as a middle-class hybrid of Lord Peter Wimsey and Bertie Wooster.

Once again, the contrast with America is evident. Jeffrey Richards argues that in the bid for box-office popularity, the British gentleman hero, usually epitomised by Leslie Howard, was pitted against the macho appeal of 'bad guy' stars such as Clark Gable, James Cagney and Edward G. Robinson: 'They had no equivalent in the British cinema and therefore gained a considerable following, particularly among working-class audiences' (1984: 240–1). However, while the British cinema of the 1930s could not replicate the perceived virility of either American films or performers, the beginnings of a transition in the construction of British masculinity is evident from the middle of the decade onwards.[11] If, as Andrew Higson suggests, individual films 'often serve to represent the nation to itself as a nation' (1995: 7), then it is possible to detect a series of cultural anxieties emerging in response to the changing political climate of the decade. Three films, *Royal Cavalcade* (Thomas Bentley 1935), *Forever England* (Walter Forde 1935) and *First Offence* (Herbert Mason 1936), encode both these anxieties and a corresponding narrative of reassurance, and in each case it is John Mills who stands as representative of the nation's youth.

'SOME FAR CORNER OF A FOREIGN FIELD': SACRIFICING MILLS FOR THE NATION

The most direct address to the anxieties of the mid-1930s is found, appropriately enough, in the semi-documentary form of George V's silver jubilee film, *Royal Cavalcade*. It is also here that the most blatant efforts are made to reinscribe recent history, in an effort to assure audiences that potentially destabilising and threatening events, such as the general strike, were only superficial scuffles obscuring a much deeper bond uniting class and nation. Mills's role in *Royal Cavalcade* is nothing less than the representation of the 'lost generation'. He first appears, sporting a jaunty striped blazer, in an idyllic recreation of pre-war England. Sitting in a boat with the girl he plans to marry, Mills evokes the Rupert Brooke of Georgian poetry, and the cinema audience could not have failed to anticipate his fate.[12] Together the couple listen to a waltz called 'Destiny', which will become a leitmotif for sacrifice within the film. Almost immediately after the depiction of their idealised romance, the film cuts to the 'shadows over Europe', as men queue to enlist and crowds cheer the prospect of war. Mills, clutching the lucky penny given to him by his girl, is among those seen embarking – a symbol of the nation's youth and promise.

The montage that follows tells the official story of the national war effort: casualty lists, women workers, munitions, planes and factories. Then the film returns to its emblematic soldier, now somewhat dishevelled, showing a photo of his sweetheart to another young lieutenant. When a volunteer is required for a raiding party, the two men behave like school boys, tossing the 'lucky' penny for the adventure of death. Mills, the winner, puts 'Destiny' on the gramophone, and pauses, pensive, turning the lucky penny in his hand. His death, which follows, is inevitable, but its depiction bears further scrutiny. The deployment of the 'Destiny' waltz immediately translates his death from the realm of contemporary politics to the realm of the mythical fates. Agency and responsibility are removed and the soldier's death in war becomes a timeless sacrifice, pre-ordained and unavoidable. The displacements enacted in this comforting anodyne are further compounded by the script. As the camera pans across battlefield graves, the narrator intones, 'Who dies if England lives?' Individual loss is worthwhile in the name of a wider community and a greater good. The echo of Brooke's later poem 'The Soldier' is clear:

> If I should die, think only this of me:
> That there's some far corner of a foreign field
> That is for ever England.
> (Brooke 1932: 150)

And with this evocation the film sets its conservative epitaph upon Mills's first incarnation as a symbol of nation.

   Royal Cavalcade is a difficult film to watch, particularly in sequences such as this, where the visual montage is so at odds with the commentary. The often shocking images of air-raids, and of civilian and military casualties, are accompanied by a script that, in its references to 'ever-smiling armies' and the Tommy's 'unfailing sense of humour', mobilises the clichés of national identity in the construction of a myth of communal solidarity. Perhaps recognising the contradictions of its own narrative, the film moves swiftly on from war to the dawn of 'a new world of high hope', and presents the spectator with a scapegoat for past losses and contemporary ills in the shape of the war-profiteer. It cannot have been an easy task for Thomas Bentley and the Associated British Picture Corporation to make an uplifting 'celebration' of a reign that incorporated the First World War, the general strike, and a devastating economic collapse. However, they achieve something of their objective through the repeated depiction of unity in adversity – even if this unity flies in the face of logic and fact. The scenes from national life that the film chooses to represent suggest the extent to which class remained a fraught issue in interwar Britain. The filmmakers strive to assuage middle-class anxieties by showing the bitterness of unemployment and strikes as nothing more than surface detritus obscuring a deeper truth of national loyalty. This is most clearly evident in the account of the general strike, which is depicted as a plucky pulling together of the nation in time of need. The comparison with the war evoked by this construction positions the strikers as the enemy, but having rendered them 'other', the film immediately moves to recuperate and rehabilitate them, making them safe through a discourse of national belonging. In a short scene set on a bus, a middle-class man attempts to perform the job of a bus-conductor. He is clearly incompetent and, in frustration, a striking bus conductor helps him out. In so doing there comes a moment of recognition – the two men fought together in the war: they share a loyalty to a national ideal that is represented as standing above class – and in the warm glow created by this happy coincidence, they settle down to talk about old times. History, even recent history, represents a secure space for the deployment of ideological freight, and throughout *Royal Cavalcade*, crisis is utilised like ghosts in a bed-time story: the spectre is raised, only to be immediately banished with reassurances of solidity.

   The film thus works to suggest that in time of crisis the nation, irrespective of age or class, will pull together for the greater good. Its repeated emphasis of this point, however, gives clear indication of just how much fear there was amongst the middle classes. Fear of class unrest was accompanied by anxieties regarding the priorities of the nation's youth and the influence of new mass cultures upon its children. Reports into the pernicious influence of cinema were plentiful, as were articles decrying the intellectual dangers of popular fiction and mass culture.[13] This degree of cultural paranoia forms a significant backdrop to *Forever England*, the second film of 1935 to sacrifice Mills in the name of national unity. Once again, the middle-brow cinema works to assuage class anxiety through the depiction of working-class loyalty, but in this case the message is accompanied by a warning to an older generation careless of their responsibilities.

The film, based on C. S. Forrester's novel *Brown on Resolution* (1929), had impeccable mainstream credentials, and before its opening was given a private showing to George V and Queen Mary. Mills's autobiography provides an account of the unprecendented scale and ambition of the project:

> *Brown on Resolution*, I discovered to my satisfaction, was intended to be the largest and most expensive production ever tackled by a British studio. Location work had never before been attempted on such a scale. A small, rocky island was bought off Falmouth, and for the first time in history the Admiralty, having approved the script, gave their full co-operation. (Mills 2001: 180)

Forever England (as the film was later retitled) is set during the First World War, and it tells the story of Able Seaman Albert Brown, the illegitimate offspring of a cross-class liaison between a naval lieutenant and a working-class girl. Mills played the central heroic role of Brown, and this performance, more than any other of the 1930s, worked to establish him not only as a potential leading man, but also as an exemplar of a particular mode of British masculinity. Brown is the embodiment of 'English' virtues: courageous, resourceful and quietly competent, and full use is made of Mills's physical appearance to construct a narrative of the plucky underdog's victory against the odds. The little man, serving on a rusty old ship, is not afraid to take on a bigger enemy, whether it be the much larger German sailor that Brown boxes in a pre-war bout, or the battleship that he will effectively sabotage with only his sharp wits and a rifle. Brown's selfless heroism and death are framed by a narrative of class constraints that give a degree of ambiguity to the film's celebration of a 'national' hero, but as Jeffrey Richards has observed, the screen presentation of a working-class hero is in itself significant (1997: 131). The repeated, lingering, half-profile and full-face camera shots of Mills looking alert, attentive and thoughtful clearly construct him in heroic rather than comic mode – a highly unusual event for a working-class character, whose potential for heroism in the thirties would generally be accidental if it existed at all. This combination of qualities associated with middle- and upper-class masculinity in a clearly defined working-class body made him an encapsulation of a community ideal that would be reactivated by filmmakers some five years later in the service of a nation once more at war.

To a certain extent, the film is a fictional reworking of the themes that dominated *Royal Cavalcade*, and ideologically it works to negotiate the tensions created by developments in Europe and the evolving threat of a second world war. By 1935, Hitler was not only chancellor, but also head of state, and Germany had withdrawn from the League of Nations. Although conscription had been introduced in Germany, in Britain the predominant mood of both government and country favoured appeasement, and *Forever England* undoubtedly speaks to this policy in its impeccably even-handed depiction of the German sailors. Both the captain of the German warship *Zeithen* and the English Captain Summerville are depicted as men who must mourn the loss of their sons to war, while the pre-war boxing match provides the opportunity for considerable homosocial bonding between the sailors of the two nations. The friendship between Brown and the German sailor Max contributes to the film's tendency to show the war as a sporting contest writ large, and the captured English sailors are treated with a level of courtesy that would have given no trouble to censors anxious to maintain good relations with Nazi Germany. Yet once again, history is being deployed as reassurance, and in an attempt to win consent for contemporary policy. The depiction of the German officer class as men of honour embraces the popular belief of the 1930s that at some point Hitler would be dealt with by the military elite. This is what the nation desired, and in depicting the Germans as 'men like us', the film endorses this desire. However, in other key respects, the film works morally not to avoid, but to prepare for war – and it does this through its portrayal of British masculinity. The construction of Albert Brown as man and hero forms a countercurrent to the dominant depictions of masculine stardom discussed above, and as such emerges as a symbolic rearmament of the nation.

If, as Herbert Wilcox suggested, the First World War could be regarded as a factor culturally inhibiting the development of a virile national masculinity, then *Forever England* works to reinscribe the cultural import of the war. The same war that deconstructed the myth of imperial masculinity here works to reconstruct an alternative mythic ideal. Albert Brown is an absolute exemplar of heroic masculinity. The original title of the film spoke to his fundamental qualities in its evocation of resolution. He is stalwart, determined, cheerful and modest; but in terms of class, physicality and attitude he could scarcely be further removed from the British heroes of the pre-First World War era. The imperial ideal was not comprised of little men. Bulldog Drummond never lost a fight in his life.[14] Albert Brown is an underdog, and in his symbolic progress from losing the fight to winning the battle, he suggests the emergence of a reinvigorated but necessarily muted masculinity. England, says this film, might be slow to anger, but she has reserves upon which to draw. Any reluctance to fight is not effeminacy, but rather an essentially peaceable nature, and a preference for the privacy of home. England as imperial nation is conveniently overlooked in the tactical reconstruction of England as a shorthand for home and domesticity, a process assisted by the early characterisation of Albert Brown as a man devoted to his mother.

There is a metonymic relationship between the love of mother, home and country. The domestic feminine space of home is also the soil to be protected, the motherland, a territory that usually requires the guiding hand of a system of governance gendered male. This governance, or political superstructure, is notably absent from *Forever England*. Charles Summerville (Barry Mackay), the well-to-do young gentleman who fathers Albert Brown, offers to marry the lower-class Elizabeth Brown (Betty Balfour). She declines out of noble self-sacrifice, censoring her own desires on account of the rigid class barriers that divide them. Yet although this is presented as Elizabeth Brown's choice, and her relationship with her son is depicted as close to the point of incestuousness, when Brown is killed, the film focuses ultimately not on her loss, but on Summerville's. Men, it suggests, should take more care of the precious commodity that is their sons. Fathers have responsibilities that are both personal and political. In touching, albeit fleetingly, upon the derogation of this duty, *Forever England* taps into cultural concerns regarding the state of the nation's youth and joins the ranks of the many films of the decade that problematise the relationship between fathers and sons.

'England Made Me': Man-Making in *First Offence*

In spite of being abandoned by his father, Albert Brown represents the ideal son, but other films of the decade were rather less optimistic about the new generation. In the context of the popular perception that a generation had been sacrificed to the mistakes of old men, it is perhaps not surprising that heightened anxiety surrounded the nurturing of youth. The 'maternalist ideology' of the interwar years placed considerable emphasis on the duties of motherhood (D'Cruze 1995: 74), but once adolescence was achieved, responsibility shifted to the father. Man-making, like law-giving, was man's work. Yet Mills's films of the 1930s suggest a degree of anxiety regarding the performance of this work in their catalogue of variously absent, ineffectual or positively malevolent fathers. However, the presentation of this problematic parenting might also be regarded as somewhat disingenuous. *Forever England, Tudor Rose, First Offence* and even *The Green Cockatoo* expose personal failures in fathering only to reassure simultaneously through the revelation of a concept of national parenting. Ultimately, the sins of the individual father become irrelevant, because 'blood will out'. It is the soil of England that in some mystical manner acts as the crucial determinant of character.

In his influential work on national character, first published in 1927, Sir Ernest Barker proposes a sedimentary model of national identity. He uses the image of a palimpsest to suggest a process of constant reinscription that over-lays, rather than erases, the past (1948: 3). Revising the work in 1948, Barker turns to the image of the iceberg to confirm this sense of change as incremental rather than radical, and to assert that there is something rooted in the historic past that continues to shape the present:

> Much may change on the surface, as the exposed summit of an iceberg may melt, and even dislodge whole blocks which fall into the forgetting sea. But just as it has been calculated that only one ninth of an iceberg appears above the surface, so it may be agreed that the great mass of national character rides as it were underseas, with a steady permanence. (p. xiii)

Whether this 'steady permanence' emerges from the material factors of soil, race and climate, or the structures and traditions of British society, Barker's writing conforms to a reassuring belief in the ephemeral nature of modernity. *First Offence* (1936) is a film premised on a very similar belief, but with one notable difference. As one of the best examples of Mills's alternative screen persona of the 1930s, the transgressive youth, it has turned the iceberg of iden-tity upside down. Eight-ninths of the film is a celebration of superficiality and the modern world; one-ninth is the 'steady permanence' of Englishness that will eventually redeem the criminal hero. The film is effectively a *bildungs-roman*, marking the passage of boy into man, and it is set in a user-friendly French underworld where the temporary criminality of the hero, Johnnie Penrose, is legitimised by being distanced from home. In the playground of Paris the discourse of man-making carries an implied national dimension, and the growth in stature of Mills's character represents a heroic assertion of decency and fair play, qualities assumed to be fundamentally and exclusively British. But before these core values emerge, Johnnie Penrose reveals himself to be a youth of distinctly dubious character. A spoilt child, enjoying an extravagant lifestyle of cocktails, fast cars and women, he rebels when his father sells his car to pay off his debts. Bereft of the symbol of his social standing and power, Johnnie seizes an opportunity to steal back the car – an act that brings him to the atten-tion of a gang of rather more professional thieves. In his new profession he falls in love with Jeanne (Lili Palmer), a key member of the gang, who reveals her reluctant involvement in a life of crime only after we have watched her flawless execution of a wide range of scams. As the romance blossoms, Johnnie enters into an Oedipal struggle with his adopted crime boss 'father' (Bernard Nedell) over the possession and future of Jeanne, and the film culminates in a dramatic confrontation between police and car thieves, in which Jeanne's amiable but weak brother Michael (Michel Andre) is killed. Johnnie and Jeanne, however, escape to Marseilles, where they take passage to a new life.

In the construction of this storyline, *First Offence* is walking a moral tightrope. Johnnie steals out of lust rather than necessity – the car is the route to the girl – but it is difficult to discern whether the audience is meant to read this transgression as youthful high spirits or reckless criminal amorality. What is clear, however, is the sub-Oedipal level of his thinking at this stage: for Johnnie, manhood is most definitely measured by the size of your motor.[15] This immaturity undoubtedly makes Johnnie a morally ambiguous hero, a figure not welcomed by the censorship regulations of the period. However, the example of *First Offence* suggests that the form of the *bildungsroman* permits a relative freedom in the depiction of crime and punishment. Inherent in the structure of the 'boy into man' narrative is the possibility of atonement and redemption, in which a wayward younger self is replaced by a responsible and mature adult self. This undoubtedly takes place here, and perhaps accounts for the production's change of title from the ominous and irredeemable *Bad Blood* to the rather more cautionary *First Offence*. But although the film embraces a transformation, its moral message remains unclear, primarily because of the question of motivation. *Forever England* begged the question of whether Albert Brown became a good sailor because he was his father's son, or because his mother raised him to be a dutiful citizen. Similarly, *First Offence* poses a dilemma in the fate of Johnnie Penrose: does he reform because of his inherent national virtues, or is it the love of a good woman that makes him a better man?

Although uncertain how to account for its hero's virtues, *First Offence* is forthright in its attribution of blame for his failings. The film opens with a title frame that announces: 'When a young man lives in Paris – when his father is indulgent and his time is not occupied – then it's odds on he'll accelerate into trouble.' The relevance of the pun is made immediately obvious by the sequence that follows. A car swerves through the streets of Paris, narrowly avoiding traffic and pedestrians before screeching to a halt, inches from a large glass trophy case. The sequence is shot from the perspective of the driver, creating an edgy impression of precipitous control. Although at this point Johnnie is still on the right side of the law, this exhilarating vicarious ride symbolises the attractions of his later criminal career. Danger is thrilling – it is a drug to which Johnnie becomes addicted – and the potentially fatal consequences of addiction to such thrills are revealed through the character of Jeanne's brother Michael, who will act as a sacrificial lamb in the narrative of the hero's redemption. For a compromised hero to be rehabilitated, some punishment is required, and in this case it will be Michael who suffers for his refusal to recant his heretical belief in the religion of crime. Michael is a man who has lacked the guiding hand of paternal authority. While his profession is that of a car thief, his hobby is stealing neckties, a pastime he indulges simply for the thrill of the chase. Jeanne, as a surrogate mother, has done her best, but she cannot compete with the authority of the gang. The attractions of crime as both a father figure and a creed are made clear from the dialogue. Introducing the world of thieves to Johnnie, Michael describes it as a creative organisation, a parallel, seemingly meritocratic, world in which imagination and initiative receive immediate rewards. The drug-like properties of crime are also suggested in the narrative trajectory: a first flush of pleasure is followed by a more sordid reality. When things go badly there is no honour amongst thieves and behind the superficial freedom lies a violent, hierarchical structure every bit as oppressive as that of the legitimate world.

In genre terms, the crime drama of *First Offence* follows the pattern of other popular genres, such as comedy and melodrama, in that it permits the expression of transgressive desires before it moves to re-establish the status quo. Thus full reign is given to the anarchic comedy of Leslie Fuller or Old Mother Riley before their narratives move to an inevitable consensual conclusion, and in melodrama the wayward woman meets her inevitable death, after first having pleasured herself mightily. In following a similar pattern, much of the pleasure afforded by *First Offence* lies in its sharply edited and neatly performed caper routines. The bulk of the film is devoted to the depiction of a series of increasingly ingenious criminal scams, and its glossy lack of concern with the morality of its subject matter is further highlighted by the time spent on a range of relatively ambitious car chases and stunts, and the cheeky performances of the principal players, especially Lili Palmer. Far more attention is devoted to the process and pleasures of being bad than the business of punishment and redemption.

That such a range of bad behaviour should be acceptable is attributable at least in part to the location of the film. By setting the narrative of an Englishman's disobedience in the playground of Paris, the true weight of his crimes is diffused: after all, it is foreigners (and comedy foreigners at that), not Englishmen, who are being robbed of their cars. The French setting also serves to distance the social threat embodied by the counter-cultural society of the gang. When it happens elsewhere, crime is exotic, rather than sordid – and this context also helps to explain why the transgressive behaviour of the hero becomes, if not acceptable, then at least comprehensible. The Englishman abroad is not himself, and the city of Paris is substantially to blame for his aberrant behaviour. Here, as would be the case in the later *The Green Cockatoo*, the urban environment is implicated in the corruption of youth. It is, in consequence, no surprise that Johnnie should decide to give up his life of crime while trundling through rural France on a haycart. After he and Jeanne nearly lose their lives in a furious cross-country car chase, a realignment of values becomes imperative, and in the tranquillity of a miniature rural idyll, Johnnie's core values reassert themselves.

Vita Sackville-West puts her finger on this central tenet of national self-perception in her 1947 essay on 'Outdoor Life':

> Statistics may readily and coldly prove the population of England to be by majority urban rather than rural; industrial rather than agricultural; yet we shall submit . . . that some peculiar and essential virtue of the English character sucks up its life from the roots buried in that baffling, contradictory, yet unwavering product of centuries, the countryman. (Barker 1976: 408)

That the countryside restores and regenerates is a familiar trope of English literature, and the association of the nation with the rural would become a central concept of propaganda during the Second World War. The same assumptions underpin the conclusion of *First Offence*. Urban environments corrupt – they are full of temptations that obscure fundamental values. Rural environments, by contrast, reveal the value of tradition, they symbolise the 'steady permanence' invoked by Barker. Back on the haycart, Jeanne reveals she was coerced into a life of crime: the urban sophisticate metamorphoses into the good self-sacrificing woman. And who better to ensure that the Englishman grows to maturity? In this situation it does not matter that Jeanne is French, not least because women act as conduits for, rather than bearers of, national identity. A woman's nationality is absorbed into the nationality of her husband, and as such the good woman does not threaten the space of national identity. In *First Offence* the 'rural' Jeanne becomes a combination of mother and damsel in distress, and in the process of rescuing her, Johnny will be redeemed, as his father recognises in his final words to his son: 'Tell her I hope she succeeds where I failed – perhaps she can make a man of you.'

However, the juxtaposition of the rural and the urban is not the only motif through which the film develops the national character of its hero. *First Offence* is deeply concerned with man-making, but the type of man being constructed in Johnnie's journey to maturity is very much an Englishman. Having argued with his father, Johnnie finds himself with a far harsher surrogate parent in the boss of the crime syndicate. Appropriately the two of them fight over access to Jeanne, who is both a key asset of the crime family, and the object of Johnnie's desire. As the Oedipal triangle struggles for resolution, the attempts of the boss to lay down the law are met with resistance from Johnnie. When the ill-gotten gains are divided up, Johnnie reveals himself to be imbued with the archetypal English characteristic of a belief in 'fair play', arguing for the workers' right to have a bigger share of the criminal pie. Here, as in so many of his later films, Mills's role constructs him as a man of the people.

Ultimately, what is suggested by *First Offence* and *Forever England* is that core values, related either to an uncorrupted rurality or to the nurturance of a woman metonymically tied to the nation, are crucial to man-making. The process also benefits from sacrifice, either in the shape of war or of hard work. Unlike Johnnie Penrose, however, Albert Brown was in no need of redemption. His death stands as a moral lesson to fathers careless of their sons' welfare – a lesson that also reveals a crucial flaw in the man-making process; namely, the reticence and inarticulacy of the Englishman. Captain Summerville never spoke to his son; Dr Penrose exhibits great difficulty in communicating with his. How are values to be transmitted without a viable language connecting fathers and sons? The preoccupation with youth, blood and nurture displayed in these narratives reflects some of the anxieties surrounding gender, generation and the changing political climate that permeated the culture of the late 1930s. That Johnnie Penrose survives to work his passage into adult masculinity is perhaps as much to do with the conventions of genre as the merits of his case, but here, as in *Forever England*, there is reassurance built into the narrative. If all else fails, England will act as a corrective force, the 'steady permanence' of the national character miraculously working on English youth to ensure their ultimate loyalty and obedience [Fig. 2.4].

FLAGGING MASCULINITY: READING MILLS IN THE 1930S

By the end of the 1930s Mills's screen persona had achieved a bizarre co-existence as dutiful doomed youth and redeemable teenage rebel, and both of these roles have significant implications for the discourse of national masculinity which he would come to embody in the 1940s. Mills's personification of beautiful youth, usually destined for sacrifice, co-existed with a more transgressive, assertive mode of performance, a repeated depth narrative that can be found beneath the surface of such superficially different films as *First Offence* (1936), *Tudor Rose* (1936) and the Will Hay vehicle *Those Were the Days* (1934).[16] These films, generically running the gamut from musical comedy to early action picture, all encode a critical encounter with the father, and represent a mode of man-making that, even when they end in an appropriate acceptance of patriarchal authority, still stand in marked contrast to the almost feminised dutifulness of *Forever England* and the public school, war-as-a-game ethos of *Royal Cavalcade*.

The significance of the modes of masculine and national self-definition worked out in these contrasting narratives is, however, not confined to the 1930s, and an examination of these films also does much to explain why, despite an absence from the screen of several years, Mills was able almost immediately to evoke a particularly British masculinity in the 1940s. Developing a concept he terms 'banal nationalism', Michael Billig argues that the day-to-day maintenance of national identity within established nations involves a 'complex dialectic of remembering and forgetting':

Fig. 2.4 Steady permanence? *First Offence* (1936).
British Film Institute/London Features International

[N]ational identity in established nations is remembered because it is
embedded in routines of life, which constantly remind, or 'flag', nationhood. However, these reminders, or 'flaggings', are so numerous and
they are such a familiar part of the social environment, that they operate
mindlessly, rather than mindfully . . . The remembering, not being experienced as remembering, is, in effect, forgotten. (Billig 1995: 38)

Over the course of the 1930s films such as *Royal Cavalcade* and *Forever England* work to construct a discourse of nationhood, based around a resonant set of characteristics perceived to be 'national'. By the 1940s, these cultural products have attained the status of 'forgotten reminders', dormant memories that are reactivated by Mills's return to the screen. As Chapter 1 suggested, actors are cumulative cultural products, carrying with them the traces of their previous performances – especially when those roles are preserved on celluloid – and their performances portray not the real, but the familiar; a set of conventions habitually understood to convey culturally meaningful information. In the words of Richard Dyer: 'What is represented in representation is not directly reality itself but other representations. The analysis of images always needs to see how any given instance is embedded in a network of other instances' (Dyer 1993: 2). Thus it is that Mills's performances of the 1930s construct him in the 1940s as an immediate 'flag' of national identity. He had already been seen, in *Forever England* and *Royal Cavalcade*, as an exemplary soldier hero, a representation tempered by the modernity of his other persona as a putative British tough guy. To adopt another phrase from Billig's suggestive analysis, Mills operates as a 'metonymic stereotype', a particular 'presented to represent the whole country' (1995: 102). He acts as a signifier that, within the rhetoric of cinema, stands for a raft of cherished, self-congratulatory 'national' characteristics: pluckiness, self-sacrifice, decency, loyalty and fair play. By the end of the 1930s, Mills the actor bore all the unwaved flags of English national identity, flags that would be picked up and waved in his deployment by filmmakers from 1940 onwards. It is also the case that, ironically, the regular sacrifice of Mills in films of the 1930s enabled his survival in the 1940s. By carrying the cultural memory of the futile and gratuitous sacrifice of the young in the First World War into the reluctant arena of the Second World War, Mills reactivates the sentiment of 'never again'. His survival in the 1940s becomes a symbolic preservation of a certain set of core 'national' values and an enactment of the particularly British fantasy represented by the triumph of the underdog.

I also think there is another reason for Mills's persistent survival in the 1940s, and this demands the acknowledgement that the reinscription of national masculinity through the character of Albert Brown is not as straightforward as it seems. The 'problem' of Brown's heroism resides in the disjuncture between his gender and his subordinate class status. Anne McClintock argues that women and the working classes are linked through their construction as atavistic repositories of national values, and this has the potential to put a rather different perspective on *Forever England*.[17] Indeed, it suggests the possibility that in this role Mills is *not* performing masculinity. Rather he is posited as a feminine symbol of nation. He is feminised by his class position and by his intimate association with the mother (who is herself an archetype of feminine self-sacrifice for the greater good of the nation). Set alongside my earlier reading, this presents a paradox; but it is one that the film quite cheerfully overlooks in its drive to construct Brown as the epitome of Englishness. In order to reinvigorate and reinscribe a national masculinity that had been vitiated by the First World War and which had become associated with an affluent leisured class, the working classes were drawn upon as uncontaminated by decadent values. Simultaneously, however, the working classes remain a subordinate group – politically feminised through their relative lack of agency, and like women, usually homogenised into a body perceived as troublesome and irrational.

So although Albert Brown performs heroic masculine actions, the camera's focus on the face and body of Mills is equally a process of constructing a feminised embodiment of nation; a passive symbol of decency and honour. It is this duality that creates another reason why Mills must not 'die' or be sacrificed in the Second World War. He is not only a useful class hybrid encoding a variety of masculine forms, he is also an embodiment of feminine vulnerability. He is that which must be protected as well as that which protects. His embodiment of nation contains elements of both base and superstructure – the home for which we are fighting, and the man who fights.

That Mills, of all the actors who came to prominence in the British film renaissance of the early 1940s, should have had the capacity to embody the nation in this way, is perhaps best illustrated through a return to the Cagney connection. By the end of the Second World War the careers of both actors had evolved to the point that a contributor to *Picturegoer* magazine could imply that the relationship between the two men was self-evident, a matter of fact upon which wider cultural conjectures could be built:

> [A]bove all John Mills typifies the ordinary British man. I think no surer proof of this is needed than the remark that 'John Mills is the British James Cagney'.
> For just as Cagney's tough, bustling warm-hearted qualities are the essence of the American, so Mills's modest, enduringly cheery courage is the backbone of the Britisher. (Lieut. G. Rowell, 'My Man Mills', *Picturegoer*, 29 September 1945)

By the time of Rowell's article, Cagney's screen persona had itself undergone something of a transformation. The 'public enemy' of the 1930s had fought a decade of typecasting to emerge in 1942 as 'Yankee Doodle Dandy', and although the hoodlum image never wholly left him, Cagney undoubtedly evolved into a symbol of the American virtues of toughness and self-reliance

(McCabe 2002: 300). Similarly the very characteristics that undermined Mills's pseudo-American gangster in *The Green Cockatoo* – understatement, sincerity, reserve – would be identified by both filmmakers and public as epitomising something integral to ideals of Englishness in the very different cultural climate of the 1940s.

NOTES

1. Ironically, for Michael Redgrave, looking to build a career on the stage in the 1930s, the opposite problem applied: 'Tall actors were not unknown' records his biographer Richard Findlater, 'but they were not encouraged' (1956: 17).

2. Perhaps inevitably, the earliest example of the Mills/Cagney comparison can be attributed to Noël Coward. In 1931, after his appearance in the stage version of Coward's *Cavalcade*, Mills was offered a seven-year contract with Fox in Hollywood. Coward's response was brutal:

   > There are two roads ahead of you – let's take the Hollywood road first. It offers you, as you say, financial security and, as you are a naturally good actor, a successful career as a Hollywood film star with all the trappings. You will have no choice of parts, however. You will play exactly what they choose you to play. They make personalities, not actors. And in my view you will end up as a cross between Jimmy Cagney and Johnnie Garfield, and not as good as either of them, because they're American and you're English. (Mills 2001: 161)

   Mills's recollections might not be entirely trustworthy, given that Cagney's first film, *Sinner's Holiday*, was released only in 1930, but it is nonetheless noteworthy that the 'master', who was to exert a considerable influence on Mills's early career, should have remarked upon both that which connects and that which divides the two actors.

3. Richards records that critics and a high percentage of audiences found British films in general to be 'rigid, class-ridden, stage-bound and slow-moving' (1984: 33), but goes on to observe that there was an audience for British films, particularly those starring such popular favourites as Jessie Matthews, George Formby and Gracie Fields.

4. The Cinematograph Act of 1927 was one of a series of Acts designed to protect the British film industry from Hollywood domination by encouraging the growth of domestic production. The Act required exhibitors to include a legal minimum of British films on their schedules, and thus ushered in the era of the infamous 'quota quickie' – a low-budget, hastily constructed film designed more to fill space than attract audiences (Landy 1991: 24; Street 1997: 7–17). The Act of 1938 attempted to undo the damage caused by the 1927 Act by establishing minimum production costs, while the 1947 Act provoked a catastrophic Hollywood boycott with its attempt to impose a duty on American films.

5. In this period, the British cinema industry's approach to the construction and promotion of stars can at best be described as erratic. There was certainly no

system to match that of the Hollywood studios. It is worth noting, however, that a little more effort was made on behalf of young female talent. The publicity stills for *Britannia of Billingsgate*, for example, describe the juvenile female leads as 'Gaumont baby stars'. Mills, as the juvenile male lead was, perhaps fortunately, spared this appellation. The gender bias of British 'star-making' again suggests, however, that the concept of stardom sat uncomfortably alongside typical conceptions of British masculinity as self-effacing and understated.

6. Richards brackets Donat's image – and appeal – with that of Leslie Howard, 'dreamer and man of action, gentleman and adventurer' (1984: 226), and argues that both actors are examples of a now vanished heroic type.

7. Mills's interest in Cagney proved prescient. Over the course of the Second World War the fashion in heroes underwent a fundamental change, and the 'debonair gentleman' metamorphosed into something altogether more pragmatic. Cagney's appeal in the 1930s, though, was also that of the anti-hero, and his films offered a 'celebration of competitive individual achievement' that was welcomed by interwar, male working-class audiences in Britain (McKibbin 1998: 433).

8. Mills's first screen role was a particularly androgynous one. He plays Midshipman Golightly, a singularly appropriate name for his adolescent character, who is neither fully boy nor man. Golightly's function is that of go-between, acting as helper to both the hero (Basil Sydney) and the heroine (Jessie Matthews). The performance culminates in cross-dressing, as Mills and Matthews exchange outfits in an attempt to divert attention from the lovers.

9. Lloyd George, 1918: 'What is our task? To make Britain a fit country for heroes to live in.'

10. Fuller's films are worthy of comment for their very direct presentation of class tension. Both *A Political Party* (1934) and *Doctor's Orders* present a narrative in which education threatens to divide a working-class man (Fuller) from his son, in each case played by Mills. In *A Political Party* Bill the chimney sweep has sent his son to Italy to become an artist, while in *Doctor's Orders*, the father is a quack and the son a fully qualified doctor, who further complicates the class equation by falling for the daughter of the hospital director. In both films an initially superior ruling elite is revealed to depend upon the contribution of the proletariat, but the potentially radical implications of the films' anarchic topsy-turveydom (the sweep becomes an MP, the quack saves the hospital) are undermined by consensual conclusions that emphasise the validity of the status quo. Nonetheless, the pressures generated within the framework of the narrative illustrate the subversive potential encoded within comic genres.

11. Evidence of British cinema's attempt to project a more manly image can be found in the promotional literature emerging from the studios. Press releases for Gaumont's *You're in the Army Now* (1937, later retitled *OHMS*) suggest a hope that machismo is contagious in their proud proclamation that imported American director Raoul Walsh liked to make 'virile pictures', while the press book for *The Green Cockatoo* claims that: 'John Mills gives a virile performance as a nightclub entertainer who uses his wits and his fists against a gang of crooks' (BFI

Collections). Nonetheless, the habit of 'making fun of heroes' was not easily shed. Thorold Dickinson's 1939 crime drama *The Arsenal Stadium Mystery* starred Leslie Banks as a police inspector more concerned with perfecting the police 'beauty chorus' than with solving the crime. Banks's eccentric creation, who demands a different hat for every occasion, conforms neatly to the pattern of outwardly foolish but inwardly acute detectives that dominated the decade.

12. Brooke's pre-war poems celebrate a timeless England of unchanging character and eternal verities: 'I only know that you may lie/ Day-long and watch the Cambridge sky,/ And, flower-lulled in sleepy grass,/ Hear the cool lapse of hours pass,/ Until the centuries blend and blur/ In Grantchester, in Grantchester . . .' (Brooke 1932: 94).

13. Anxieties regarding the influence of cinema on the young and impressionable were not confined to Britain. Jostein Grisprud observes that although the majority of surveys and studies undertaken in America in the interwar period failed to find a causal link between delinquency and the cinema, a high degree of selective reporting resulted in a prominent public debate and, from 1934 onwards, a stricter enforcement of the Production Code (Hill and Gibson 1998: 204). A detailed account of British responses to the perceived dangers of cinema is provided by Richards (1984), while Q. D. Leavis provides perhaps the most complete statement of the belief that indiscriminate consumption of fiction was an addictive 'habit' amongst the poorer classes (1978: 7). Leavis argued that the 'conditions of modern life' had produced a reading public who did not read with 'any artistic, spiritual, moral or informative purpose, but simply in order to pass time' (pp. 48–9), and she expressed concern about the potential impact of the new 'passive and social amusement' of cinema upon the 'next generation' (p. 323).

14. Alison Light observes that 'Sapper's' Bulldog Drummond stories were still selling well in the interwar years, and that we cannot assume a clear-cut or complete break with pre-war ideals of masculine heroism (1991: 65). These ideals, however, might be seen as residual and nostalgic in contrast to the modernity of the 'unmanly' detectives who dominated the interwar years.

15. It would be hard to overestimate the significance of the car as a symbol in this period, and like the cinema, its mass appeal was a cause of concern for traditionalists. Although J. B. Priestley declared in his *English Journey* of 1933 that 'the motorist was the man of the future' (1997: 10), A. J. P. Taylor suggests that not everyone found this concept reassuring, recording that 'experts', concerned about Britain's declining birthrate, feared that the 'baby Austin [had] ousted the baby' (Taylor 1992: 302).

16. *Tudor Rose*, unusually, combines the two modes of man-making, enabling Mills both to rebel against his father's authority, and be sacrificed on the altar of his father's mistakes.

17. McClintock suggests that in the nineteenth century: 'Britain's emerging national narrative gendered time by figuring women (like the colonized and the working class) as inherently atavistic – the conservative repository of the national archaic' (1997: 93).

3

Mills at War, 1940–45:
The nation incarnate?

> The soldier hero has proved to be one of the most durable and powerful forms of idealized masculinity within Western cultural traditions since the time of the Ancient Greeks . . . Intimately bound up with the foundation and preservation of a national territory, the deeds of military heroes were invested with the new significance of serving the country and glorifying its name. Their stories became myths of nationhood itself, providing a cultural focus around which the national community could cohere. (Dawson 1994: 1)

> Without those unwarlike soldiers and sailors and airmen, whose thoughts have been not of conquests but of their homes, English liberty would not exist. (E. L. Woodward, in Barker 1947: 549)

Who or what is the soldier hero of the Second World War? There is no simple or singular answer to this question, as one of the characteristic devices of British filmmaking in this period was an attempt to foster a democratic spirit. The hero became not only Everyman but also Everywoman. Moreover, heroism was no longer seen to be the preserve of the special individual but rather a quality emerging from shared values and beliefs, a powerful ideological shift that gave rise, as the war progressed, to what might be termed the 'composite' hero. The most famous early manifestation of this heroic body was Noël Coward's *In Which We Serve* (1942), a film which, in the words of Dilys Powell, 'took a handful of typically British men and women and made from their stories, ordinary enough in themselves, a distillation of national character' (1947: 27–8). The film offers three clear sites of audience identification: Captain Kinross, played by Coward himself; Chief Petty Officer Hardy, played by Bernard Miles; and Ordinary

Seaman 'Shorty' Blake, played by John Mills. These three characters offer recognisable points of human heroism alongside the greater heroism which is identified as residing in the body of the ship. This 'body' made of men, who are together more than the sum of their parts, can only function if all its components work effectively. In consequence, when Richard Attenborough's stoker panics, his cowardice is seen not as an individual failing, but as a failure of communication, for which the captain is at least partly responsible. Explaining his actions, and his organic vision of the crew, Kinross concludes, 'I will not punish a man for an action for which I must hold myself largely to blame.' In giving the stoker a second chance, the group hero is constructed as self-governing and holistic, and Attenborough's character is reabsorbed into the body of the ship, before being rehabilitated and redeemed through the classic narrative device of a dutiful death.

Shorty Blake, like *Forever England*'s Albert Brown almost a decade earlier, was a crucial role for Mills. In his autobiography he credits the role with restarting his career, and observes that the 'smell of success' hung around the film while it was still in production (2001: 256). The wider significance of Shorty Blake, however, resides in his class position and the role he is allowed to play in the drama. Aldgate and Richards observe that '*In Which We Serve* was the first film to give equal screen time to the other ranks' (1994: 208), and in casting Mills as Shorty, Coward constructed the actor as a working-class ideal. Shorty Blake was designed both to embody and speak for a significant dimension of the nation. He was tough, courageous and resourceful, exhibiting under pressure the key national characteristics of loyalty and humour. He was, in essence, a small figure with a big heart representing a small island that wanted to see itself in much the same way. Together with the captain and the chief petty officer, Shorty Blake is an integral part of a group hero embodying a very particular construct of the nation. The characters of all three men are developed through flashbacks to the family, constructing the home as the root of national belonging, and using the complexities of family life as a metaphor for wider public loyalties. Writing a year before Coward's film was released, George Orwell mobilised a similar metaphor, albeit in rather less flattering terms. The British nation, in his view, was 'a family with the wrong members in control' – 'It has its private language and its common memories, and at the approach of an enemy it closes its ranks' (1970: 88).

In Which We Serve converts the insularity of Britishness into a series of Chinese boxes: home, ship and nation are differentiated only by size, and the result is the creation of a nation defined as 'a small, self-contained, tight-knit community, a unity-in-diversity' (Higson 1995: 179). In utilising the family as metaphor, Britishness becomes a construct that can embrace the squabbling and 'petty' differences that supposedly shape domestic life, while conveniently overlooking the fact that such internal differences might be crushing oppressions for some family members. At the same time, tolerance is constructed as an integral national characteristic, suggesting by extension that Britishness is spiritually generous and flexible in comparison with the more rigidly policed identities of continental Europe.[1] The success of the group hero as propaganda thus depends upon difference. It must be, of necessity, heterogeneous, made up of characters divided by class, education and geography, but united by a common purpose. Alongside a number of representatives of middle-class England, the group will usually contain a variety of working-class types, and these characters between them will also embrace further dimensions of region and ethnicity. There will be a Celt, a cockney and/or a northerner, with an optional bookworm or toff thrown in to liven up the oppositional dynamics. The composite hero attempts to represent in microcosm the sum of those who have a stake in the nation at war – at the same time as it works, ideologically, to construct that which it claims to represent.[2] Through inclusion on the screen, a narrative of national belonging is created, whereby those who might feel little or no investment in the national destiny of a Great Britain still dominated by the values of a privileged caste are encouraged to identify with, and become part of, an extraordinary endeavour.[3]

But what is the role of the individual hero, or the star performer, in such narrative constructions? How did an actor such as Mills emerge as more than a component within an overall structure designed to embrace the diversity and complexity of the national character? What makes him stand out from the mass as a particularly resonant embodiment of the Second World War soldier hero? Perhaps the obvious answer is his survival. The dutiful deaths that were a feature of his youthful screen persona became a thing of the past. In the cinema of the Second World War ships sink and planes crash, but Mills remains stubbornly alive until the war is safely won. Once the war is over, Mills's persistent habit of survival is immediately undermined, and his characters evolve into problematic and imperilled figures, lacking the direction of a clearly defined quest and uncertain of their function in the postwar world. However, as the previous chapter suggested, Mills's roles of the 1930s had ideally placed him to embody both the nation in need of preservation and the modern masculine agent facilitating that preservation. Between 1942 and 1946 Mills was indestructible, and was repeatedly cast as a linchpin character holding the composite hero together.

Yet when war broke out, Mills was a long way from the cinematic preeminence he would achieve in the late 1940s. Indeed, the beginning of the Second World War saw him literally rather than symbolically employed in the defence of the nation. In August 1939, when it became clear that war was inevitable, Mills had asked to be released from his triumphant run in *Of Mice*

and Men, and together with his great friend Anthony Pélissier had joined up
before hostilities were even declared.[4] But it was not to be a long career, as Mills
succumbed to an ulcer and was discharged on medical grounds early in 1941.
As his autobiography tells it, his time with the Royal Engineers was frustrating,
amounting in the end to little more than playing at soldiers. Between 1939 and
1940 Sapper, later Sergeant, and ultimately Second Lieutenant, Mills was primarily deployed in the organisation of concert parties (Mills 2001: 234–40). At
some point during this period he must also have been released to make his first
film of the war years, Ian Dalrymple's propaganda-cum-recruitment comedy
Old Bill and Son (1940).[5] This film has largely been forgotten, but it is worth
attention both as a transitional film in the development of Mills's screen persona,
and as an attempt cinematically to imagine a war that was happening, but which
had not, in any clearly representational sense, yet 'happened'.

Old Bill and Son begins just before the outbreak of hostilities and, as the title
suggests, its primary narrative concerns the relationship between father
(Morland Graham) and son (John Mills). The generational conflict between
them must be overcome, and war is presented as a man-maker and match-
maker, guiding young Bill to a newly mature relationship with his father and
his sweetheart, played by Rene Ray. The film devotes considerable time and
energy to explaining the war and its likely implications, and the generation gap
between father and son is exploited to illustrate the changing nature of
warfare.[6] As young Bill displays his new battledress uniform he comments: 'We
don't sparkle with brass buttons like you did. This is meant for a job. The army's
mechanised now.' Alongside its optimistic paean to modern warfare, the film
mobilises the family unit to suggest the potential impact of this modernity on
the homefront. Young Bill's adopted sister, Sally, who doubles as his girlfriend,
joins up immediately, much to the consternation of both father and son. Later
in the film, when Sally arrives in France, young Bill's response is, 'Blimey –
Mum'll be turning up next.' She doesn't, but a swift cut to Blighty reveals her
to have become a terrifyingly efficient drill sergeant.

This, then, is war as a family affair. Home and nation are conflated, making
the defence of England the defence of a cosy domesticity, and the wider ideological implications of the conflict are not considered until the final reel, when
a brief foray into battle brings the enemy into focus. As a group of German prisoners are ushered back to camp, father and son agree that the Nazi war-machine
is nothing in comparison with the guts of free men. But, for all the film's
attempts to address change, its portrayal of warfare is still, as Robert Murphy
has noted, 'misleadingly reminiscent of the First World War' (2000: 15). This
anachronism is understandable given that during the phoney war it was difficult
to conceive of a theatre of war other than one based upon the experiences
of 1914–18, but it nonetheless gives a dated feel to the depiction of soldiers

billeted on a small French town. The uncertainty that marks *Old Bill and Son's* representation of warfare is also present in its dramatic construction. The film bears the hallmarks of 1930s filmmakers' reliance upon music-hall conventions. Morland Graham's comedy turns are reasonably well integrated into the narrative, but the need to stage a concert party arrives from nowhere, suggesting a lingering belief that a patriotic film wouldn't be complete without a good sing-song around the piano. Yet although the concert party sits uncomfortably alongside the military adventure, it does serve a purpose that anticipates a key concern of wartime filmmaking – it creates a tableau of cross-class, cross-gender and cross-national cooperation, as Canadians, women, commanding officers and commoners are brought together in the creative enterprise. This does not take the film far along the road of constructing a composite hero, but it does reveal *Old Bill and Son's* attempt to create a degree of low-key realism in its depiction of ordinary people. The film also strives to build an ideologically powerful narrative of belonging and inclusivity through its assertion of a brave new world of possibility emerging from the constraints of war. War, indeed, is presented as the ideal job opportunity for the feckless lower classes. The army makes a man out of young Bill, and he is kept happy in his work by the promise of advancement. His best friend is conspicuously middle-class and well-educated, suggesting that a privileged upbringing does not mean preferential treatment, and the film does nothing to contradict young Bill's belief that he can become an officer.

But what contribution does *Old Bill and Son* make to the construction of Mills as a national Everyman, and how does it add to the development of his screen persona? Mills begins the film in a familiar performance mode. He is the disaffected son, slightly at odds with the law; self-centred and immature, rather than irredeemably criminal. When he first appears, he is every inch the working-class wide boy, sporting a wardrobe that could have been recycled from *The Green Cockatoo*. He lounges against Old Bill's taxi like a prototype spiv; a seedy, 'fly' young man in a ludicrously wide-lapelled, ill-fitting pin-striped suit and a jaunty trilby hat. Mills keeps his elegant hands in his pockets, and talks with cocky certainty about a prospective job managing a funfair up north. Both characterisation and costume verge on a parody of the masculinity portrayed in *The Green Cockatoo*, suggesting the film's desire to redesignate the parameters of toughness. *Old Bill and Son* is constructed to perform a transformation in which the pseudo-American, streetwise tough guy, once the epitome of masculinity, is superseded by the newly virile British Tommy. War effectively 'ups the stakes', revalorising the criteria upon which masculinity is judged, and setting new standards of behaviour. *Old Bill and Son* thus becomes an early example of cinema's contribution to the construction of an approved version or template of the modern military ideal. In the course of its simple narrative, the film takes Mills, so often the troublesome teenager of the 1930s, and turns him into a prototype of the tough, practical man of war that he would more memorably depict in *In Which We Serve* [Fig. 3.1]. *Old Bill and Son* also reinscribes the rules for women. The casting of Rene Ray opposite Mills resurrects the screen partnership of *The Green Cockatoo*, and her character is similarly subject to change. In this case the concept of the hopeless, helpless female needing protection from bad men and big cities is usurped by a more war-friendly, plucky, woman who 'can do'.

By the end of *Old Bill and Son* Mills's screen persona had grown up. He was neither the doomed youth of *Forever England* and *Royal Cavalcade*, nor the semi-delinquent youth of *Britannia of Billingsgate* and *First Offence*. The final shot of the film frames Mills as the absolute symbol of the Tommy. War has made a man of him and its demands have superseded those of the conflict with the father. *Old Bill and Son* undoubtedly draws on Mills's established ability to play working-class characters, and indeed, his cockney accent has noticeably improved since *The Green Cockatoo*. The film also presents a character with no exceptional qualities, and in inhabiting this role, Mills continued to develop the 'ordinariness' that would contribute to his Everyman tag.

I have suggested that the Mills of the Second World War was, in effect, unsinkable – but there is one film that does not conform to this pattern. Anthony Asquith's comedy-thriller *Cottage to Let* (1941) was the first film made by Mills after his discharge from the army, and the only film of the 1940s in which he plays a clear-cut, unambiguous villain. Both the casting of Mills and the public response to this casting indicates the extent to which, even at this early point in the war, Mills was becoming emblematic of an English ideal. Recalling in an interview how relieved he was to find work, Mills also details the unexpected impact of his performance: 'Any job would have done but I loved playing the villain. I was remembered from before the war as a hero and I was attacked by the fans for "letting down the country" and all that stuff' (McFarlane 1997: 413).

Mills and Asquith had previously worked together on *Forever England*, the film that first constructed Mills in patriotic mode, and it is clear that Asquith's decision to cast Mills as the insouciant, carefree, casually heroic Flight Lieutenant George Perry sought to reactivate the latent banal nationalism encoded in that film. Asquith's strategy here is very similar to that of Hitchcock in his deployment of Cary Grant in *Suspicion*. He is playing on audience expectations and assumptions. Graham McCann, Grant's biographer, observes that audiences could not believe 'that a character played by Grant could really turn out to be a murderer' (1997: 140) and, in response to Asquith's spy story, Robert Murphy similarly observes: 'We cannot bring ourselves to believe that a fighter pilot – particularly one played by John Mills – could really be a traitor' (2000: 45).[7]

Fig. 3.1 Thoroughly modern Mills: *Old Bill and Son* (1940). British Film
Institute/London Features International

Unlike Hitchcock, however, Asquith was free to play his 'double bluff', and the
revelation of Mills's treachery is a truly shocking moment in a film that otherwise veers slightly uncertainly between farce and thriller [Fig. 3.2].

The plot of *Cottage to Let* is a straightforward 'who's going to do it', featuring an eccentric inventor, John Barrington (Leslie Banks); his even more

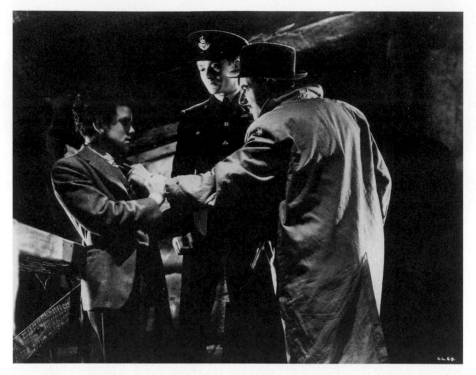

Fig. 3.2 'Letting down the country': Mills shows his dark side in *Cottage to Let*
        (1941). British Film Institute/London Features International

eccentric wife (Jeanne de Casalis); his mild-mannered assistant, Alan Trently
(Michael Wilding); a suspicious stranger, Mr Dimble (Alistair Sim); Mills's
wounded pilot, Perry; his attractive nurse, Helen Barrington (Carla Lehman);
and a cockney evacuee obsessed with the exploits of Sherlock Holmes (George
Cole, in his film début). All the characters behave suspiciously, but technically
the ending should not come as a surprise. The pilot's untrustworthiness is clearly
signposted, and available to be read by those who can see past the emblematic
heroism encoded in Mills's performance and persona. Nonetheless, Asquith
could not have found a better way to bring home the message regarding the
threat of Fifth Column activity. The characters in the film, like the audience in
the cinema, were looking for heroes and following the Battle of Britain there
would have been a cultural desire to read the pilot as saviour not sinner. The
very uniform of the RAF can be seen in this period to encode a heroic 'excess',
affording the wearer an instantaneous aura of dignified glamour. The already
heroic status of the pilot is further intensified by the casting of Mills. If someone
as personable, charming and 'British' as Mills's screen self could be a traitor, then
the nation would truly need to be on its guard.

   Cottage to Let was the first of three films that Mills would make with Asquith during the war, and it provides several early examples of the skill with which the director filmed Mills in particular and his actors in general, although it does not deploy the close-up to the same telling effect as the later *We Dive at Dawn* and *The Way to the Stars*. *Cottage to Let* presents a number of 'baiting' scenes in which the ultra-confident and smoothly plausible Perry plays with the anxious, clumsy Trently, exploiting Trently's romantic desires for Helen Barrington. These scenes usefully illustrate Asquith's ability to make the most of his actors' corporeality. Trently is played by Michael Wilding, a broad-shouldered, handsome actor who is also much taller than Mills. However, the natural authority that might be given to Wilding by his physical attributes is undermined by a combination of heavy glasses that obscure his eyes and a number of pratfalls that encourage the audience to see him as gangly and uncoordinated rather than tall and well-built. In contrast Mills's eyes are as open, clear and trustworthy as ever, and he appears compact and self-assured in uniform. He is bustling and purposeful, moving more easily when wounded than Wilding does when fit. Power and authority are thus seen to reside not in the physical shape of the body, but in the way that body moves and the manner in which it is filmed.[8] Asquith also allows Mills to make good use of what James Naremore has termed 'expressive objects'; that is, props that are manipulated by an actor in order to assist in the emphasis or construction of an emotion. Naremore explains:

> Part of the actor's job . . . is to keep objects under expressive control, letting them become signifiers of feeling. Sometimes the player's dexterity is foregrounded (as when Chaplin does a 'dance' with dinner rolls); but more often it is hardly noticeable, lending emotional resonance to the simplest behaviour. (Naremore 1990: 87)

   Mills is not only skilled at the manipulation of external objects, he is also good at using his hands as subtle but complex signifiers of emotion. This ability would be much more powerfully deployed in his later films for Asquith, but even in *Cottage to Let* there are effective examples. In an early 'baiting' scene in which the confident Perry taunts Trently the nervous 'back-room boy', Mills plays with a spoon and a richly symbolic bowl of cherries that has been specially provided for him by Helen. He turns the spoon round in his hand, gently pushing the cherries around the plate, suggesting the extent to which he is manipulating both Trently and Helen. The camera work and lighting also encourage distrust of the character. The room is dark, lit only by an anglepoise that throws light onto Mills, seated in bed. The potential weakness of this position is turned into strength by camera angles that leave Trently in the dark, entering the room as a supplicant to serve the wounded hero. As Trently blurts out his secrets in an attempt at self-validation, Mills's measured manipulation of his expressive objects acts to imply that Trently is supping with the Devil.

One of Asquith's strengths as a director is his depiction of interiority. His projects are often intimate and their impact is greatly heightened by his detailed attention to the body. In examining Asquith's technique it is useful to draw a comparison with that of David Lean, whose work with Mills will be discussed in Chapters 4 and 7. Lean, famous for the scale of his productions, is a much more expansive director than Asquith. While Asquith focuses on the body of his actors, for Lean the actor is a small part of a much larger visual spectrum – the spectacle or panorama. Mills as Pip in *Great Expectations* is seldom seen in the intimate close-up that we might expect a director to lavish on the central protagonist. Rather he is often a small figure, jostled, bustled, dwarfed by the enormous, sometimes threatening vigour and energy of his surroundings. By contrast, the young Pip (Anthony Wager) is shot far more intimately, especially in his encounters with the convict, Magwitch. This is, perhaps, appropriate to a story concerned with alienation from self, but the focus on Magwitch is also, like the close-ups of Charles Laughton in *Hobson's Choice* (1954), indicative of Lean's fascination with the grotesque. Lean's close-ups emphasise distortion and threaten to rupture the realist mode, whereas Asquith can be seen to use the technique as a mode of depicting emotional truth, of allowing an actor to create a performance that is, in his own words, 'realler than the real thing'.[9] Discussing the relationship between documentary and feature film, Asquith argues that, even in films attempting the documentary recreation of the ordinary, when it comes to the leading characters, an 'actor' is required:

> sometimes without any sacrifice of outward realism his imagination will be so fired by the subject that he will give something more real than the real thing. That is to say he will express more of the man's inner personality, show us more facets of his character, present us, in fact, with a rounder, more living figure. (Asquith 1945: 26)

For Asquith, then, it is indeed the case that 'a good deal of the meaning of the fiction film is borne by its actors and their performances' (Thompson 1978: 55), and in his two critically acclaimed service pictures *We Dive at Dawn* (1943) and *The Way to the Stars* (1945), it is Mills who acts as the linchpin giving substance to an emotionally subdued but newly inclusive national masculinity.

CLOSE ENCOUNTERS: *WE DIVE AT DAWN*

In *We Dive at Dawn* Mills plays Lieutenant Freddie Taylor, captain of the submarine *Sea Tiger*. Superficially, Taylor is an insouciant, self-confident member of the upper middle classes. He has a manservant and a string of female admirers – although none of these women appears on screen due to the rather more pressing demands of war. Yet Mills's Freddie Taylor is not a toff; neither is he the kind of aloof, paternalistic commander portrayed by Coward in *In Which We Serve*. Rather he is, in Andrew Spicer's words, altogether more 'modern and classless':

> Taylor, alert and determined, with his stubbly beard and crew-necked sweater, is ordinary and down-to-earth, almost the same as his men. *The Times*'s reviewer saw him as, 'by no means one of those carelessly heroic captains who can solve all difficulties with a studied flippancy and an order bellowed down the speaking tube. He is a man of nerves, which he can control, but not altogether conceal.' Mills's more naturalistic performance style constructs Taylor as a tough man of action who has absorbed the democratic ordinariness of the People's War. Taylor is a competent, merit-ocratic professional, not a breezy amateur. (Spicer 2001: 10)

Some of this democratic ordinariness must, however, be put down to the par-ticular demands of the submarine service. The press books for the production emphasise its authenticity, and this concern with appearance extended beyond technical detail to a concern with the veracity of crew behaviour. A technical adviser sent from the service was primarily concerned to convey to audiences an appropriate degree of scruffiness: submariners, in their cramped, claustrophobic conditions, are not inclined to stand on ceremony. Nonetheless, Spicer is right to draw attention to the relative classlessness of Mills's performance. Indeed, as I indicated in the introduction, the ability to play across the classes is a key feature of Mills's career and an important determinant in his classification as an Everyman figure.[10]

In *We Dive at Dawn*, however, the class dynamics are shaped as much by con-trast and context as by individual performance. The crew framework presents a composite hero from which four characters emerge: Mills's officer, Freddie Taylor; a cynical Yorkshireman, Leading Seaman Hobson (Eric Portman); a slow-speaking Irishman, Petty Officer Mike Corrigan (Niall MacGinnis), and Reginald Purdell's cockney Chief Petty Officer Dabbs. These four characters provide a range across the ranks, and each has a narrative outside the 'action' story at the centre of the film. Hobson is embittered by a failing marriage, Corrigan is the reluctant bridegroom, uncertain whether he can commit himself to marry the daughter of CPO Dabbs, who himself is involved in a doomed comic attempt to win the attentions of the lovely Gladys. These stories, along with Taylor's abortive string of dates, form a frame narrative that seeks to give substance to the composite body of the crew. The crucial combination, though, is the contrast between Mills and Portman, who together are called upon to embrace as much of the class spectrum as it is possible for two men to do. The film is particularly disingenuous in relation to Portman's character, Hobson, who remains, in class terms, a conveniently loosely-defined signifier. Although he is only a leading seaman, in an early interview with the captain the question is raised as to why he has not 'made more of himself'. He speaks several languages, but it is suggested that he picked these up from 'knocking about' a bit, rather than from a formal education. He has a regional accent, but is not a provincial caricature, a combination which further obfuscates the question of class origin. He begins the film firmly below decks, but he is not part of the working-class community depicted there. Both Portman's performance and the demands of the role set Hobson up as a loner, yet this does not prohibit him from being part of the wider community of the ship. Indeed, by the end of the film he has proved himself so invaluable that he becomes a de facto officer, present on the conning tower for such key scenes as the return to port and the revelation of the mission's success.[11] The ambivalence of Hobson's class position, combined with his emergence from the ranks to take a proactive role in the prosecution of the mission results in the construction of a very flexible locus for audience identification, and this in turn facilitates the construction of a double head for the composite hero. When, as happens at several key junctures, Portman and Mills are framed in semi-close-up, one on either side of the screen, the construction of Spicer's modern meritocracy is complete [Fig. 3.3].

The action narrative of *We Dive at Dawn* is straightforward. The *Sea Tiger*, back from an uneventful tour of duty is almost immediately dispatched to hunt the German battleship *Brandenburg*. As captain and crew struggle to sink the ship, they come under attack and are forced to stage their own sinking in order to escape, without knowing whether they have succeeded in their mission. Short of oil, they refuel during a daring raid on a Danish port before sailing home to the news that they did indeed sink the *Brandenburg*. This fantasy of resurrection, in which a crew literally returns from the dead, is carefully built into the ostentatiously realistic appearance of the film to create an upbeat tale of survival against the odds, but nonetheless *We Dive at Dawn* closes with caution. As another submarine leaves the harbour to continue the fight, the film situates its heroic narrative within the discourse of 'business as usual' that dominated constructions of Britishness during the war years. As the anonymous submarine cuts through the waves, a closing voiceover announces: 'One comes in, another goes out – just like running a ruddy bus service.'

There is nothing remarkable about this story – although a spectator might be forgiven for believing that two films have been inadvertently spliced together, such is the difference in tone between the intense realism of the submarine sequences, and the altogether more fantastical 'boy's own' adventure of the Danish raid. What makes the film significant is Asquith's claustrophobic rendition of life on a submarine and the performances he elicits from his actors. To

Fig. 3.3 Composite heroism: Mills and Eric Portman in *We Dive at Dawn* (1943). British Film Institute/London Features International

establish the other-worldliness of the submarine, Asquith frames the action with the romantic back-stories described above, and he facilitates the shift between the two arenas through three long sequences which feature Mills making the transition from submarine to depot ship. In these extensive panning shots that form a marked contrast to the close-up and semi-close-up used to film the cramped submarine conditions, Mills's character is transformed from careful captain to carefree dilettante and back again. Descent from the submarine conning tower requires care and can be done only slowly. The steps to the depot ship, however, present no such problem and Mills bounds up them with a youthful vigour reminiscent of his roles of the 1930s. And indeed, once aboard he re-encounters his younger self, fixing dates before heading off for a massage to get himself in shape for the rigours of his leave. The beard that acted as a marker both of his maturity and the priorities that obtain beneath the sea, is shaved off, returning him to a much more youthful appearance. When the ship's personnel are recalled, Asquith enacts the sequence in reverse.[12] The jaunty young Mills leaves the depot ship to emerge in the conning tower as the quietly authoritative captain.

Once he is aboard the submarine, however, Mills's performance is built around stillness and sound. Both the camerawork and Mills's central prop, the periscope, work to disrupt familiar patterns of viewing, and this, combined with the absence of incidental or dramatic music, foregrounds the aural as a mode of perception. The submariner has only limited vision. The images brought down by the periscope are unstable and he depends upon the sounds perceived by the hydrophones, and his own knowledge of the sea-sounds that come through the hull. The construction of a constrained and threatened world is in part achieved through a rigorous adherence to the submariner's point of view. Prior to the attack on the Danish port there are very few cuts to the surface and the narrative provides no information regarding the success of the mission or the scale of the danger beyond what can be perceived by the crew. The press book records:

> Complete realism of undersea conditions were [sic] obtained by the per-
> sistence of Asquith in confining all camera movement to the cramped
> space of the submarine's hull. Natural obstacles to the action, such as tor-
> pedoes, bulkhead doors, iron ladders . . . are not removed to facilitate the
> camera viewpoint, but remain in picture, so that from a cinema-goer's
> angle, the impression of being imprisoned under the sea is exceptionally
> real. (BFI collections)

The representation of confinement and the sensory imbalance of the sub-mariner are further augmented by Asquith's use of partial or decentred close-ups. When Mills is away from the periscope, he is shot in such a way as to suggest both his preoccupation and his role as the 'head' of a delicate mechanical 'body'. Asquith situates him to the left or the right of the screen, leaving other activity visible behind him. Mills's gaze in these shots is left without an object. He looks upwards, perhaps at an instrument, perhaps at the invisible but omnipresent sea, perhaps into the middle-distance of preoccupation, but the effect is not unlike a conversation with the blind in its disruption of the eyeline. When he is working at the periscope, the prop itself contributes to the destabilisation of Mills's features, obscuring one eye, and throwing curious patterns of light and shade across his face. In working with this 'expressive object' Mills is as restricted in the gestures available to him as Asquith is with his camera angles, but although he scarcely moves from the periscope, he nonetheless gives a performance of remarkable psychological detail. In an article for *The Cine-Technician*, Asquith recalled the process and impact of the performance:

> He [Mills] had a long solo which consisted of nothing but a string of
> technical orders quite unintelligible to the layman . . . on paper, the

> speech which had not one personal touch in it, looked a very grim prospect for the actor . . . what made it exciting was the imaginative way in which Mills drew the picture of a man whose brain has, so to speak, to be in two places at once. That is to say he has to issue orders which apply to the moment while his mind is already concentrated on the next move. The weight of his thought is never behind the spoken word which is really only the mechanical physical expression of what he had been thinking a moment before. (Asquith 1945: 27)

It is indeed an exemplary sequence. The lights are dimmed and the camera centres on Mills at the periscope. His face is eerily illuminated and the only other visible part of his body is his hands. He is almost completely still apart from tiny facial tics that betray his nervousness: from time to time he slowly bites at his lower lip, or moves his tongue across it in a gesture of concentration. His voice, meanwhile, remains crisp and authoritative, although there is no eye contact with those to whom he issues orders, as his gaze is entirely fixed on the scope. As the periscope sequences extend, a characteristic hand gesture becomes noticeable: a ripple of the fingers, as if to release some of the coiled-spring tension within his body. Suddenly frustration gives an edge to his voice, he snaps, steps back and sighs, quickly running his hand through his hair – a small gesture that seems enormous within the microcosmic scale of the performance. Throughout the chase, Mills's staccato orders into the void are punctuated by the clicking of his fingers. This non-verbal cue for periscope movement accentuates urgency and augments the spectator's sense of watching an other, linguistically differentiated world. Finally, as the *Sea Tiger* closes in on its prey, Asquith raises his camera angle, looking down on a Mills whose stillness now becomes that of a predator ready to pounce.

The close-up of Mills at the periscope has become one of the most familiar film images of Second World War cinema, and his portrayal of Freddie Taylor deservedly won him considerable critical approval [Fig 3.4]. Throughout the film Mills's body language works to convey the complexity of inhabiting the 'idealized masculinity' of the soldier hero (Dawson 1994: 1), and crucial to the success of his performance is the ability to display vulnerability in concert with authority. Indeed, it is this combination of qualities that does so much to make Taylor an integral part of his crew. The evident effort involved in his command is a unifying factor that detracts from his class position without undermining his authority. Vulnerability is a fundamental dimension of screen masculinities, and the depiction of this quality would be equally crucial to Mills's performance in his next film for Anthony Asquith, *The Way to the Stars* (1945).

Fig. 3.4 Close encounters: Mills and expressive object in *We Dive at Dawn* (1943).
British Film Institute/London Features International

THE SURVIVAL OF THE ORDINARY: *THE WAY TO THE STARS*

On first appearance, Mills's new character, Pilot Officer Peter Penrose, bears a
superficial resemblance to his predecessor, Freddie Taylor. In the role of
Penrose, Mills's task is to exhibit emotional vulnerability behind a mask of
appropriately masculine stoicism, to create a hard shell protecting the airman
from feeling the pain of loss. The ability to deny or disguise emotions is a
crucial dimension of traditional patriarchal masculinities. In the words of
Stephen Frosh:

> Rationality and self-control . . . go together as aspects of masculine
> mastery: in both cases, they treat experience as controllable and homoge-
> neous, amenable to domination and to the power of the will. Masculine
> ideology idealises the life of the rational mind, fetishising organised activ-
> ity: moving forward, making progress, thrusting with force into the future,
> untrammelled by emotion, liberated from the confusions of womanly
> feeling, balanced, critical, self-assertive, free. (Frosh 1994: 103)

Unfortunately – or perhaps, fortunately – this is easier said than done, and what most often draws attention to the construction of this protective shell are the cracks in its façade. Freddie Taylor's nervous tics and Shorty Blake's relentless humour all draw attention to the fears, anxieties and desires that have been repressed, but not removed, by the imperatives of heterosexual, patriarchal masculinity. In *The Way to the Stars*, however, the construction and maintenance of this mask is problematised, and we are made to question its validity. Unlike most earlier war pictures with a service context, this film is concerned not with action but with its aftermath, and the logic of its narrative demands that men learn not to be afraid of an emotional dimension that they can neither control nor articulate. As societal prohibitions continue to work against any manifestation of feeling between men (except in situations of extreme danger or extreme alcohol consumption), and as the masculine myth demands that masculinity be absolutely uncontaminated by the feminine, the film in a sense demands the impossible. It celebrates stoicism, understatement and reserve, but it also suggests the price of these qualities. Men must remain men, with firm ego boundaries, but they must also become family men, admitting the unstable element of the feminine into their lives. Behind this paradox lies a problem that would come to prominence in the films of the 1950s: the spectre of redundancy that always haunts the soldier hero in peacetime.

In its desire to problematise survival, *The Way to the Stars* presents a very different approach to the subject of war. Although the film covers the period 1940 to 1944, there are no battle scenes or representations of the enemy in the narrative, and this is indicative of the changing priorities in operation at the time of the film's production. Germany and Nazism, have, in effect, ceased to be the problem. What matters now is reconstruction and the future. This shift in priorities results in a film that gives far more weight and screen time to reaction shots, and scenes recording the impact of sudden death on those left behind. The pace of the film is not the only contrast. The politics of *The Way to the Stars* are very different from those of *We Dive at Dawn*, or indeed of any of the films previously examined. The film was made at the very end of the war as a tribute to Anglo–American cooperation, and as such it also carries a complex series of messages regarding national identity, most of which are conveyed through the juxtaposition of contrasting masculinities.[13] This is a tribute to cooperation that simultaneously encodes a number of attempts to reassert a specifically British mode of masculinity in the face of overwhelming heroic colonisation by the Americans.

The film tells the story of two bomber squadrons, one British and one American, based at the richly symbolic Halfpenny Field, a site so old it featured in the Domesday Book. Opening with a shot of a battered sign declaring 'Royal Air Force Station', the camera pans across a landscape of barbed wire and derelict buildings before the voice of the narrator introduces us to the control tower and crew room. A flock of sheep moves across the screen, reasserting the rural identity that was extensively deployed as a symbol of Britain during the war, and claiming the pastoral as a norm to which the nation has reverted. This sequence introduces a flashback to 1940 when Peter Penrose stands on the threshold of a new life. Framed in the doorway of a transport plane, he scans his new environment before leaping down with eager enthusiasm. In Penrose's case, *The Way to the Stars* revisits the coming of age narrative, beginning as it does with his effective 'emasculation'. Arriving at Halfpenny Field as a '15 hour sprog', he is immediately established as the epitome of the ordinary. The man who will be his mentor, David Archdale (Michael Redgrave), is underwhelmed to discover that Penrose has passed out only 'average' from his class, and when introduced to the commanding officer (Trevor Howard), it is quickly established that he has no useful connections. Penrose does not belong in this world, and his feeble attempt to assert himself by talking up his flying experience ends in humiliation. By making the character a secondary school teacher the film aims to construct a figure at the epicentre of middle-class values, a model modern citizen and an ideal representative of a nation whose obsession with the Beveridge Report had forced the government to recognise social reconstruction rather than restoration as a positive war aim.[14] The pilot figure that had carried such potency in the early years of the war is now consciously demythologised, not least by the decision to base the film around a bomber, rather than a fighter, squadron. The casual heroics of the 'fighter chaps', while admirable, have no place in a bomber, where every pilot is responsible not just for himself, but for his crew. The emphasis, then, is upon the squadron as a team or unit, and here, as would be the case in his next film, *Great Expectations*, Mills's role is to act as a pivot – the quiet centre around which the more obviously dramatic narratives rotate.

Part of the achievement of *The Way to the Stars* lies in its hybridity. It successfully marries a narrative of war with what might be termed a 'woman's picture'. Its other linchpin character is 'Toddie' (Rosamund John), proprietor of the Golden Lion at Shepley, and wife of David Archdale.[15] Toddie acts as a counterpoint to Penrose, in that she is illustrative of the emotional journey demanded of women in wartime, and as such is obliged to survive the death of the two men she loves: her husband and the American pilot, Johnny Hollis (Douglass Montgomery). Archdale and Hollis are doomed romantic heroes, and their deaths form emotional peaks within the film, but the narrative emphasis is concerned as much with moving on as it is with mourning these monumental figures. And they are, quite literally, monumental. Redgrave, in particular, towers over Mills. When they first shake hands it could be a meeting between father and son, while the 'dressing-down scene' that follows Penrose's brief attack of bravado resembles nothing so much as an encounter in the headmaster's study. Asquith makes no effort to disguise the disjuncture, and indeed, deploys Mills's lack of height to comic effect later in the film. Inevitably, then, Penrose–Mills looks up to Archdale–Redgrave, the latter becoming a father figure and friend to the infant pilot.

Being pitched at a dual constituency, this film, more than any of those previously discussed, seeks to represent and to a certain extent interrogate gender relations. In so doing it inevitably reveals much about the ideological preoccupations shaping British society at the end of the war. Jeffrey Richards records that: 'the critics almost universally praised the film for its realism, Englishness and emotional restraint. In a sense, they were equating all three' (1997: 88). This cuts to the heart of the film's depiction of national identity, but it is also crucial to an understanding of its construction of masculinity. Within *The Way to the Stars* a fundamentally homosocial community is shown. Only exceptional men such as Archdale and Hollis actually seem capable of forming relationships with women. The other airmen remain in the schoolroom, and their banter, along with Penrose's attempts to negotiate his relationship with the shy and browbeaten Iris, acknowledge the extent to which English masculinity is an inarticulate mode of being.[16] While understatement and emotional restraint were considered to be key national characteristics, *The Way to the Stars* suggests that for English men this extended to an absolute inability to express themselves directly, particularly when it came to grief. Within the film David Archdale is credited with the composition of John Pudney's famous poems, 'Missing' and 'For Johnny'. The first of these is recited by Archdale in the privacy of Toddie's kitchen, a safe, private space where masculine defences can briefly be lowered. Archdale has just lost his close friend Squadron Leader Carter, but the grief he feels cannot be directly expressed. Instead he recites the poem, explaining afterwards: 'I try and say things I feel that way sometimes. Sort of hobby.' Archdale's poetry is a secret – indeed, he stresses to Toddie that nobody must know about this strange habit – and in describing his writing as a hobby, he connects this reticence to the particular form of British masculinity. In 'The Lion and the Unicorn', George Orwell observed that the English are a nation indifferent to the arts, but addicted to hobbies, obsessed with an individual's right to pursue whatever eccentric pastime he might choose within the privacy of home or spare time (Orwell 1970: 77–8). Emotionally, then, Archdale effects a double displacement that is, according to Orwell, typical of national cultural attitudes. His feelings are only legitimised – or rendered safe – through translation into verse, while the artistic activity of writing verse is itself only legitimised by its redesignation as a hobby.

Archdale, however, is far ahead of his compatriots. He can find words, even if he cannot openly acknowledge them. None of the other British male characters in the film can find words to express their grief, while women, it is tacitly suggested, do not need to. The film mobilises a traditional binary opposition through which women are constructed as essentially pragmatic, while men are the dreamers and idealists. The film encodes the ideologically potent suggestion that women are better at letting go of the past because their 'real' role is to guarantee the future through the production of the next generation.[17] This is not to suggest that Toddie is not grieving, rather the film implies that she is able to accept her loss and move on, a process symbolised by her careful placing of Archdale's lighter and poem in a discreet bureau drawer. She has become the embodiment of Archdale–Pudney's poem, 'For Johnny', her actions answering the verse's injunction to 'keep your head/ and see his children fed' (Gardner 1999: 77). As the film progresses, Pudney's poem becomes something of a mantra, mobilised to facilitate the impossible expression of male grief. Toddie asks a deeply uncomfortable Penrose to read the poem, and later gives it to the Americans Hollis and Friselli as a mechanism to facilitate the exchange of emotional pain.

In *The Way to the Stars*, women – as metonymic representations of an ideologically validated heterosexual family life – force emotional engagement upon men who feel safer staying within the protective shell of playground cameraderie and homosocial banter. In his relationship with Iris, Penrose can be seen to be emerging from this arrested development and seeking to emulate his 'father's' emotionally mature relationship with Toddie. The film comically deploys a conspicuous contrast between Archdale's passionate embrace of Toddie, and the chaste, childlike peck swiftly exchanged between Iris and Peter. However, Peter's emotional development is brought to an abrupt halt by the death of Archdale, after which he concludes that an airman has no right to marry or have children. At this point Penrose goes into emotional cold storage, erecting rigid boundaries in order to maintain the public façade of masculinity. He had planned to propose to Iris, but the pain of losing his 'particular pal' prevents him from making the transition from a secure, known homosocial economy to the unknown parameters of the heteronormative ideal. This is a crisis which the film insists Penrose must resolve: it is as much his duty to regenerate as to defend the nation. The emphasis on family structures within the film is indicative of its postwar preoccupations, and these values shape the scenario of *The Way to the Stars*, irrespective of the period of the war actually being represented.[18]

The death of Archdale is one of the key emotional events of the narrative, but perhaps appropriately for a film so focused upon emotional restraint, it receives no verbal articulation. Rather the death is conveyed through the use of an expressive object. In the opening scenes of the film we learn that Archdale has a talisman, a lighter that he is loath to fly without [Fig. 3.5]. Before his final, fatal mission, this lucky charm cannot be found. As usual, we see nothing of

Fig. 3.5 Objects speak louder than words: Mills and Michael Redgrave in *The Way to the Stars* (1945). British Film Institute/London Features International

the mission. Instead there is a montage showing the faces of those on the ground as they listen to the sound of the squadron departing and returning. The camera then cuts to the crew room, focusing on the door as a subdued group of flyers walks through it in total silence. There is no incidental music, and the silence continues as the camera slowly moves through them to focus in close-up on a box of matches on the chimney-breast. When the box is in the centre of the frame, a hand reaches out for it, pauses, then discovers Archdale's lighter, hidden behind a piece of paper. The close-up stays on the hand as it picks up the lighter and brings it to meet the other hand. The hands are delicate, and they turn the object with contemplative care. Slowly the lighter is raised to reveal not Redgrave's face, but Mills's. His hair is tousled, he has smuts on his forehead and a five-o'clock shadow. An unlit cigarette hangs from his lip. The camera position does not change as, with the minimum of movement, the cigarette is lit and the flame blown out. Taking the cigarette out of his mouth, Mills looks up for the first time. His mouth is tight, his brows slightly furrowed. Smoke rises past his face as the camera pans back to reveal him putting the lighter in his pocket, before giving an almost imperceptible shake of the head and walking out of the frame, which holds for a moment on the empty room. Thus, without words or music, Archdale's death is announced.[19]

This is an extremely powerful scene that retains its emotional impact after nearly sixty years, and it is immediately followed by a further intense encounter in which we watch Mills build up the defences of traditional masculinity. As friends come to commiserate with Penrose, we watch him move from the absolute stillness of abstracted grief to the briskness of denial, culminating in repressed anger as he recounts the unprofessional mistake that killed Archdale. The voice of the aggrieved son can be heard protesting about the betrayal represented by the father's death when Penrose observes: 'He should have evaded after dropping his bombs . . . used to tell us to do it often enough.' The hero, then, does not have a heroic death, and Archdale, for all his admirable qualities, is reconstructed as a figure of the past. From his excessive moustache to his slangy talk of 'ruddy near pranging the kite', he is part of the myth that must be laid to rest. Mills, his child, survives as a less flamboyant model of the hero who establishes his masculine credentials through the rejection of excess, be that in words or in manners. Mills's ordinary modern hero anticipates an as yet unrealised age of the common man, but the resolutely middle-class milieu of the film ensures the parameters of this transformation are, to say the least, limited. However, the process of cementing this new mode of national masculinity is not primarily achieved through comparing types of English hero. Rather it emerges from the culture-clash scenario that shapes the second half of the film. In 1942, the USAAF takes over Halfpenny Field, initiating a narrative of bemusement and conflict that gradually mutates into an idealised image of international tolerance, cooperation and mutual benefit.

Initially, though, the emphasis is on difference. The transitional scene takes place in the room once shared by Penrose and Archdale, and although it is very definitely played for comedy, there are ominous, almost uncanny implications in the depiction of Johnny Hollis. Hollis is the first American we meet and an ideal ambassador. Polite, friendly and whistling cheerfully, he looks around the room much as Penrose did two years previously. However, his enthusiasm for Archdale's old German 'Lavabo' sign links him more closely with the doomed hero and, although the spectator will not realise it until later, the conversation that develops includes an exact premonition of his death. For this scene Mills is equipped with a squash racquet and dressed in a simple white shirt and dark trousers: the English sporting amateur incarnate. He and Hollis make peaceful first contact, but this tranquillity is short-lived, and the old order of things is radically disrupted by the arrival of Joe Friselli (Bonar Colleano, Jnr). Friselli is the epitome of brash, over-confident America, and he strides into the room loudly declaiming his inability to comprehend the

Fig. 3.6 The sporting little nation: *The Way to the Stars* (1945). British Film Institute/London Features International

British [Fig. 3.6]. Mills, who is packing to leave the room, stands quietly in the margins, looks Colleano quizzically up and down, and says nothing until he is introduced by Hollis. Throughout the scene he is polite and reticent, giving only tiny amounts of information and allowing Colleano's character to talk himself into an embarrassing misapprehension. In terms of both visual impact and dialogue, national difference is embodied by the two actors. Colleano is taller. He physically dominates the room and takes up a confident territorial pose with one foot on Mills's bed. Each time Mills needs to get from the chest of drawers to his suitcase he must comically circumnavigate the expansive Colleano, who talks as much with his hands as with his voice. Colleano, meanwhile, is scarcely aware of Mills, having dismissed him as non-operational. The painful truth of this in political terms is, however, diffused by the pantomime quality of the sequence that instead invites the audience to share the joke of the inexperienced Friselli's patronising behaviour towards a man who has completed forty-three missions. Colleano punctuates his mono-logue with energetic hand gestures that force Mills to come to an abrupt halt each time he tries to pass by. Brought to a dead stop, Mills stares down at the flailing hand or pointing finger as if it were a creature with a life of its own. Again he says nothing to indicate that the American is in the way, or that he is talking rubbish. Instead he simply scratches his cheek and waits his opportunity to nip past. The encounter avoids confrontation by the combination of Colleano's obliviousness and Mills's small stature – his gaze is fixed on the American's hands rather than his face – and the skirmish ends in a British 'victory'. As Colleano offers Mills a ride in his aeroplane, Mills reaches down the flying jacket that symbolises his considerable experience and leaves the room with a jaunty put-down.

Although softened by comedy, the defensiveness and resentment of the British position is clear. The discovery of Penrose's credentials undercuts the over-confidence of the parvenu Americans and challenges their assumption of national superiority. Here Mills, as an emblem of Britishness, stands for a nation of long experience and history in contrast to the 'newness' of America. Britain has already been there and done that, and it does not need to boast of its achievement. Naturally, as the film progresses, the rude and irritating Friselli is revealed to have a heart of gold. Indeed, he is instrumental in freeing Iris from the chains of her hideous aunt. However, his attempt to woo the English rose ends with another example of British self-validation. As Iris dances with the exuberant American, she looks up and sees Penrose, in full flying kit, framed in the doorway. Reminded of her real love and loyalty, she runs from the dance floor, reassuring the audience that British women can see beyond good times and silk stockings, and the dutiful British man will be suitably rewarded for his wartime efforts.

Yet these low-key attempts to raise the profile of a British nation losing power and authority to its American allies are set within an overall context that celebrates the sacrifices made by the Americans. The principles of community and consensus promoted in earlier realist war films are here expanded to suggest that a shared cause can bring not just different classes, but different nations together.[20] By the end of the film, British masculinity has accomplished a tiny evolution. It has come to tolerate, even to embrace, the otherness of America. In the process, however, it has also consolidated its self-definition as stoical and reticent, and has constructed a new mode of hero who, while notably more demotic, also represents a regression in terms of emotional articulacy. Penrose is no more adept at conveying his happiness than he was at speaking his grief. In spite of being told what to say by Toddie, when he attempts to propose to Iris he proves himself absolutely incapable of getting the words out, asking her instead whether she would be willing to 'take on forty-nine and ninepence a day', that being the pay of a squadron leader with a marriage allowance. In his magnificent inarticulacy, his diffident heroism and his unproblematic ordinariness, Penrose is Everyman as the middle classes might desire him. He is just sufficiently modern to give hope for the future, and more than traditional enough to reassure those who nonetheless fear change. Like Shorty Blake and Freddie Taylor he puts duty above everything, suggesting that Everyman is ultimately indistinguishable from the good soldier, a figure for whom the demands of the public sphere will always override personal considerations. However, the extent to which Mills's screen persona had come to embody reassurance and stability is most clearly manifest not in such visions of conformity as Peter Penrose, but rather in a much less well-known and rather more transgressive performance from 1945. War may have papered over the cracks that divided Britain into the two nations of the rich and the poor, but the division had not gone away, nor had the fundamentally different priorities attendant upon such a divide. In Sidney Gilliat's *Waterloo Road* (1945), these conflicting demands resurface and are ultimately contained only by the elasticity and accumulated trustworthiness of Mills's screen persona.

EVERYMAN FOR HIMSELF: MILLS IN *WATERLOO ROAD*

Waterloo Road (1945), like *The Way to the Stars*, is a war film about home, and like *The Way to the Stars* it constructs women as progenitors of a new postwar society. It also pre-empts Asquith's film in depicting the British male hero as woefully inarticulate, but this is where the similarities end. Where duty dominates the middle-class milieu of Asquith's airforce picture, Gilliat's study of a working-class soldier, his wife and her admirer is far more concerned with desire. The result is a film that negotiates not only the transgressive potential of female sexuality, but also the disobedience of the subordinate soldier, and in so doing it celebrates the re-emergence, in a 'realist' context, of the individual hero.

Although condemned by association with the 'fairytale' world of Hollywood, the individual hero did not go away in wartime. Rather, the type co-existed with the more respectable group hero of realist war narrative, providing illicit pleasure through the avoidance of social responsibility. In the early 1940s audiences were hungry for narratives that endorsed their experience of war, but this appetite declined as the conflict progressed, and a degree of war-weariness made the fantastical escapism of costume melodrama seem ever more appealing. This transition is evident in the massive popular success of Gainsborough studios's costume drama cycle. Films such as *The Man in Grey* (1943), *Madonna of the Seven Moons* (1944) and *The Wicked Lady* (1945) were loathed by the critics, but loved by audiences who turned up in their droves to see transgressive desires writ large across the screen.[21] Sue Harper argues that some of the potency of these films resided in the contradictions 'between the verbal level of the script and the non-verbal discourses of decor and costume'

(1994: 119). At the levels of both production and consumption, these films provided a vital outlet for a sensibility at odds with wartime propaganda:

> Gainsborough provided a site for a carefully costed expressionism whose practitioners had been unhappy working in the theatre or other studios because of the dominance of a realist orthodoxy; it was through this visual expressionism that the audience's fears or desires could be rehearsed. (Harper 1994: 119)

Waterloo Road was also a product of Gainsborough studios, but visually it conforms entirely to the parameters of realist representation.[22] However, the ambiguity that permeates the film nonetheless arises from a conflict between documentary and escapism. Although frequently cited as a film operating within a critically approved realist framework, the stories it tells repeatedly resist the hegemonic narratives of duty and self-sacrifice. Andrew Higson argues that one of the functions of wartime propaganda was to ensure that every citizen understood the importance of doing his or her duty, and cinema had a role to play in 'securing the consent of private citizens to the national cause' (1995: 213). This should be achieved, he continues, 'by demonstrating the irresponsibility of holding private, and particularly romantic, interests above the national interest' (p. 213). This is something that *Waterloo Road* singularly fails to do. Instead it performs something of a 'Jekyll and Hyde' transformation on the idealised Everyman at the centre of group heroics, causing him to abandon public duty in favour of heroic self-assertion within the private sphere.

On its release in January 1945, *Waterloo Road* achieved the rare double of being a critical and box-office success. The critics called it 'grown-up', 'unpretentious but accomplished' (*Daily Mail*, press book (BFI collections)) and 'a tough, exciting little story, told with sympathy and humour' (*Daily Telegraph* 15 January 1945). Like many films of the Second World War it is a narrative of reassurance, of justice and just deserts, but its focus is on the 'enemy within' rather than the external forces of evil represented by Nazism. However, it is also a 'late war' film, and as such is no longer concerned with warning against the perils of fifth-column incursion. Instead, *Waterloo Road* categorises the enemy within as the spiv, a figure whose power lies in the illicit temptations of the black market, which by 1945 was seen as a far more enticing proposition to a war-weary nation than any political ideology. But the narrative is also about gender trouble, and begins, like all good patriarchal stories, with the temptation of Eve. Here the serpent assumes the guise of Ted Purvis (Stewart Granger), an ex-boxer turned opportunist racketeer, who tempts the innocent Tillie Colter (Joy Shelton) with the forbidden fruits of luxury and a good time, while her soldier husband, Jim (John Mills), is away at war. The story hovers between comedy and melodrama, emerging as a hybrid that might be described as a carnivalesque comfort blanket.[23] Jim Colter goes AWOL, evading the military police in a series of comic chases, before eventually confronting Ted Purvis and fighting him for possession of the home territory of his wife. The film ends with one of the most celebrated fight scenes in British cinema, after which Colter dutifully returns to his regular job of fighting the Germans, having paused just long enough to lay the seeds of future regeneration in the shape of Baby Jim junior.[24]

Waterloo Road is not a complicated story, and its success in pleasing both middle-class critics and working-class audiences is probably attributable to its marriage of fantasy and realism. The depiction of recognisably ordinary lives on the screen is combined with a splendid piece of film tinsel in which John Mills gets to act out and resolve the anxious fantasies of every frustrated serviceman cut off from home and family. On the surface, then, this is a straightforward homosocial competition between good soldier and bad spiv for possession of the culturally valuable female. Yet there remains a deep dichotomy within the film. For a wartime narrative of reassurance, *Waterloo Road* is overwhelmingly and surprisingly concerned with transgressive desires, a number of which it acts out for the pleasure of the audience. In a succinct and perceptive analysis of the film, Tony Williams has argued that *Waterloo Road* 'raises the spectre of sexual desire only to expel it from the narrative' (2000: 83). However, sexual transgression is only one dimension of the dangerous topsy-turveydom mobilised by the narrative. As Sue Harper's reading of the Gainsborough melodramas suggests, a film's impact can never be confined to the ideology of its resolutions. Events within the film, its patterns of visual representation and verbal discourse all combine to present a very different set of possibilities from those valorised by the hegemonic morality of the conclusion.[25] The Pandora's box opened by *Waterloo Road* can thus be seen to embrace the evasion and defiance of authority in the chase sequences, the vicarious satisfaction of watching violent confrontations in the fight scenes, and, in the relationship between Tillie and Ted Purvis, the indulgence of prohibited desires.[26] Arguably, Tillie's desire is rendered safe by its context. A flashback sequence establishes that her unhappiness derives from her cautious husband's refusal to give her a baby before going off to war. A woman without a baby, the narrative suggests, constitutes a social problem – but, thankfully, it is a problem with an easy solution! However, although the back-story works to close down the transgressive potential of Tillie's desire, visually the film pushes on regardless. Tillie does not finally change her mind about Ted until after she has given the audience the pleasure of a substantial screen kiss, and for some spectators, this was no small pleasure. Andrew Spicer quotes one of Granger's female fans: 'When Stewart Granger is kissing the heroine (in any film he has been in), I experience a real thrill . . . If only that could happen to you, something inside me seems to say' (Spicer 2001: 13).

Waterloo Road is thus much closer to a Gainsborough melodrama than it might at first appear. This is a film about desire as much as duty. Id takes over from superego, and for the space of eighty minutes everybody follows their desires and everybody desires what is taboo; be it a supposedly unobtainable married woman, the thrill of adultery, or taking 'French leave'.[27] Given this proximity, and the fact that Gainsborough melodramas were generally greeted with a substantial degree of critical disdain, it seems odd that the transgressions of *Waterloo Road* should have met with such critical sympathy. A possible answer to this enigma lies in the film's eminently forgettable frame narrative.[28] The story of the Colters is contained within a flashback provided by the film's only middle-class character, Dr Montgomery (Alastair Sim). Sim's grouchy, absent-minded and irreverent pseudo-philosopher has plenty of comic elements, but the film's press book makes it clear that this character is meant to be taken seriously, concluding its summary of the plot with the following homily:

> The wise old doctor realises that Jim and Tillie have found a solution of their troubles in the child and hopes that other young couples will learn to know that amidst the uncertainty of war family life is still strong . . .

Judging from responses to the film cited in J. P. Mayer's survey of *Picturegoer* readers, it seems more likely that most young couples switched off after the fight, and emerged from the film with either a renewed conviction of Stewart Granger's desirability, irrespective of role, or with the consoling fiction of the underdog's superiority (a message physically encoded within the body of John Mills). However, the frame narrative is important, as is the class status of Dr Montgomery. As almost the only representative of traditional structures of authority within a film about working-class characters taking the law into their own hands, Dr Montgomery acts to reassure the other half of the cinema-going public: the middle classes. In his opening voice-over he reminds spectators that people were under enormous strain. His endorsement of the Colters as a family gives middle-class approval to the potentially destabilising rebellion symbolised by Jim's running away to home. Indeed Montgomery effectively orchestrates Jim's revenge – getting him to do the dirty work of punching the man that he, as a representative of the law-abiding citizenry, would like to see punished.[29] He tells Jim where to go to find Purvis, and in advising him on Ted's susceptibility to an upper cut, effectively gives Jim the weapon with which to defeat him.[30]

The film is walking a tightrope in its presentation of loyalty and disloyalty and the familiar face of Sim is one of the techniques it uses to counterbalance the presentation of transgression. The other key technique is the casting of John Mills as the soldier who goes AWOL. Barry King's observation that an actor 'always pre-signifies meaning' (1985: 37) is particularly relevant here: by the time of *Waterloo Road*'s production Mills was redolent with emblematically national characteristics. The ability to portray loyalty and devotion to duty, established as far back as 1935 in *Forever England*, and developed in *In Which We Serve* and *We Dive at Dawn*, is deployed in *Waterloo Road* as an absent presence. The audience associates Mills's screen persona with reliability and trustworthiness, even when he plays a character who patently does not behave in a reliable manner. Consequently, when Mills as Colter gives his word that he will go back to camp as soon as he has sorted out his problems, the audience believes him, even if the officer he is addressing does not. In *Waterloo Road* Mills's performance mobilises all those characteristics that had earned him critical plaudits in his earlier war films: he oozes an inarticulate integrity, a gritty desire not to burden others with his problems and a drive to get the job done, whether it be cleaning up the home front or the Germans.

The complexities introduced by the screen persona of Mills are paralleled by the resonances carried by the body of Stewart Granger. Physically, the two stars could not be more dissimilar [Fig. 3.7]. Granger was a significant heart-throb in the process of rising to stardom through the careful management of

Fig. 3.7 Fighting for the postwar nation: Mills and Stewart Granger in *Waterloo Road* (1945). British Film Institute/London Features International

Gainsborough studios (Richards 1997: 112), and here his reputation in costume drama is deployed and undermined to suggest a sensibility gone to seed. He embodies decadence and corruption. The tall, athletic, broad-shouldered Granger sports a costume designed to highlight both his physique, and his essential untrustworthiness. His wide-lapelled suit is an affront to utility design, while his loud bow tie appears similarly dissonant – an almost feminine affectation – amongst the grey conformity of wartime life.[31] By contrast, Mills's Jim Colter is almost never seen out of uniform, and his uniform, as a private soldier, is as plain as they come. His clothing here is functional and symbolic of duty. For Granger's character, however, image and appearance are crucial to his opportunist business, and an integral component of his narcissistic exhibitionism. Throughout the film Ted is associated with mirrors – a warning to the audience that Tillie is nothing more than a vanity project for Ted's self-worship and thus has little to gain from a relationship with him. His pleasure comes from knowing that Tillie, and others, are looking at him, and his desire to 'have' Tillie resides solely in the perception that she is 'hard to get', and that her possession would increase his standing as a competitive male.

Waterloo Road thus returns us to John O. Thompson's contention that 'a good deal of the meaning of the fiction film is borne by its actors and their performances' (1978: 55), and on these terms the film becomes a site of conflict. While the frame narrative works to close down the transgressive potential of the film, this potential is immediately reopened by its visual dynamics. Granger is a heart-throb actor, and although Mills may get the girl, he does not get a love scene like Granger. Yet the conflicting sites of desire are not the only ambiguities opened up by the film. For all the protestations of 'wise old' Dr Montgomery, it is hard to believe that the future will belong to the Colters. At a series of key points in the film, the *mise-en-scène* tells a story quite different from the ostensible narrative of the soldier's quest. In the opening scene of Dr Montgomery's flashback we see Ted Purvis watching Tillie Colter in his shaving mirror. But just as Tillie is unaware of Purvis's reflected gaze, so Purvis is unaware that he is being watched by Montgomery. The camera does not linger on the disapproving gaze, but it is enough to indicate the antipathy not so much between the characters as between what they represent. This initial impression is confirmed by events at the centre of the film. The mid-section of the narrative is comprised of cuts between Jim's pursuit of Ted and Ted's seduction of Tillie. Throughout these scenes Jim has little or nothing to say. He is the archetypal, inarticulate working-class male, the man of few words who gets the job done. When he is taunted at the Lucky Star, Ted's amusement arcade, his frustration spills over, suggesting that he can only speak with his fists.[32] He is quick-witted and tough, but his skill is in his hands, and his lack of words taps into a long-held cultural distrust of the man who speaks too much. The virtuous working classes are silent.

Those who talk too much have ideas above their station, as is demonstrated by Ted Purvis. His loquaciousness stands in marked contrast to Colter's difficulty with words (a difficulty shared by Tillie in the flashback to their honeymoon), and forms an uneasy parallel with Montgomery's verbosity. In a telling juxtaposition of scenes, Ted talks Tillie into doing the exact opposite of what she had wanted to do, just after the film has shown Dr Montgomery's stream of plausible rhetoric deflecting attention from Colter by bamboozling a rather dim policeman.

Thus in *Waterloo Road* only two characters have any significant linguistic power – Dr Montgomery and Ted Purvis – and the film is as much an account of their battle as it is of Jim Colter's. In a few key scenes, Montgomery identifies Purvis as a threat to the status quo and, having identified his enemy, in Jim Colter he finds the weapon to defeat him.[33] While the surface text presents the apolitical narrative of two men fighting over a girl, the encoded text that emerges from the margins is a conflict between middle-class hegemony and subcultural transgression, a conflict for control and dominance of the community. Commentators have rightly observed the prescience of the film in its portrayal of the spiv (Murphy 1989: 149) but the film is also prescient in its depiction of the degree of confusion and disempowerment that awaits the archetypal British hero in the postwar years. Throughout the film, the Colters have been infantilised – described as 'good kids', doing their best – and while their lack of power might situate them as Mr and Mrs Everyman, it also suggests that Everyman still needs the watchful eye of a paternalistic government. The long-repressed desires unleashed within *Waterloo Road* thus act as a smokescreen behind which those in power before the war attempt to control the postwar succession; a conclusion that suggests that while wartime cinema was happy to depict consensus, it was reluctant to envisage the long-term consequences of wartime change.

It is hard not to see a reactionary dimension in the contradictory messages of *Waterloo Road*. The film constructs the working-class man as hero only to undermine his authority and render him the silent cypher of established structures of power. This, along with the remorselessly middle-class preoccupations of *The Way to the Stars* suggests that already in 1945, elements of British film culture were demonstrating a conservatism at odds with the political climate of the nation. But it is nonetheless the case that *Waterloo Road* makes a hero out of a disloyal working-class subject, and within such a framework, the Everyman ideal inevitably emerges as a more ambiguous construction. Mills is the actor most commonly associated with the Everyman ideal (Richards 1997: 131; Spicer 2001: 27; Macnab 2000: 103), but even within his supposedly definitive performances, there remains a considerable structural incoherence within the type. While the upper-middle and middle-class characters he portrayed were undoubtedly rendered more ordinary and accessible by his benchmark performances, it is not clear whether Everyman status was ever able fully to embrace the working-class hero. Mills had the ability to perform working-class masculinities, but the contexts in which these perfomances took place made the working-class hero endearing rather than empowered. Even Jim Colter's self-assertion is framed within a legitimising paternalism that seeks to neutralise the potentially disturbing subtexts of the film. Nonetheless, in representational terms, the deployment of Mills in *Waterloo Road* entails risk as well as reassurance. At the same time that his screen persona works to render Colter's transgressions safe, the film's narrative sows the seeds of doubt, undermining the spectator's faith in the model of duty embodied by the actor. Mills's performance as Jim Colter thus destabilises his wider cultural status as Everyman by suggesting that every man has his limits. Jim Colter's disobedience suggests that, given enough time and sufficiently *personal* motivation, even Shorty Blake might abscond from the navy. The Everyman construct seeks to homogenise British masculinity. It claims that all classes have equal investment in an equally rewarding national family, and it does this by depicting the ordinariness of the top and the trustworthiness of the bottom in a model where everyone's priorities are the same. Such a fantasy could only cohere in wartime and, by 1945, the joins were starting to show. The eruption of the personal into the narrative of war thus becomes a questioning of consensus and authority, and not least of *Waterloo Road*'s potential to disturb lies in its suggestion that the seeds of rebellion and discontent were present even within the national body of John Mills.

Waterloo Road leaves much unresolved, particularly in its suggestion that community is limited, and ultimately Everyman must look after himself. On one point, however, the film is emphatic. In the early and middle years of the war, British cinema struggled to suggest that women could be Everymen too. Films such as *The Gentle Sex* (1943) and *Millions Like Us* (1943) worked to undermine the traditional association of women with the inward and domestic through their depictions of very public, female versions of the group hero. In the new era of Everyman for himself such ideas were firmly forgotten, and Everyman became, once again, a mono-gendered construct. Tillie Colter's future horizons were clearly designated as the kitchen sink and the pram, but Jim Colter's fate was less clear. The 1950s would see the breakdown of consensus, and cinema would be crowded with narratives of readjustment and masculine crisis. But first would come a period of national renegotiation, in which Britain, and her cinema, struggled to construct a viable new sense of self in radically straightened circumstances. Mills's roles in the late 1940s give a clear indication of the near impossibility of such a task.

Notes

1. Jeffrey Richards usefully distinguishes between 'individuality (characteristic difference)' and 'individualism (a philosophy of the self)', and suggests that wartime filmmaking privileged a 'collectivity of heroism' built on tolerance and cooperation (1997: 89). Individuality also makes space for the cherished concept of eccentricity in definitions of the national character.

2. It should be noted, however, that the diversity of the composite hero had its limits. Representatives of the Empire were conspicuous by their absence, and racial diversity was confined to the ethnic groupings of Britain and Ireland. Americans appeared, but this is consonant with a desire to emphasise the imperilled status of Britain. In the construction of an effective propagandist vision of Britain the emphasis had to be on the opposition between homely underdog and tyrannical Reich, with the result that the British Empire was overlooked in favour of the 'English' nation.

3. This concept is obviously not confined to the work of Mills. The group hero was fundamental to the 'story-documentary' that developed in the late 1930s and reached its apogee in such wartime films as *Target for Tonight* and *Western Approaches*, films which, according to Higson, combined the public gaze of montage with the private point-of-view perspective to explore 'the place of the individual within the nation' (1995: 208). The influence of the documentary idea on feature film production is discussed by Higson (pp. 186–212), while Robert Murphy illustrates the construction of the group hero in his account of *One of our Aircraft is Missing* (2000: 93–4). The composite hero is a key feature of such diverse and critically acclaimed films as Charles Frend's *The Foreman Went to France* (1942), Leslie Howard's *The Gentle Sex* (1943), and Carol Reed's *The Way Ahead* (1944), to name but a few. All of these works, however, can be seen to fall on the realism side of Michael Balcon's infamous distinction between 'realism and tinsel', and it is in the tinsel tradition of more melodramatic story-telling that individual heroes and heroines continued to thrive.

4. According to Mills, this was harder than might have been expected, with neither Navy nor Rifle Brigade showing any desire to recruit an actor of the advanced age of 31 (Mills 2001: 224–5). It is worth noting, however, that although Mills had had little significant film work since the end of his unsatisfactory contract with Gaumont British (1937), in joining up he was abandoning a burgeoning stage career.

5. Mills's autobiography is misleading with regard to this film. Mills remembers it as one of a group of government films he made in 1941, but it was clearly constructed at an earlier point in the war, as is evident from its release date, thematic preoccupations, and style.

6. There are elements here of the debate between Spud and Candy enshrined in Powell and Pressburger's infinitely more subtle *The Life and Death of Colonel Blimp* (1942). Overall, *Old Bill and Son* is torn between the modern and the nostalgic, praising the practicalities of the new army, while still seeking to endorse the ongoing value of the sporting individual.

7. McCann's observations are quoted in full in Chapter 1.

8. In a three-way scene with Helen, the camera finds its line on Mills and Carla Lehman, who are very similar in height, pushing the taller Wilding out of the frame.

9. Asquith and Lean worked together on a number of projects in the late 1930s, the first being Gabriel Pascal's production of *Pygmalion* (1938), and Lean's memories indicate something of the different weight the two directors would come to place on the actor's performance:

> While Puffin [Asquith] was a good director, he could have been a first-rate director if he hadn't had this diffidence. He almost let his actors do too much on their own – an actor could get away with murder on one of Puffin's pictures because Puffin would feel he shouldn't push his ideas. But I learned a lot from him. (Brownlow 1997: 123)

By contrast, Kay Walsh, Lean's second wife, describes Lean as 'a born landscape artist . . . [whose] canvas happened to be celluloid' (Brownlow 1997: 132).

10. Not everyone was convinced by these shifts. Raymond Durgnat, reviewing *The Family Way* (1967), argued:

> John Mills has been playing working-class types for over twenty years, never, to my mind, convincingly, because, intelligent and observant though he is, a middle-class sensitivity is ineradicable from his character. (Tanitch 1993: 115)

I have found no evidence of similar misgivings in wartime reviews of Mills's performances, and in general he was both accepted and applauded in roles across the class spectrum.

11. In July 1943 *Picturegoer* magazine ran a story-feature 'We Dive at Dawn', 'Freely adapted from the film by Marjory Williams'. What is interesting about Williams's somewhat incoherent version of the film's narrative is her decision to tell the story entirely from Hobson's perspective, turning the film into a narrative of individual heroism, in which the public activity of war facilitates private romantic resolution. After Hobson, 'heavy-eyed, unshaven, but mentally at concert pitch', has provided the impetus to save the ship, he returns to face his wife, where 'reconciliation newly-dyed in blood and tears, fluttered like a flag between them' (Williams 1943: 14).

12. The third and final use of the sequence occurs when the triumphant *Sea Tiger* returns to port, bringing a pleasing symmetry to the film's closure.

13. A full account of this international collaboration can be found in Aldgate and Richards (1994: 276–98). However, the publicity stills held by the BFI also indicate the extent to which the production was designed as an exercise in Anglo-American relations. Many stills focus on the various dignitaries, British and American, who visited the set during filming, and there are more photographs of the American-Canadian star Douglass Montgomery 'relaxing' off set, than there are of his actual performance. The film's press books are also instructive in terms of target audience. Alongside actor biographies and accounts of the production are such items as 'What the Modern Girl should Wear' and a series of photographs of Rosamund John and Renee Asherson modelling outfits from the film. Clearly

the distributors recognised the degree of war-weariness that had overtaken British audiences and aimed to pitch their film at the romance as well as the service market.

14. The Beveridge Report was a foundation stone of the welfare state and emerged from a commission on health insurance established in 1942. On first publication the report sold a remarkable 635,000 copies, and the evident popularity of the proposals enabled Labour ministers within the cabinet to push ahead with recon-struction legislation before the end of the war, most notably in the case of the 1944 Education Act (Mackay 1999: 60–4, 151–4).

15. Posters and publicity for the film sold it as: 'The story of "Toddie" the girl whom the world will take to its heart', a description that may have had marketing value, but is strangely at odds with the film's construction of Toddie as a businesslike and responsible woman.

16. As I indicated in Chapter 1, 'banter', a mode of discourse that affirms 'the bond between men while appearing to deny it' (Easthope 1992: 88), is perhaps the only acceptable means of articulating intimacy between men.

17. Female war workers, a staple of the early forties film diet, are conspicuous by their absence from this film.

18. Although filmed in 1945, the film covers the period 1940 to 1944. Archdale dies in 1942, when the forming of new family units would have been a lower prior-ity for propagandists.

19. Naremore, on the subject of expressive objects, observes that: 'Once these objects have entered into social relations and narrative actions, they are imbued with the same "spirit" as the humans who touch them' (1990: 87), a comment that seems singularly appropriate to the role of the lighter in this film.

20. The most significant manifestation of this is, of course, the death of Johnny Hollis, who turns down the opportunity to go home because he feels that 'if a guy didn't get here until the middle of things, maybe he should stick around until the end'.

21. For accounts of critical responses and contrasting audience reactions to Gainsborough melodrama see Richards 1997: 111–17; Higson 1995: 212, 215; and Harper 1994. Harper in particular cites an impressive catalogue of critical oppro-brium, including the *Tribune's* memorable indictment: 'Because I am, by inclination at least, an historian, *The Wicked Lady* arouses in me a nausea out of all proportion to the subject' (1994: 123).

22. Helen Fletcher in the *Sunday Graphic* enthused that: 'The miracle has happened . . . an English company has made an absolutely natural film about the ordinary life of ordinary people in wartime London' (Press Book for *Waterloo Road*, BFI Collections).

23. In many respects *Waterloo Road* conforms to the pattern of a genre identified by Andrew Higson as the 'melodrama of everyday life' (1995: 262) – that is, films that purport to deal realistically with British life, but which are often ambiguously sit-uated between a discourse of community and inclusivity, and a conservative desire for the restoration of the status quo.

24. This fight really caught the attention of both public and critics. A. E. Wilson in *The Star* rather splendidly described it as 'one of the most vigorous displays of fisticuffs and furniture smashing I have ever seen on the screen' (Press Book for *Waterloo Road*, BFI Collections).

25. As Clare Whatling has argued, the cinema creates a 'fantasy space' within which the spectator has considerable freedom to appropriate screen representations and to read across or against the dominant discourse of the film. Describing the experience of queer spectatorship, Whatling suggests that cinema viewing is a 'transformative process' in which 'interpretation lies largely (though not exclusively) with the desire of the spectator' (1997: 2, 6), and this model of spectatorship resonates strongly with the arguments for trangressive desires encoded within non-realist British films of the 1940s.

26. These chases are more transgressive than they might at first appear, as they do not simply comprise the errant individual evading authority. Early on in the 'adventure' Colter is befriended and assisted by Duggan, a Canadian soldier, who has become a sort of professional absentee and who exists as part of a sub-culture of those living outwith the bounds of the law. Duggan has his own routes and modes of existence, but also inhabits the legitimate public world, appearing in bars and cafés alongside other soldiers and civilians. Both visually and in narrative terms he opens up an unresolved liminal space. When he sees his regiment being shipped off to fight, he tries to rejoin, but immediately gets into a fight with his officer, and once again becomes an outlaw. His disobedience is neither punished nor resolved within the narrative, except insofar as, having refused to sit through the boring bits of war (training), he is denied the opportunity to participate in the exciting bits (actual combat). It is hard to believe, though, that many spectators would have subscribed to this belief in the thrill of war.

27. This phrase has interesting implications for the perception of national character. Putting private desire above public duty, going AWOL, is considered a very 'un-British' act and consequently characterised as French. The film's concern with the unleashing of the emotions perhaps accounts for Helen Fletcher's fascinating statement in *Time and Tide*: 'If *Waterloo Road* were not so English it would be French' (20 January 1945).

28. One of the devices through which, in Williams's words, the film 'desperately attempts to impose a "normalcy" solution upon past and present events' (2000: 83).

29. The desire to see Ted Purvis punished is not confined to the middle classes. The concluding fight takes place during an air-raid and is interrupted by an ARP warden – who cheerfully gives his approval for it to continue when he realises who is being beaten. But nonetheless, it is the middle rather than the lower classes who stood to gain most in the long term from the repression of the sub-culture represented by Purvis.

30. 'I sometimes think the remedy [to the ills represented by Purvis-Granger] is in your hands . . . I mean the hands of the people you represent . . . You make the sacrifices. Fists don't solve anything – but in this case . . .'

31. The bow tie is also a uniform of sorts, and is sported by Purvis's lieutenants. As Robert Murphy has observed, the spiv was the point of contact between two worlds – the legitimate and the criminal – and as such needed to be easily recognisable (1989: 150).

32. The only exception to this is when Colter opens up to Lewis, the military policeman who has been chasing him. Lewis can be seen as a father figure, but unlike Montgomery he comes from Colter's own class, and communication between the two is facilitated by their shared homosocial community, the army.

33. Montgomery does not mince his words with regard to the spivs, and his description of Purvis as 'the symptom of a general condition' effectively identifies him as a disease that threatens to corrupt the body politic.

Part II

4

A Cautionary Note:
Great expeditions and the postwar world

It cannot be said that it is war, it cannot be said that it is peace, it can be said that it is post-war; this will probably go on for ten years. (Stevie Smith 1979: 13)

In literature England speaks today with many voices, and some of the writers seem to be speaking only to themselves . . . No great English poet at present sees life steadily and sees it whole; the Lady of Shalott's mirror has splintered into hundreds of jagged fragments, in each of which glimmers a tiny part of the national consciousness. This disintegration of vision may indeed reflect the confused and troubled mind of the age. (James Sutherland, in Barker 1947: 319)

The day before sailing the Royal Geographical Society entertained Scott and his party at luncheon . . . The president, Major Leonard Darwin . . . congratulated Captain Scott on having such a well-found expedition and . . . said that Captain Scott was going to prove once again that the manhood of our nation was not dead and that the characteristics of our ancestors who won the great Empire still flourished amongst us. (Evans 1924: 22)

The transition from war to peace is neither tidy nor immediate. VE day was in May 1945, VJ day in August, but for some members of the armed forces, demobilisation took years to achieve. For these men and women, and for the countless families deprived of homes by blitz or doodlebug, peace was an absence of threat, rather than a return to anything that might once have been conceived as normality. For many, there was no desire to return to the status quo of the 1930s; indeed, the nation's wish for fundamental social and political change found eloquent expression in the Labour Party's landslide election victory of 1945. Yet these reformist sentiments co-existed with anxiety about what reform might mean, and with practical desires for stability and reward. Above all, the people wanted an end to upheaval, restrictions and stoicism. The Mass Observation archive records starkly contrasting reponses to the end of the war – from euphoria to anti-climax – while Michael Sissons and Philip French's seminal essay collection *The Age of Austerity* suggests that in most areas of life, things got worse before they got better.[1] The war was won at a tremendous cost to the nation, and in its aftermath the very concept of Britain became subject to fundamental revisions. Historians continue to debate the nature, the extent and the timing of these changes, and a succinct summary of the forces that ultimately defeated the impetus to rebuild the Empire is provided by P. J. Cain and A. G. Hopkins:

> The question of why the Empire became unstuck so soon after it had been reglued has engaged many minds and stimulated much excellent research. It is probably fair to say . . . that most historians favour a multi-causal explanation which features, with varying emphases, the decline of British power, the rising costs of empire, the loss of imperial will, the irresistible force of colonial nationalism and the pressures of international opinion, including of course the attitude of the United States. (Cain and Hopkins 1993: 285–6)

Yet the 'facts' of imperial reconstruction and the move towards decolonisation stand in complex relation to how these events were perceived. Kumar suggests that the Empire was integral to constructions of British identity, even though it was seldom articulated as such. Citing Billig's banal nationalism as a model, he proposes that: '[R]ight through to the 1950s . . . the fact of empire [was] strongly present in the national culture' (2003: 195). To see this powerful symbol of British authority begin to be dismantled, as from 1947 onwards, it slowly but surely was, must have had an impact on the nation's sense of self. It would be premature, in the immediate aftermath of war, to invoke the concept of decline discussed by Colls (2002: 143–4), but there is no doubt that the late 1940s delivered a significant series of blows to Britain's overseas authority. The crisis in Palestine, the departure from Burma, the bloody partition of India all combined with economic recession at home to generate a significant degree of cultural anxiety about the state of the nation. Churchill, typically, put things more bluntly, decrying in December 1946 the 'steady and remorseless process of divesting ourselves of what has been gained by so many generations of toil, administration and sacrifice', and concluding that the only appropriate term for this state of affairs was 'scuttle' (Hennessy 1993: 229–30).

An overstatement, perhaps, but Churchillian rhetoric always left a mark, and few in Britain could have doubted that the nation's status as an imperial and an international power was changing.[2]

In this context of uncertainty, the poet Stevie Smith's conception of a temporal construct of 'postwar' seems singularly appropriate. The late 1940s formed a nebulous border zone between the two more familiar states of war and peace. This transitional state could not but impact upon cinema production and consumption. In terms of popular demand, signs of change had been evident since at least 1943, with audiences turning their backs on realism and seeking release from the pressures of wartime in the escapism of Hollywood and the Gainsborough melodramas. By 1945, it is possible to observe the beginnings of a bleak, consciously anti-heroic 'spiv' cycle in British screen drama,[3] and both these developments indicate the advent of what would be a major shift in patterns of cinema heroism. However, the substantial change of the postwar cinema era – the transition from the relatively unambiguous, clear-cut heroics of wartime to the disillusioned anti-heroics of the early 1950s – did not materialise overnight. Rather there existed an uncomfortable interim period in which the concept of the hero came under increasing pressure, revealing cracks and uncertainties, self-doubt and poor judgement. This chapter consequently also acts as a border zone within the wider structure of the book, tracing the tension between optimism and pessimism, celebration and cultural mourning that manifests itself in three strongly contrasting films of the immediate postwar period. All three films provided major starring roles for John Mills, and all three used his established screen persona to develop patterns of ambivalence and anxiety within their narratives.

1946–49 might have been the 'age of austerity' for the nation, but for John Mills it was a period of plenty. If box-office receipts can be used as a gauge of success, then the late 1940s were amongst the best years of his career. His success, however, was critical as well as popular, and much of this can be attributed to his starring role in David Lean's 1946 production of *Great Expectations*. But although *Great Expectations* brought him unprecedented success and international recognition, it is important to note that his casting in this landmark film was fundamentally indebted to the cumulative effect of his wartime 'Everyman' roles. Peter Penrose, the ordinary man in extraordinary circumstances, was an essential pre-requisite of Pip. But it was not simply the quality and high profile of Lean's adaptation that boosted Mills's career. In the immediate postwar years he undertook a phenomenal amount of film work, and *Great Expectations* was rapidly followed in 1947 by *The October Man* and *So Well Remembered*. *The October Man*, a tightly constructed thriller, directed by Roy Ward Baker, provided Mills with the first of many damaged hero roles, and in the process captured something of the fundamental shifts taking place in representations of masculinity. It was critically well received and added useful lustre to Mills's reputation. Edward Dmytryk's *So Well Remembered*, by contrast, deployed a hero of almost inconceivable virtue. An adaptation of a James Hilton pot-boiler, the film is, perhaps deservedly, forgotten – but nonetheless, this ambitious Anglo-American co-production is notable on at least two grounds. First, it provided Mills with a substantial leading role, playing the supremely worthy small-town newspaper editor George Boswell from youth to late middle age. And second, the film gave notice of the shape of things to come in terms of gender politics. George's wife Olivia, played by Martha Scott, is a precursor of a key 1950s stereotype: the vain, vicious, power-hungry, self-centred and suffocating woman who is wholly unable to understand either the ethics of civil society or the needs of men.

This prodigious output was followed in 1948 by *Scott of the Antarctic*, a prestige production, some years in the planning and execution, that drew heavily upon Mills's reputation as an embodiment of heroic virtues. The film presents a celebration of an imperial tradition threatened by both the events and the films of 1939–45, and as Charles Barr (1993) and Jeffrey Richards (1997) have noted, it chooses not to comment on the series of mistakes that led to the failure of Scott's expedition. The 'semi-documentary' resuscitation of the Scott myth at this time has considerable implications for understandings of masculinity and national identity. Once again, Mills is drawn upon as a symbol of nation, but the public-school, gentlemanly ethos of this particular incarnation seems to represent a reactionary desire for the resurrection of a pre-war mode of British masculinity in the face of an uncertain postwar world. Yet the film was not universally well-received, and many of those involved, including Mills, were uncomfortable with the compromised nature of its characterisations. *Scott of the Antarctic* thus sits uneasily as both a memorial to heroism and a monument to futility. It could only partially capture the mood of the nation, and it is interesting that Mills's first performance as an imperial hero should come at a time when that mode of masculinity was coming to be seen as outmoded and undesirable.[4] For the first time, the heroism performed by Mills looked backwards rather than forwards.

Nonetheless *Scott of the Antarctic* and the myth it enshrined had sufficient prestige to be chosen for the Royal Command performance in 1949. But in box-office terms it was not the popular success that might have been hoped for. Mills's reputation as actor and star, however, was untarnished by the film's lacklustre performance, and J. Arthur Rank, the biggest man in the British film industry, was sufficiently pleased with the financial potential of his home-grown star to offer him a generous seven-year contract to write, act and produce. On the basis of this, Mills ended the 1940s with his first, and only, films as a producer: *The History of Mr Polly* (Anthony Pélissier 1949) and *The Rocking Horse*

Winner (Anthony Pélissier 1950). Both films broke the heroic mould so long inhabited by Mills. Both would be critical successes and box-office failures. In *The History of Mr Polly* Mills enjoyed the freedom to experiment with comedy, undermining his familiar persona, making himself conspicuously dowdy as the oppressed fantasist Polly. In *The Rocking Horse Winner*, a bleak and powerful adaptation of a D. H. Lawrence short story, he yielded centre stage to the child actor John Howard Davies, taking only a small supporting role in the film. The public, remembers Mills, did not approve of either strategy:

> I began to receive letters from irate fans. They apparently didn't want to see me playing, for the first half of [*Mr Polly*] at least, a rather angry, petulant, hen-pecked husband with a quiff and an untidy moustache. I was stuck with the hero image and hadn't realized it. (2001: 298–9)

Yet the heroic image of which Mills writes had undoubtedly undergone a transition since 1945. The cracks in the façade of national unity that had started to appear in *Waterloo Road* became increasingly evident as the decade progressed, and these tensions can be traced not only in the bleak and muted world of *The October Man* and the documentary horrors of *Scott of the Antartic*, but also in the exuberant, celebratory tapestry of *Great Expectations*.

REALISM AND TINSEL: *GREAT EXPECTATIONS*

> I remember seeing *Great Expectations* and thinking it looked like no other film I had ever seen. It was extremely stylised, and yet it had a savage realism missing from British literary adaptations. (Brownlow 1997: 209)

Great Expectations, by its very title, promises a narrative of new beginnings. What Dickens's 1861 novel provides, however, is an altogether bleaker fable. In his *bildungsroman* about a blacksmith transformed into a gentleman, Dickens ruthlessly exposes the pernicious class politics of Victorian society, and he concludes his narrative with an ambiguous ending that questions whether it is ever possible to escape the past or atone for our mistakes. His protagonists, Pip and Estella, end the novel older, wiser and infinitely sadder. They might have a future together, but the novel offers only the faintest suggestion of this possibility. Dickens's *Great Expectations* is a story of self-deception, disappointment and disillusion. Pip's ambitions are built on sand, and as such the novel does not immediately present itself as a fable for a new world order. Yet David Lean's film adaptation constructs the narrative as precisely this. Part of the enduring power of the 1946 film lies in its renegotiation of the ambiguity that permeates Dickens's novel. Lean re-envisages Pip as a hero appropriate to his age and reconstructs *Great Expectations* as a postwar social allegory.

This is not to suggest that Lean abandons Dickens. The film does ample justice to the writer's dramatic scope and his grotesque characterisations, while in visual terms, the realisation of the vast eery emptiness of the estuary land-scapes powerfully captures the vulnerability of the child Pip. Throughout the film Lean, like Dickens, proves himself unafraid of hyperbole. Through the use of devices such as forced perspective, silhouette lighting, pathetic fallacy and surreal montage sequences, *Great Expectations* negotiates a boundary between the stylised and the realistic that captures much of Dickens's own somewhat ambivalent relation to classic realist fiction. Lean's biographer, Kevin Brownlow, records the director's memories of the film's striking opening sequences:

> We made everything larger than life, as it is in a boy's imagination . . . As far as the scenes with Pip are concerned we were not aiming at reality. What we wanted to create all the time was the world as it seemed to Pip when his imagination was distorted with fear. (1997: 210–11)

Traces of this approach persist throughout the film, resurfacing in particular whenever the convict Magwitch appears in the narrative.[5] Yet the film also remains brutally true to the class politics of Dickens's novel and as Pip's brave new world turns into a nightmare return of the repressed, it is difficult not to see the promises of postwar Britain evaporating into an ominous re-establishment of the status quo. However, this pessimism co-exists with an altogether more optimistic narrative which posits individual empowerment as a weapon against social disenfranchisement. While such a message can hardly be regarded as radical, it makes sense within the context of the film's produc-tion. In a world of demobilisation and the resumption of interrupted lives, powerful feelings of uncertainty circulated within society. Old jobs could not easily be resumed. Women left behind had transformed into something new and potentially threatening and, for some ex-servicemen, leaving the army meant an instant and unwelcome loss of structure and status. The character of Pip, however, has the potential to negotiate this territory.[6] Arbitrarily removed from his natural environment, he is shaped by forces unknown to him and exposed to previously unimaginable influences. Rudely awoken from the dream of instant class empowerment, he must fight to assert his values and beliefs against the indolent power of a destructive old order symbolised by the spectral Miss Havisham.

In possibly the most significant shift of emphasis within the film, Miss Havisham becomes villain rather than victim. She is presented as a repository of false values who would emasculate all men through the deployment of her chosen weapon, the 'heartless' Estella. It is left to Pip to reassert masculine agency, which he does in two sequences more redolent of the thriller than the classic adaptation. Hero and villain meet in two violent encounters. After the first, which will be discussed in greater detail later, Miss Havisham is dead but not defeated. The hero himself is wounded – collapsed beside the smoking body of his nemesis – and still the villain's power lives on. Structurally, this is the thriller's necessary masochistic setback, after which the hero will return, all the stronger for his suffering, to inflict the inevitable final defeat upon his enemy. This scenario is enacted in the final scenes of the film, and is the point at which film and book most definitively part company.

The final confrontation takes place in the house where once Miss Havisham (Martita Hunt) presided over the torment of Pip, and where Estella (Valerie Hobson) now sits alone, trapped in the past of her mentor. Voices from the early scenes of the film echo across the soundtrack, while visual clues link Estella to the sterility and stasis of Miss Havisham's clock-stopped world. She is slipping out of the symbolic order of time into the realm of madness: 'How long have you been here?' asks Pip; 'I don't know,' Estella replies. Mills's heroic version of Pip enters the house as a symbol of the future who must fight the now ghostly force of Miss Havisham's past. Kevin Brownlow reports that Mills was delighted with the revised ending as it gave him the opportunity to tear down curtains while declaiming: 'I have come back Miss Havisham, I have come back – to let in the sunlight!' (1997: 208). As the protagonists thus move from symbolic darkness to healing light, the set is exposed as a room bizarrely hung with tattered drapery, that looks like nothing so much as the streamers of a victory parade. Against this backdrop, Estella is forcibly brought back into the realm of the social through the power of masculine command: 'Look at me,' repeats Pip until she does so, and is instantly, miraculously, freed from her chains.

The melodrama of this sequence is obviously a radical departure from Dickens's novel, but it is not the end of the film. The final shot is a rear view of Pip and Estella running through the garden of the house like the children they once were, before slipping through the gate to freedom framed by the title 'Great Expectations'. This curious return to childhood evacuates the passion that had been implicit in the previous scene in favour of a further revision of Dickens's ambiguous closure. The voice of experience, provided by Mills's voiceover, is absent from the final sequence. It is no longer necessary because the sites of innocence and experience have been reversed. Having exposed the Garden of Eden as a sham, Pip and Estella step out into the world, ready to start afresh. They have been liberated from the mistakes of the previous generation and are free to begin again in a postwar, post-Havisham classless society. It is not difficult to see the contemporary parallels implicit in Pip's *bildungsroman*, nor to recognise the proximity of his fate to that of the struggling Everyman. In this context it is perhaps not surprising, then, that David Lean should have turned to John Mills, the nation's pre-eminent Everyman, for the role of Pip.

As the previous chapter suggested, Mills's wartime fame emerged from his capacity to represent the 'ordinary' person made extraordinary by the circumstances of war. He evolved into an Everyman figure, in both senses of the word. He was a representative example of the ordinary man and a mundane hero who must overcome a series of obstacles in order to achieve salvation. As the earlier characters of Peter Penrose and Jim Colter had revealed, being Everyman was an achievement as much as a representative act. Nonetheless, by the end of the war, Mills was recognised as an embodiment of national virtues. 'The most popular of English actors' (Noble 1947) had become a convenient cinema shorthand for Englishness – recognised by both directors and audiences as somehow speaking to and for the nation – and a number of factors contributed to this synonymity. One of the most significant of these, and perhaps the one that most suited him to the role of Pip, was Mills's ability to play across the class barrier. This unusual class mutability was facilitated by his physical slightness, eminently trustworthy face and understated naturalistic performance style. He was the ideal choice for rendering potentially threatening figures safe and, when manifest in Mills, the working classes became loyal components of the national body. By embodying the masculinity of the underdog, irrespective of the class he was performing, Mills had found himself in absolute ideological alignment with the propagandist vision of Britain as a plucky little island.

In terms of his screen persona, Mills had become the poster-boy of 'poetic realism', valorised by the middlebrow critics and ineffably linked to the 'quality film' product.[7] But while one category of critics applauded the promotion of this national masculinity, public taste had, most emphatically, moved elsewhere. By 1944 *Picturegoer* magazine, Britain's primary organ of 'star-gazing', had pronounced itself well and truly war-weary. Editorials from 1944 and 1945 repeatedly stressed the need for escapism, and in consequence the magazine paid no attention whatsoever to the production of *The Way to the Stars*, Mills's last film prior to *Great Expectations*. It was not a case of bad publicity – indeed, the magazine gave the film a good review – but rather a case of uninterest. There was no advance publicity, there was no fanfare on release, and little local attention was paid to its impressive line-up of stars: Michael Redgrave, John Mills, Rosamund John and the Canadian actor, Douglass Montgomery. *Picturegoer* is not a wholly reliable indicator of the popularity of any given actor or film, but it does provide valuable information about the extra-filmic dimension of star construction and about changing tastes in screen masculinities.[8] By 1945, then, the magazine's pages were devoid of uniforms, and its editorials were demanding a different sort of entertainment, a demand that was readily satisfied by the phenomenally successful Gainsborough studio melodramas. Films such as *The Man in Grey* (1943), *Fanny by Gaslight* (1944) and *The Wicked Lady* (1945) were loved by audiences and loathed by highbrow critics. They also made undisputed screen stars out of their heroes: James Mason, usually appearing as a violent, sadistic, sexually transgressive figure, and Stewart Granger, generally embodying the sometimes doomed and sometimes rewarded romantic hero. Mason's stardom in particular bears scrutiny: Peter William Evans, in a recent article on the actor (Babington 2001: 112–17), links him to Byronic models of masculinity. He is predatory, menacing, emotionally detached, and yet also, paradoxically, he embodies an almost feminine beauty. And although, generally speaking, he is punished by death, this seldom occurs until after he has given expression to an aggressive sexuality which usually involves the physical punishment of his female co-stars. Whether this can be read as symptomatic of cultural crisis or of tensions within the construct of masculinity is unclear, but *Picturegoer* readers loved it, voting Mason best actor of 1945 for his transgressive performance in *The Man in Grey*.

In comparison with this, Mills's star status was at best ambiguous.[9] He had risen to prominence in a series of films that conspicuously downplayed everything that might be associated with the concept of stardom. Personal desires, individual motivations, even charisma – all were subjugated to the greater goal of duty. Everyman was very much a 'team player', and when Lean cast Mills in *Great Expectations*, he was consciously mobilising the accumulated freight of the actor's screen persona. Kevin Brownlow records the director's approach to his 'star': 'You know, Nob, I want you to do this [play Pip in *Great Expectations*], but it's a coat hanger for all the wonderful garments that will be hung on you' (Brownlow 1997: 211). This speaks volumes about Mills's screen persona in 1945. Coat hanger suggests a necessary structure that is nonetheless obscured by an altogether more interesting or vibrant cover; and for at least the first half of the film, the role of Pip demands exactly this. The character of Pip is a passive object through which the desires of others are enacted, and Mills, in consequence, is called upon more to react than to act. He has no significant speeches and spends much of his time listening to the expositions of others. As Lean had predicted, his performance underpins the more eccentric and extravagant performances of Martita Hunt as Miss Havisham, Francis L. Sullivan as the lawyer Jaggers, Bernard Miles as Joe Gargery and Alec Guinness as Herbert Pocket. Yet he also embodies the coat hanger as a trope. Pip's 'authentic' identity is that of the blacksmith: he is a working-class figure upon whom the outward trappings of a gentleman have been hung. Indeed, as befits a man being used as a coathanger, Mills looks deeply uncomfortable in Pip's new clothes, which in the first scenes after his transformation are subtly excessive, giving the impression of a slightly foolish class imposture. When we first see Pip in these new clothes, the camera pans slowly up his body. Patent shoes shine with the unyielding brightness of stiff new leather, the suit seems constraining and uncomfortable, suggesting that the blacksmith has literally been incarcerated in his new identity, and the ensemble is topped off by a ludicrous bow, behind which Mills's neck disappears. Resplendent in his new garb, he heads for Jaggers's chambers, where he is framed against the diminutive figure of Wemmick (Ivor Bernard). In the forced perspective of Bryan's interiors, Mills appears as a working-class Alice in Wonderland, utterly disorientated by his surroundings [Fig. 4.1].

Although he is destined for property and is being made into a gentleman, the early adult Pip is profoundly powerless, and the film puts great emphasis on the extent to which both he and Estella are the victims of an experiment in social engineering. 'We are not free to follow our own devices, you and I,' observes the acquiescent Estella, and throughout the narrative both she and Pip are manipulated, watched over and controlled by the previous generation. As a neophyte gentleman and a passive recipient of good fortune, Mills's performance opportunities in the first half of the film are predominantly corporeal and based around the process of listening. The bewildered, slack-jawed concentration with which he listens to Jaggers emphasises his naivity, disorientation and lack of self-confidence, while the scene in which Herbert Pocket (Alec Guinness) tells the story of Estella facilitates subtle physical comedy. Pocket's narration takes place at the dinner table and he breaks off at key points to correct Pip on points of etiquette. Here, as in his earlier films, Mills makes effective use of expressive objects.[10] As he listens to the story, he eats remorselessly but absent-mindedly, filling his mouth with a large potato, which he proceeds to chew throughout the scene. We see the muscles of his face moving in a huge effort that suggests the relationship between eating and understanding: Pip has too much to digest. Later his listening is put to a further test in the epiphanic sequence in which the convict Magwitch (Finlay Currie) returns and explains, at length, that it is he (and not, as Pip had believed, Miss Havisham), who is his benefactor. Lean's sense of the Gothic is foregrounded in this scene. Elemental forces rage through the night, and these sounds posit Pip's room as a sanctuary. This safe space is then shockingly invaded by the equally elemental force of Magwitch, bringing unpalatable truths and exposing the construct of the gentleman. This sequence is significant not only for the effectiveness of Mills's shocked under-reaction – only the sound of a breaking glass registers his horror – but also because it marks a turning point in Pip's narrative, his role in the film and, by extension, Mills's performance.

The Everyman concept that had shaped Mills's wartime stardom was an ideal screen persona for the Pip of the film to this point – and indeed, it might have continued to suffice for the Pip of Dickens's novel, whose redemption is a long and painful process. But it will not suffice to explain the Pip that emerges in the final section of Lean's film. This Pip shakes off his snobbery and self-delusion in a moment. After the shock of the encounter with Magwitch, Mills's character undergoes a fundamental and immediate transition from boy to man.

Fig. 4.1 The actor as coat hanger: *Great Expectations* (1947). British Film
Institute/London Features International

From the ordinariness of an everyman, subject to the will of others and end-
lessly manipulated, he mutates into an altogether more dangerous and assertive
new man, reminiscent not of democracy and equality, but rather of the powerful individual hero of the Gainsborough melodramas. Halfway through *Great
Expectations*, then, John Mills magically metamorphoses into James Mason, and

although the comic dimensions of his performance still appear in alternating scenes, it is as an action hero that he ends the film.[11] From the scene that follows Magwitch's revelations onwards, the shift in performance is immediately apparent. Mills speaks differently. His voice is now that of the voice-over: the truly adult Pip. It is deeper, carefully measured and more forceful. There is no hesitancy and his face is set. This is a prelude to agency; for the first time in the film, Pip will act rather than react. And in this context it is interesting to note how Mills himself interpreted Lean's instruction to be a coat hanger. His autobiography records:

> He warned me that Pip was a 'coat-hanger' for all the fantastic characters that Dickens had woven around him, and the part would need everything I could give it to prevent our hero from being swamped. I was more than ready to take the chance. (Mills 2001: 284)

The scene is set, then, for an act of man-making. The coat hanger fights back, and he does so by confronting Miss Havisham and Estella in the room where he was humiliated as a child. This dramatic reversal is a pivotal scene within the film. Pip takes control of the narrative, talking rather than listening and gives voice to his anger, articulating emotions he had not until now felt free to admit. The scene opens with Mills's entrance, swathed in an extravagant dark cloak and holding a candle. His face is set. There is no smile of greeting and his voice has the cold authority of a lawyer setting out his case. There is little movement amongst the actors. What emotions they have are again conveyed through verbal modulation and expressive objects. Miss Havisham stamps on the floor with her stick, Estella knits remorselessly – a mechanical action that emphasises her detachment from the emotions surrounding her and which provides an eerie soundtrack to the confrontation between Pip and Miss Havisham. Estella departs before the scene is over, leaving Pip free to assert his independence:

> You may dismiss me from your mind and conscience, but Estella is a different case – and if you can ever undo any scrap of what you have done amiss in keeping part of her very nature away from her it will be better to do that than to bemoan the past through a hundred years.

The encounter ends with an imposing costume departure: boots, cloak and a slammed door, after which Miss Havisham is immediately engulfed in what might be seen as the flames of retribution. The sequence is, to borrow a phrase from Peter Evans's account of James Mason, 'the return of the repressed'. The working-class Pip, having been manipulated, abused and feminised by the affluent Miss Havisham, here reasserts his masculinity, but it is not a working-class masculinity that he displays; rather it bears all the hallmarks of the class authority to which his benefactors have exposed him. To Miss Havisham he must look something like Frankenstein's monster, the creation with the power to destroy its creator. Within the context of the film's production we might also see it as the return to self-determination of the male, who during the war years has been subject to the arbitrary control of others. Within the film narrative, however, Pip's repressed can more specifically be seen as a combination of his 'natural' virtues, buried as a result of the social experiments to which he had been subject, and an assertive adult masculinity that has not previously been able to develop because he has had no free will. Here, as ever, masculinity is premised upon a concept of agency as opposed to a femininity rooted in subjection.

Mills's speeches in this scene are by far his longest and most significant in the film to date, and they are given additional weight by the *mise-en-scène*. He stands above Estella and Miss Havisham, in a position that rejects the power they have held over him, while the guilty women are seated below and exposed to the full glare of the firelight. They are interrogated by him, bathed in the light of his vengeful righteousness. Throughout, the camera works to emphasise his authority and dignity. His costume (the cloak) and deportment evoke the dominance of a James Mason, rather than the familiar obliging Everyman. His voice in his address to Miss Havisham is that of the prosecutor, cold and clinical. In relation to Estella it is kinder, with touches of passion and anger, but even when his voice is raised, his body and face remain almost motionless and impassive. The scene thus combines masochistic self-control with sadistic verbal flaying. He is in pain because of the women, but he inflicts pain through his words. He will no longer be controlled by them and a harsh masculinity replaces his feminine vulnerability. After Estella's revelation that she will marry Bentley Drummle, he turns his back on the women, and the camera angle works to make his presence brooding, monumental and unusually tall. In conception and in execution, Mills comes to inhabit the spirit of Gainsborough masculinity, even to the point where the film metonymically associates him with the sadism characteristic of Mason's film successes. There is a clear implication of cause and effect in the scene's concluding punishment of Miss Havisham. Mills strides to the door and as he slams it behind him, a coal falls from the fire and ignites his tormentor. He is the agent of her destruction[12] [Fig. 4.2].

In the final third of *Great Expectations*, then, there is a remarkable shift in Mills's heroic characterisation and performance style, and this cannot be ignored in considering the success of the film as a whole. In contrast to the actor's previous service films, *Picturegoer* magazine demonstrated great interest in the making of *Great Expectations*. It trailed the production with stories and put the stars on the cover of the magazine (4 January 1947). Reviews of the film in general were excellent, and *Picturegoer* was no exception. It credited the

Fig. 4.2 Dominant masculinity: Mills asserts himself in *Great Expectations* (1947).
British Film Institute/London Features International

film with technical perfection and cited Mills's performance as brilliant. And
in 1948 Mills won the *Picturegoer* gold medal for his performance as Pip. *Great
Expectations*, more than any of his previous films, had made Mills a 'star'.[13] This
was his only victory in the 'gold medal' competition, and it is significant that
he should have achieved this success for the role that links him to a mode of
performance he seldom had the opportunity to develop – in other words, for
the role that brings him closest to the fantasies embodied by James Mason.
Great Expectations won a number of awards, but Mills won the *Picturegoer* poll
not because he was in a Dickens adaptation or a 'prestige' picture, but because
he was starring in a costume drama, an ironically legitimate example of the
Gainsborough melodramas the public had been flocking to see for the past
three years. And he won it because it is a picture in which he, as hero, was able
to be both James Mason and Stewart Granger, both violent masculine agent
and suppliant romantic hero.

So although Mills got the role of Pip because of his relationship to the
Everyman concept (the coat hanger), he emerged from the film with a very
different star profile on account of *Great Expectations*'s proximity to the

costume pictures so popular during the last years of the war. The film was rig-orously promoted in this category. In an advertisement for *Life* magazine, readers were encouraged to have 'great expectations' of 'throbbing romance', 'thrilling action', 'breathless suspense', 'thundering adventure' and 'heart-warming charm'. Rather bizarrely, the final caption accompanied a picture of Estella and Miss Havisham whispering over the head of the young Pip, but inaccuracies aside, the promotional material played more on transgressive desires than on ideas of prestige and quality. However, for an actor such as Mills, roles such as Pip were few and far between[14] – and the situation was not helped by the crisis in British film production that developed at the end of the decade. Mills's next picture was *Scott of the Antarctic* (Charles Frend 1948), and although this was a very prestigious production, in terms of his encounter with mass popular stardom it has to be seen as a regressive step. *Great Expectations* took him out of the crowd, whereas *Scott* put him back into the group ethos. He may be the heroic leader, but the qualities being celebrated are those of understatement and endurance rather than pleasure and excess. It is also the case that *Scott* remorselessly returns Mills to a predominantly homosocial envir-onment, within which desire could at best be a transgressive subtext. Mills once famously remarked that he had had more submarines than leading ladies, and perhaps in the end it is because of his screen persona's fundamental association with a particularly British mode of muted homosociality that his status as a romantic star was relatively short-lived. In the 1950s, with a few notable excep-tions, it would be action adventure that provided his roles.

Great Expectations can thus be read as a narrative of man-making that restores the individual hero to a pre-eminent position. In the postwar context, however, it must also be seen as a narrative of nation-making, or national rebuilding. In its presentation of 'gentlemen' and the grasping bourgeoisie, it operates as a vali-dation of working-class values, and Lean's adaptation does everything it can to boost the potentially vulnerable postwar male ego. However, it is impossible not to read a degree of ambiguity into the story itself. Is class aspiration wholly invalid? Or viable only if roots are remembered and respected? Are the upper classes pointless and doomed? Or will happiness best be achieved by all knowing and staying in their places? Estella and Pip both represent 'illegitimate' figures groomed for a new class position. That their 'education' has, in both cases, been a perverse one, does not necessarily suggest an essentialist view of class politics. But it does act as a warning for a 'new' postwar society and a government with a mandate for change. For all the class critique built into its narrative, Dickens's *Great Expectations* ends with the personal and introspective. Lean's, by contrast, ends with a tearing down of the fabric of the past in which old structures are abandoned for an as yet undefined new world. This is not a narrative of inte-gration, but of resistance, in which those new to positions of authority find an authentic voice that can challenge the hidebound and destructive orthodoxies of the past. It is, then, a version of the text that strives for optimism, uniting the hybrid characters of Pip and Estella in an open-ended vision of new beginnings and hope for the future. The same could not be said of Mills's next film, *Scott of the Antarctic*, which in its uncompromising narrative of failure and death presented a rather more pessimistic fable to the postwar nation.

Flogging a Dead Hero: *Scott of the Antarctic*

> Much patience and much hard work go into the making of any film. Into *Scott of the Antarctic* went more besides, for in the same way as that wonderful evergreen story of human courage and endurance has gripped the imagination of every Briton and become part of our national being, so did the filming of it seem to everyone concerned to be something out of the ordinary run of film-making – an honour, rather, to participate in. (James 1948: 116)

Why retell the story of Captain Robert Falcon Scott in 1948? Why revisit one of Britain's greatest myths of heroic failure in the immediate aftermath of the nation's great, if economically and emotionally devastating, victory in the Second World War? There is no straightforward answer to these questions, but their interrogation has the potential to expose the anxiety shaping constructions of Englishness in the postwar period. David James's entertaining account of the film's production describes the Scott story as 'part of our national being' and frames the project in terms of a patriotic endeavour. Making *Scott* is somehow a service to the nation, and in adopting this perspective his book further preserves and develops the mythical dimension that has surrounded the story since its inception.

That the myth was widespread and powerful becomes evident from a survey of the press coverage at the time of the film's release. A general feeling of critical disappointment greeted the film, although there was no particular consensus about what was actually wrong with it (some praised the first half and loathed the second, others took a diametrically opposed view). In terms of both praise and criticism, the film reviews suggest that engaging with Scott is culturally fraught territory. In part this emerges from a general problem associated with the subject of national heroes. Everybody has their own Scott, Nelson or Wellington, and feels a particular investment in the maintenance of aspects of the myth. Any attempt to 'fix' the story in a film narrative will inevitably lead to some degree of disappointment or resentment. Yet the critical debate about the technical and emotional accuracy of the film was further complicated by the powerful national dimension of the Scott myth. Writing in January 1949 – a month after the first wave of criticism – Ewart Hodgson of the *News of the World* (2 January 1949) felt the need to fight back on behalf of the film:

> This race to which we belong can claim no monopoly in courage. But we have an odd approach to courage, for, while abhorring boastfulness, we bow to no nation in our capacity for understatement and self-effacement. And it is those two national characteristics that this film has so triumphantly captured . . . I see that there has been criticism in some quarters . . . Another carper, doubtless embedded in a fireside armchair, pipes up that the film stands convicted of melodramatic banality when Scott sums up the Antarctic thus: '*Great God, this is an awful place.*' Such fault finding revolts me . . . Let me repeat that 'Scott of the Antarctic' is a towering motion picture which could have been made only by Britons.

For Hodgson, Scott himself is secondary: to criticise *the film* is anti-British. Paradoxically, by constructing a monument to self-effacement, the film itself achieves heroic status. It is a cinematic representation of Britain and, as a result, any criticism of its achievement must be read as unpatriotic. The *News of the World* might not have been in step with the more highbrow critics, but it remains a significant barometer of popular opinion and indicates just how important heroes are in the construction of national identity in general, and national masculinities in particular.

But what position does Scott hold within the national imagination? Jeffrey Richards situates the explorer as part of a 'tradition of Englishman as gallant loser', observing that 'many of the great mythic events in British history have been heroic defeats' (1997: 53), and it is indeed the case that Scott's story persists as triumphant in the face of overwhelming odds: namely, the failure of the mission, the death of the principals and the overwhelming evidence of bungled preparation and poor leadership that has gradually emerged over the years.[15] This paradoxical celebration of failure is ongoing: only recently Scott could be found gracing a 68-pence stamp as part of a series commemorating 'Extreme Endeavours' (29 April 2003), and it is, perhaps, the very monumentality of his failure that makes the myth so potent. For Roland Huntford, Scott's most critical biographer, it is the totality of his failure that saves him from both ignominy and historical obscurity. The sanctity of death drew a discreet veil over the expedition's blunders and a 'party line' was established that enabled him to become a legend overnight:

> Scott was a monument to sheer ambition and bull-headed persistence; he was, after all, the second man at the South Pole. His achievement was to perpetuate the romantic myth of the explorer as martyr and, in a wider sense, to glorify suffering and self-sacrifice as ends in themselves. (Huntford 1979: 563)

Through death, then, Scott is saved from public scrutiny, rehabilitated before anyone had noticed his fall from grace. But irrespective of the state of Scott's reputation, how much appeal could the war- and postwar-weary public find in the narrative's glorification of suffering and self-sacrifice? Certainly this is what the government was continuing to demand of a jaded population, for, as Susan Cooper records, the postwar transformation was very slow in coming. Rationing was worse than in wartime, rehousing projects were proceeding at a snail's pace, there were power shortages and, to cap it all, in 1947 along came the most vicious winter of the century. Much was promised, but by 1948, little had materialised:

> Wars end tidily in the history books, with the moment of signing a document. But there was no single finishing line for the shortages of food, clothes and fuel, and all the aspects of austerity which gave a dull grey tinge to post-war life. (Cooper 1986: 41)

The nation was exhausted, facing a process of reconstruction in which the high hopes of wartime seemed bogged down in a succession of crises and, given the still prevailing audience enthusiasm for fantasy and escapism, it seems unlikely that the dogged detail and documentary realism of Scott's journey would have had immediate popular appeal. Indeed, the film does not sit comfortably within the trends of postwar British cinema production, where a different sort of group hero was emerging, namely the comic ensemble, epitomised by the anarchic groups of Ealing's *Passport to Pimlico* (1949) and *Whisky Galore* (1949), and Gainsborough's Huggett family sequence, which began in 1947 with *Holiday Camp*. Nonetheless, the suffering of the sympathetically portrayed characters within *Scott of the Antarctic* is undoubtedly designed to affect the audience, and may well have provided a cathartic site for the negotiation of feelings of grief and loss permeating British society. Michael Balcon recalls that 'Charles Frend had been looking for a long time for a subject of genuinely epic dimensions' (1969: 171), and this desire to produce an epic in the aftermath of the war suggests a process of displaced memorialising: a commemoration of the dead made more manageable by the distancing process of time.[16]

But the story of Scott is also an imperial narrative, and the film's determination to respect Scott's journals and the feelings of the expedition's survivors ensured that it conformed to patterns of heroism established in the nineteenth century. Jeffrey Richards observes that:

> the Empire was seen and promoted as a vehicle for the operation of British character at its best, a character that was a cross between evangelical commitment, strength of purpose and hardwork and chivalric ideals of leadership, service and sacrifice. (1997: 33)

One might also argue, on the evidence of Scott's planning, that this model equally promoted the virtues of amateurism. The notion of character described by Richards speaks to an ideal of divine inspiration and purpose, wholly at odds with conceptions of professionalism and training. The concept of the English 'all rounder', whose 'character' is such that he can turn his hand to anything, is evident in the contrast between Amundsen's pragmatic selection of men who could ski, and Scott's inclusion of men with no experience of Polar conditions whatsoever, but with sufficient 'give it a go' enthusiasm to cross continents on the off-chance of adventure.[17] The role of imperial hero was not something that could be learnt, rather it was something that, to the right sort of Englishman, just came naturally. The fundamental importance of concepts of good sportsmanship and fair play to the construction of Englishness is made painfully evident in the film version of the story. The news of Amundsen's decision to head for the South, rather than the North, Pole is greeted with cries of dismay from the crew. 'Not very sporting I must say,' comments Oates. It is hard to ignore the implication that with his competent skiers and hundreds of dogs, Amundsen was somehow on the verge of 'cheating'. Certainly the Norwegian is presented as failing to understand the 'rules of the game', which suggest that uncharted territory has a default status as part of the British Empire. As Teddy Evans (Kenneth More) comments on hearing of Amundsen's presence in the Bay of Whales: 'He's got some cheek – we found this place first.'

The colonial context, however, was also redolent with contemporary significance. In his fascinating cultural history *I May Be Some Time: Ice and the English Imagination*, Francis Spufford observes that both 'in 1901 and 1910, Scott sailed to Antarctica down a corridor of Britishness' (1996: 250) and it is impossible to ignore the proximity of the film's production to the traumatic partitioning of India and the loss of what was once regarded as the 'jewel in the crown' of Empire. To revisit Scott in this context, then, is to evade the collapse of the imperial ideal through the resuscitation of a comforting narrative in which a mythical victory is snatched from the jaws of a practical defeat. *Scott of the Antarctic* confronts the uncertainty of the present political climate with the mythologised security of the past. There is, in the fascination of the story, an attraction and a terror that Spufford very appropriately describes as sublime. Writing of the romance of catastrophe, he observes that: 'The whole existence of something called the sublime, devoted to spectacles of grandeur and terror, testifies that our appetite for tragedies somehow hides an odd species of enjoyment' (Spufford, 1996: 27). The men are dead. They have failed, and there is nothing to be done but celebrate the manner of their failing. In 1948, however, the Empire was only beginning to break down. The full extent of the crisis and the manner, dignified or otherwise, of its demise, remained to be seen. It could not yet be imagined, but the pain of the initial loss could be counteracted by the displacements of history and the return to the comfortable and reassuring spectacle of glorious English defeat. A failure that is always already well done. Scott's story, then, is a transcendent failure – a failure that touches on the intimate terrors of national decline and facilitates the negotiation of an unbearable truth.

These factors offer some explanation of why it was in Scott that Frend found the 'subject of genuinely epic dimensions' for which he had been searching. The myth was resuscitated because it provides, in Spufford's words, 'a skeleton ready to be dressed over and over in the different flesh different decades feel to be appropriate' (1996: 4). This contention is born out by 'Teddy' Evans' *South with Scott* (1924) which tells the familiar story as an adventure narrative for the benefit of 'Britain's younger generations', and offers an uncompromising celebration of the homosocial bond to set against the 'post-war days of general discontent' (p. 64). The hint of generational anxiety that creeps into Evans's post–First World War narrative can also be found in the margins of the 1948 retelling. Mills himself, writing the foreword to David James's *Scott of the Antarctic: The Film and its Production*, presents a pessimistic perspective in which the film is perceived as a national rallying point, a cause that can unite a nation fragmented in the aftermath of the war:

> We have tried and *really* tried to do justice to one of the greatest stories in
> the world. Those men – all of them – surely showed to what magnificent
> heights of courage, heroism, unselfishness and gallantry men could rise in
> the face of impossible odds. There was a feeling – a general atmosphere
> in the studio that I have never encountered before. Everyone concerned
> with the production – chippies, painters, sparks, make-up – all of them
> took a deep personal interest in the film. They were all desperately anxious
> for the result to be worthy of the great subject, and surely a story that can
> uplift and inspire is badly needed in these very troublesome and worrying
> times in which we live. (Mills, in James 1948: 12)

In the light of this cooperative vision it is not surprising that Spufford suggests that the 1948 version of the Scott myth can be read as 'a postwar fable of class integration, apt for the austerity era' (1996: 4); but although this is in many respects apposite, it oversimplifies the film's negotiation of the myth and the tensions that underpin its straightforward retelling of the 'official' story.

As the previous chapter and the reshaping of *Great Expectations* suggested, 'fables of class integration' belonged to the Second World War itself. The power of these fables diminished rapidly under the pressures of austerity, and as the 1950s approached it was class antagonism rather than integration that threatened to shape the national psyche.[18] Consequently, it is rather the case that the

1948 *Scott* contains a nostalgia not just for class integration, but for a whole sense of national purpose that was rapidly disappearing over the horizon of the war's end. The oft-repeated final lines of the film bear a further repetition:

> We took risks, we knew we took them. Things have come out against us – and therefore, we have no cause for complaint. Had we lived, I should have had a tale to tell of the hardihood, endurance and courage of my companions that would have stirred the heart of every Englishman.

These lines, directly taken from the 'Message to the Public' that concludes Scott's journals, are singularly appropriate for the moment in which a new mythology is being born: the myth of the nation's finest hour that is the popular memory of the Second World War. The 'musn't grumble' attitude of 'no cause for complaint' invokes the stoicism of wartime survival, while the boys-own endorsement of the Polar party's heroism sets the scene for the wartime adventure narratives that proliferated in the 1950s. The film is nostalgic rather than contemporary both because it mourns what has been lost in the aftermath of war, rather than celebrating an ideal which has been discovered, and because it returns to a conception of masculine heroism that validates the supremacy of officers and gentlemen.

The question of why Scott, however, naturally begs the further question, why Mills as Scott? As with Lean's *Great Expectations*, he was immediately perceived as fitting the role, not least because of what David James describes as 'a very strange physical resemblance' to the explorer (1948: 64). Michael Balcon, the film's producer, recalls:

> My first choice to play the part of Scott was John Mills and I think it was one of the finest performances that fine actor has ever given. John worked hard, as a very young actor, to make the grade . . . he is of that rare company of actors who never fail to give a good performance. He is a pleasure to work with – professional to the fingertips – and his sincerity comes through in everything he does. (Balcon 1969: 175)

Balcon's eulogy is interesting in its emphasis on effort and reward, an emphasis repeated in the biographies that accompany David James's story of the production. 'Few actors,' we are told, 'have had a longer and tougher fight to achieve success than John Mills . . . and even fewer stars have maintained top-ranking position so steadily and for so long as he has done' (1948: 128). The effect of these descriptions is to suggest that Mills, as a man as much as an actor, is worthy of the role. Both physically and in terms of character he already embodies something that is appropriate to the depiction of Scott.

This returns us to the shifting patterns of Mills's screen persona. It was his 'Everyman' status that facilitated his casting as Pip in *Great Expectations*, but

Scott was no Everyman. Nonetheless, it seems likely that the Everyman legacy again had a role to play in his casting. Balcon's stress on Mills's status as a merit-ocratic film star, someone who has had to struggle long and hard to make it on his own, suggests a desire to utilise an actor who could somehow democratise the potentially autocratic figure of Scott. The perception of Mills as a tough man of the people and the extra-filmic knowledge of his struggle for success are seen providentially to equip him for a role which demands an inordinate amount of suffering and sacrifice, while his deployment also makes it possible for the filmmakers safely to reinhabit a myth which, in terms of class and national self-perception, was becoming increasingly difficult to maintain. In this sense, then, Spufford is right to associate the film with 'class integration'. In the casting of John Mills, if not in its narrative, or ultimately the perfor-mances of its principal actors, the film seeks to create a democratic spirit within the austerity era.

There is a distinction to be drawn in the film's construction between the actual Scott story, which harks back to an imperial ideal associated with the Victorian and Edwardian eras, and a more immediate nostalgia for a lost wartime homosocial community that pervades the *mise-en-scène*. This commu-nity, however, belongs to the men Scott leads. In spite of his carefully empha-sised long-standing friendship with Wilson, within the film he is never presented as wholly belonging to the group, and this apartness is significant. Here, as was the case with *Great Expectations*, we can see Mills's body and pre-existing screen persona standing in opposition to the demands of the role and the actual performance he gives. Although pre-signifying a democratic ideal, Mills's performance comprises the aloofness of class and authority. His face, even in the early scenes, contains none of the boyish enthusiasm that charac-terised Pip, and none of the vulnerability that marked out his officer-class por-trayals in *We Dive at Dawn* and *The Way to the Stars*. Indeed, the filmmakers' decision to establish Scott's character in a scene in which he sits for a bust being sculpted by his wife, is surely significant in contributing to the creation of a somewhat unyielding and not wholly sympathetic character [Fig. 4.3]. The scene has the obvious practical purpose of introducing both Scott and his wife, and showing her at work is a convenient short-hand indication of her status as an exceptional woman. However, in order to pose, Mills's Scott must sit ramrod straight, his face reduced to the minimum of movement. The effect created is to reduce the perception of intimacy between the couple. They each prioritise their own work, and Scott's fixity of body is used to imply a fixity of purpose. The scene also constructs an ironic foreshadowing of the mythic dimension of the story about to be told. Even before the expedition leaves port, Scott is being shaped as an iconic figure, part man and part symbol: a monument in his own lifetime. There is, then, a tension to be read between the meanings encoded by

Fig. 4.3 A monument in his own lifetime: Mills as Captain Scott (1948). British
Film Institute/Canal+ Image UK Ltd

Mills's body, the actual performance he gives, the role of Captain Scott as
written for the film, the letter of the law upholding the Scott myth, and the
shifting meanings of the masculine group between 1911 and 1948.

The tension between the myth of the imperial hero and the myth of the
people's war is perhaps most effectively illustrated in Mills's subtle depiction of
Scott's apartness. This distance from the men he leads is fundamental to the
film's negotiation of the somewhat reactionary imperial ideal I discussed earlier.
Graham Dawson, discussing the British soldier hero, contrasts the public presentation of the nineteenth-century hero Henry Havelock with that of the
twentieth-century's T. E. Lawrence:

> [W]hereas Marshman's [Havelock's first biographer] Havelock was a care-
> fully cultivated public image with the controversial and contradictory
> elements of both his public and private lives edited out, Lawrence of
> Arabia was the product of twentieth-century mass media which actively
> seek out the controversial aspects of the private man and expose his 'secret
> lives' to the public gaze of ever-widening audiences. (Dawson 1994: 208)

Dawson's distinction provides a useful framework for reading Balcon and Frend's re-creation of Scott. Although the film is constructed with a respect for detail and authenticity that firmly situates it within the documentary tradition of Second World War British cinema, the treatment of character attempts an unproblematised return to a Victorian model of hagiography.[19] Scott is constructed as 'an embodiment of desirable, British masculine composure in the face of adversity' (Dawson 1994: 150), a properly heroic 'adventurer and christian soldier' (p. 144), with 'elements of both his public and private lives edited out'. The filmmakers were masochistic in their pursuit of authenticity and verisimilitude and, as has been recorded elsewhere, they ran into some difficulties negotiating the sensibilities of surviving relatives and members of the expedition. The result was a script and storyline that read strictly by the book, namely, Scott's journals. This, as Mills comments in his autobiography, left little room for exploring the characters.[20] However, it is impossible to ignore the extent to which criticism and complexity inhabit the margins of the film, and this dimension emerges both from the filmmakers's visual acknowledgement of mistakes that receive no verbal articulation,[21] and from the degree of discomfort in the performances of the principals. Mills's performance reveals that his pre-existing screen persona could soften, but could not wholly disguise, Scott's distance from the men he led. In the aftermath of a war in which officers and men moved into ever closer proximity, Scott is presented as a man apart, and at key points throughout the film, his exclusion from the homosocial community of men is subtly but effectively conveyed [Fig. 4.4].

A key scene within which the performance of the principals complicates the process of hagiographic representation comes during the final journey to the Pole. The twelve remaining men enjoy a Christmas dinner comprising extra rations of pony and a sweet. They are in good humour, with Oates (Derek Bond) comically planning to fake a fit in the hope of getting a tot of brandy. As Taff Evans (James Robertson Justice) tells a joke, the camaraderie of the group is emphasised by a slow tracking shot that moves around the men. Pleasant anticipation can be read on the faces of Bill Wilson (Harold Warrender), Oates and Lashly (Norman Williams). As the camera reaches Scott, however, Mills is not already smiling or half laughing at Evans' story. Rather, his face is fixed. The lines on his forehead are sharply etched against his black weathered skin, suggesting preoccupation with weightier matters, and this determined set of the features is emphatically not the face of a man listening to a funny story. When the punchline comes and the others laugh, his lip twitches in the ghost of a smile, but the effect is that of a man smiling because he knows he is supposed to, rather than a man who actually gets the joke. A similar pattern of characterisation emerges in the earlier Midwinter Day celebration scenes.

Fig. 4.4 Not quite one of the boys: *Scott of the Antarctic* (1948). British Film Institute/Canal+ Image UK Ltd

While the men carouse, Scott slips away to the quiet of the stables, where he talks about Amundsen with Oates. Although low-key and constrained by the demand that the film be respectful to dead heroes, Mills succeeds in presenting a performance of singlemindedness and obsession that has the capacity to un-settle if not actively disrupt the master narrative of heroism.[22]

The filmic presentation of the Scott story, then, is riven with tensions emerging from the power of the myth and the national investment in its preservation.[23] It is also caught in the uncomfortable complexity of the postwar moment. The 1948 *Scott* encapsulates two struggling modes of national self-perception. On the one hand it revisits the hero of Empire, and in so doing uses Scott's failure to negotiate the doubts and anxieties circulating as a product of Indian independence and the change in Britain's status as an imperial power. In this context, the race for the Pole can also be read as a rehabilitation of Empire, or a sort of 'Empire-lite'. Struggling across Antarctica has all the hallmarks of colonial adventure, and all the attendant benefits of territorial expansion and potential triumph in international competition, but miraculously it offers these benefits without the troublesome cultural dimension. Colonising an ice-covered continent inhabited only by penguins maintains a framework for the formation of national masculinity, without the conflicts developing from indigenous resistance to Empire.[24] Graham Dawson observes that colonial adventure remained 'an attractive and exciting narrative form well into the twentieth century' (1994: 151), but while the Scott story draws on this obvious appeal, it is also important to see Scott's reserved, dignified and graceful 'defeat' as proposing an 'English' response to the changing character of the postwar nation. However, at the same time as it grapples with contemporary uncertainty through the presentation of a historical failure, the film also mourns a loss from the more recent past. *Scott of the Antarctic* yearns for the lost masculine ideality of wartime, and even although Mills's Scott sits uncomfortably amongst his men, in their banter and bonding lie the remnants of a group hero and a national unity fast disappearing from the narratives of British society and its cinema.

For the main part, then, *Scott of the Antarctic* is a profoundly nostalgic film, but there is one dimension in which the film might be seen as forward-looking: namely, its presentation of gender. *Scott's* entirely Edwardian depiction of home as a paradoxical space of nurturance and emasculation, and the contrasts it establishes between domestic confinement and masculine adventure, eagerly anticipate the gendered tensions that would come to characterise British film narratives in the 1950s. The postwar readjustments of returning service men and the perceived female failure to understand the male experience would be far more bitterly dealt with in films such as *The Long Memory* (1953) and *Carrington VC* (1956), but nonetheless they are fundamental to the psychological explanation of Scott's motivation. The early scenes of the film introduce us, in short succession, to Scott's atypical wife Kathleen (Diana Churchill) and Wilson's all-too-typical wife Oriana (Anne Firth). After travelling to Scotland to recruit Bill for his expedition, Scott must first negotiate the gatekeeper and guardian of domestic security that is his wife. He breaks the news to the couple that although he got within ninety miles of his goal, Shackleton has failed in his attempt to reach the Pole. Oriana is the first to respond: 'Isn't ninety miles near enough?', to which Scott replies, 'No, because it isn't it. It's not the South Pole. That's still there waiting – and, er, I think an Englishman should get there first.' This exchange is accompanied by shot/reverse shot close-ups of Firth and Mills indicating that their contrasting points of view represent opposing sides in a battle for the masculine soul of Wilson. This scene is in marked contrast to the introduction of Kathleen Scott, a sculptor who is presented as understanding 'the fascination of making the first footmarks'. Nonetheless it is possible to conclude that the resurrection of the Scott myth in 1948 is also linked to the fear of domestic confinement that emerges in postwar culture.

The end of the war and demobilisation finally enabled servicemen to return to a home idealised by absence, but which all too often appeared compromised in reality. The home to which men returned was not that which they had left, and the women to whom they returned were similarly changed by wartime experiences ranging from blitz to evacuation to potentially liberating employment. Disillusionment was inevitable as men experienced anxieties about employment and the reconstruction of their masculinity outside the context of the military. In such a context, *Scott of the Antarctic* can be seen as a fantasy of masculine fulfilment. The exploration of the Antarctic wilderness proposes a masculine space which can be set against the feminised space of home. Significantly, in the construction of the film, home is *not* a secure environment from which Scott departs. Rather, by opening with a montage sequence recreating the return of the earlier *Discovery* expedition, the film posits home as an uncomfortable, passive, disabling space within which the hero is confined, and from which he longs to escape. As Scott finally sets sail in the *Terra Nova*, escaping from the petty pressures of fundraising, the camera cuts between a close-up of Mills's face and a symbolic seagull wheeling over the ocean: 'It is wonderful to be free at last from problems so difficult for me to handle,' intones Mills's voice-over. The constraints of the office are replaced by the freedom of the big adventure. Risk rehabilitates the male, and the escape depicted in the adventures of Scott is no less invigorating for being doomed.

The concept of home as an abject space, a site of attraction and repulsion that is paradoxically both desirable and threatening would become a familiar trope of postwar British culture. Writers from Kingsley Amis to John Osborne would exhibit a horror of the domestic, seeing it as an emasculating force, suffocating male energy and potential. In the late 1940s, however, the problems of readjustment and the loss of the 'privileged' identity of the soldier were only just beginning to be represented. *Scott of the Antarctic* engaged with these anxieties on an epic scale. *The October Man*, by contrast, approached them through a low-key realism ideally suited to the mundane terrors of postwar readjustment. This film is neither *bildungsroman* nor epic, and its protagonist, while not actually anti-heroic, is a conspicuously insignificant figure. *The October Man* anticipates the tropes of alienation and isolation that would dominate representations of masculinity in the 1950s, and its paranoid outlook and grim landscapes present a very different postwar vision from the optimistic new beginnings of *Great Expectations*.

THE OCTOBER MAN: THE SHAPE OF THINGS TO COME

Scarcely a week passes without its new film of schizophrenia, paranoia, neurasthenia and the rest. (George Graham Walker, 'Let Us Get Back to Normal', *Picturegoer*, 11 October 1947)

If *Scott of the Antarctic* was nostalgia incarnate, then Roy Baker's *The October Man* (1947), was the shape of things to come. This critically well-regarded thriller is a narrative of demobilisation disguised as a murder mystery, and it uses the concept of the wounded hero to articulate issues of postwar disorientation and disempowerment. *The October Man*, like *Great Expectations*, tells a story of new beginnings, but in this version the brave new world is a grim and unwelcoming place. The film, predominantly shot in exterior darkness or dimly-lit interiors, is set in a suburban residential hotel, and although contemporary in setting, it chooses to avoid any direct reference to the war. It is nonetheless a narrative of postwar readjustment, and opens with a traumatic accident that physically and psychologically wounds the hero, Jim Ackland, as effectively as any bomb. As Ackland (John Mills) leaves hospital after a year's convalescence, the doctor categorically warns him of the dangers: 'When you've been in a hospital a long time, the outside world seems strange and noisy. People will upset you at first – try not to let them.' Ackland represents the hero who cannot trust himself to return to civilian life, but his alienation is exacerbated by the absence of a heroic narrative, such as war, that would frame and legitimise his evidently wounded masculinity. The film's narrative could be described as the struggle to preserve Ackland's sanity, or perhaps the struggle to define his masculinity, but either way, this battle is also implicitly the social demand for a return to normality – a demand encapsulated by the supporting characters' repeated assertion, in the face of Jim's own doubts, that he is 'all right now'. *Picturegoer*, whose reviewers had exhibited a steadily increasing fear of psychoanalysis as the 1940s progressed, claimed to find no trace of such unhealthy preoccupations here, but an analyst might beg to differ; for this is a film profoundly concerned with the violent impulses that must be repressed for a civilised society to function, and the instabilities exposed by any traumatic rupture, be it accident or war.

However, the demons haunting Ackland also have an external manifestation. His return to the public world is further complicated by the bleak depiction of the community that awaits him. This is a mean-spirited and morally denuded society within which the hotel operates as an emasculating environment that persistently undermines Ackland's attempts to assert himself. The setting of the film has an uncanny quality, appearing at times to present an ominous reworking of the domestic dimension of *The Way to the Stars*, with the gruesome Brockhurst Common Hotel functioning as the dark, repressed double of Toddy's welcoming Golden Lion. The impression of a sinister inversion of what had once been a positive environment is exacerbated by the presence of Joyce Carey in both hotel lounges. As Iris's obnoxious and self-centred aunt in *The Way to the Stars* she was ultimately defeated by a fortuitous combination of factors: Joe Friselli's American charm, Peter Penrose's resilient virtues and Toddy's eventual assertion of authority. In *The October Man* she reigns unchallenged, presiding over the lounge like a spider at the centre of a sordid web of gossip. Entering the cold embrace of the hotel, Ackland is understandably demoralised. Caught in the glare of the residents' prying eyes, he retreats to the sanctuary of his bedroom; exhausted, isolated and tormented by his memories of the past. Throughout the film Ackland's traumatic memories and his suicidal impulses are encoded through the screech of train whistles and the manipulation of a white handkerchief. The handkerchief directly recalls the accident which injured him and killed a child. At the moment of impact Ackland had been tying knots in his handkerchief to make it look like a rabbit, and in moments of stress the handkerchief reappears in Mills's hands, sometimes suggesting threat – when only one knot is viciously tied – but being revealed as vulnerability when the completed rabbit emerges. In his portrayal of the agonised and self-doubting Ackland, Mills's performance is absolutely central to the film. There are very few scenes in which he does not feature, and this narrow perspective is indicative of the decline of the wartime composite hero. There is no longer a context within which such a figure could thrive, and in his place emerges the postwar paradigm of the alienated individual. This inevitably male mode of hero becomes increasingly evident, and increasingly tormented, as the 1950s progress, but in the border zone of *The October Man*, there remains the possibility of redemption through the love of a 'good' woman. Hope for the future is thus seen to reside in a combination of work, self-belief (a sort of masculine 'plausibility') and the unquestioning loyalty of woman-as-helpmeet.

Yet for all the significance of the redeeming woman, *The October Man* is a fundamentally homosocial narrative. It presents a world in which all power and all possibility of self-respect is negotiated between men. Women are not actively evil in this film, but by implication they complicate the tidy structures of patriarchal society. The film presents three significant female characters who, beneath surface subtleties, conform to a familiar set of stereotypes. The virginal redeemer is Jenny Carden (Joan Greenwood), significantly a character that Ackland encounters through the healthy world of work rather than the debilitating environment of the hotel. In this picture Greenwood appears almost impossibly young, her tiny form and delicate features making her a child-woman against whom even Mills stands tall. The diminutive physical stature of the heroine is important as, in terms of the narrative, her role is one of considerable strength. A number of scenes present her as the calm voice of authority against the incipient hysteria of Mills's Ackland. This potentially threatening empowerment is, however, safely contained by camerawork and lighting that emphasises her soft, hyper-feminine features, suggesting vulnerability where in fact there is none. Indeed, the character of Jenny retains vestigial traces of the more independent wartime heroine, but now her mission is her man – and, in what postwar society would have applauded as an entirely healthy transformation, she believes in him as uncritically and wholeheartedly as she was once encouraged to believe in her country.

In Molly Newman (Kay Walsh), by contrast, we are presented with a girl too free with her affections, who is punished for her adultery by death. Yet Molly is a very restrained, and in this sense archetypally British, version of the whore. Molly is always more victim than villain. Described by Ackland as 'a little pathetic', when her dreams begin to fade, she seeks redemption in a return to home and Woolworths. In *The October Man*, then, it is not women's sexuality that is presented as the major threat to patriarchal society, but rather its absence. The film suggests that it is the woman beyond the remit of male control, be she spinster or widow, who is far more sinister and dangerous than the whore. The figure of Mrs Vinton (Joyce Carey) is not just foolish and misguided, she is a corrupting, emasculating force eating away at a healthy heterosexual society. I described her earlier as a spider sitting at the centre of a web of gossip, and she seeks to pull each new resident into the orbit of her authority. When Ackland refuses to make a fourth at bridge, her response is telling: 'You won't play? That's very unsociable.' In a world turned upside down by war, the spinster sets the parameters of society and the wounded hero must submit or face exclusion.

Fortunately for Ackland, however, help is at hand through that most fundamental of man-making activities: work. In the absence of war, masculinity is shaped by the activity of work – a man is what he does – and long before Jenny brings her legitimising heterosexuality to Jim's process of remasculinisation, he has been set on the road to recovery through immersion in the homosocial world of work. Jim's colleague Harry Carden, and the world he metonymically represents, is a good father who provides a secure environment for the vulnerable Ackland that is established as the antithesis of the dark feminine nihilism of the boarding house. Jim and Harry are industrial chemists, building the brave new world in their bright laboratory, and through the validation of his employment, Ackland is reborn.[25] The unutterably weary Mills who first drags himself up to his room is replaced by a Mills who runs carelessly up and down the stairs, reinvigorated and well on the road to recovery. Ackland's reward for his proficiency within the masculine sphere is an introduction to Harry's sister Jenny, who becomes what Eve Sedgwick would term an object of male homosocial exchange. Jenny is part of a triangular system of desire in which the two men, while not actually rivals for her affection, nonetheless use her as an object that consolidates and seals the homosocial bond between them.[26] The pattern could also be described as Oedipal, in that Harry, the father, provides Jim, the son, with an appropriate love object that is neither the mother nor, crucially, anything that might disrupt the primary bond between the two men.

There is little dramatic tension to be found in a woman's unconditional support for her man, which is what Jenny provides when the police identify Ackland as their prime suspect for the murder of Molly Newman. Rather, the emotional betrayal at the heart of the film is a homosocial one. It is Harry, not Jenny, whose support wavers when doubt is cast on Ackland, and a key scene at the centre of the film reveals the extent to which the film presents a struggle for patriarchal acceptance. Patriarchal structures change across history, constructing and, in turn, being constructed by prevailing ideological forces. The patriarchy of late capitalism, which shaped the aspirational, competitive world emerging in the aftermath of the Second World War, was not necessarily kind to men. While it undoubtedly promoted and protected their interests, it did so at a price; namely, conformity to a set of criteria that demanded subordination to structures of authority and power, belief in a success ethos, and a particular mode of self-presentation. Men were obliged to exemplify rationality, restraint and control, all of which attributes were defined by their distance from culturally constructed notions of the feminine.[27] Ackland is imperilled because of his dangerous proximity to the feminine, which is made explicit when he expresses his fears to Jenny. In the process he also reveals the extent to which Harry acts as a patriarchal benchmark within the narrative:

> Ackland: 'What does Harry think? . . . Does he think I did it?'
> Jenny: 'It doesn't matter what Harry thinks.'
> Ackland: 'It does a bit you know. Harry's a very [pause] reasonable person. If he's not quite sure . . .'

Throughout this dialogue a rising edge of hysteria has been discernible in Mills's voice, but he nonetheless pulls back from the brink: 'I'm sorry. I'm sorry. I try to be reasonable, then I get tired and I can't hold on any more.' It is at this point that the couple are joined by Harry, whose presence fundamentally alters the power dynamics of the scene, revealing the extent to which women are incidental accessories to a series of dramas being played out between men [Fig. 4.5]. Judging Ackland to be if not guilty, then at least tainted by association, Harry turns their consensual relationship into a rivalry by attempting to take Jenny away. With his back to the wall, Ackland responds with an effort to out-perform his rival. He is more reasonable even than the force of reason posed against him. As Jenny speaks to Ackland, proposing a meeting, Jim's gaze is fixed on Harry, negotiating the handover of the woman. Jenny notices their silent communication and cries, 'It isn't what Harry wants!', but in this she is wrong. If Ackland is ever fully to regain his masculinity and be accepted as a legitimate patriarchal subject, then he must respond not to Jenny's desires, but to Harry's.

Fig. 4.5 Homosocial bonds: Erotic triangles in *The October Man* (1947). British
Film Institute/London Features International

Picturegoer's article, 'Let Us Get Back to Normal' (October 1947), proposed
that one of the redeeming features of *The October Man* was its suggestion that
the love of a good woman is all a man needs to deal with his psychological
problems. Unfortunately, closer inspection of the narrative does not support
such a reading. However much rational advice and unconditional love Jenny
imparts, it is ultimately insufficient to save Ackland. Rather, the film implies,
it is the more familiar medicine of agency that restores his masculinity. Pursued
by the police and running against the clock, Ackland sets out to solve the
murder himself, and in so doing fulfils the requirements of the thriller hero.
The thriller form depends not on institutional structures, but on individual
agency, pitting a lone figure against seemingly insurmountable odds. Thrillers
would become one of the staple forms of 1950s British cinema, their formula
ideally suited to the anxieties of the decade. In the success and survival of the
hero, the genre promotes a fantasy of individual empowerment, imagining an
escape from societal constraint and surveillance. Institutions, such as the police
or the services, are not generally presented as corrupt, but rather too large and
impersonal to respond to individual circumstances, and all too often they

misread the evidence. Ironically, Jim Ackland is misread by the police because of his association with another institution – the hospital – and having been labelled as a 'mental case', he is excluded from the society of rational masculinity. His words carry no weight as he is no longer a plausible male. Ackland's impotence cannot be healed by Jenny's belief: her word, as a woman, carries no more weight than his as a madman. His situation can be alleviated only through action and the confrontation of risk. Here *The October Man* embraces the spiritual principles of *Scott of the Antarctic*. Women are all very well, but masculinity is only secure so long as it is being constantly reasserted through action. The pattern that concludes the film is a familiar one. Ackland is physically beaten, he reasserts himself and fights back; Ackland is psychologically beaten by the disbelief of the police, he regroups by evading them and becoming the agent through which the mystery is resolved.[28]

The film ends with Mills leaning over the railway bridge repeating the line, 'I didn't give in.' The symbolic handkerchief of the past has been crushed on the rails below, and Joan Greenwood is in his arms. But, as Marcia Landy has argued: '[T]he image of [Ackland's] salvation hardly mitigates the dark and menacing world portrayed throughout the film' (1991: 270). As a vision of the postwar world, there is little positive to be found here, and the film struggles to achieve optimism in the face of uncertainty. Neither Jenny nor Harry is keen to listen to Jim's doubts, rather they overwrite them with their assertions of his normality and health. This is a society that would deny the power of the past, a society seeking to return the repressed whence it came. In its romantic conclusion it offers a fantasy of escape from dark days and darker memories, but as the narratives of the 1950s would reveal, the past could not easily be contained. In the decade after the war, past crimes and past glories would increasingly permeate British cinema narratives – either as a burden to be born, or as a myth to be inhabited. For Mills, and the particular mode of masculinity he had once represented, it was the end of an era and, not unlike the postwar period itself, his career followed a pattern of great expectations followed by disappointment and readjustment.

It was perhaps unfortunate for Mills that his most successful years in cinema to date should have coincided with the beginning of the latest, and perhaps most catastrophic, of British film industry crises. In August 1947, following a series of parliamentary debates dubbed 'Bogart or Bacon', the chancellor of the exchequer, Hugh Dalton, imposed a 75 per cent tax on American films. The Motion Picture Association of America responded with a boycott. These events occurred at a terrible time for the biggest man in British films, J. Arthur Rank, who had been wooing the American market in an attempt to get a wider release for British pictures. The Dalton duty effectively scuppered his plans and ensured a chilly reception for British pictures abroad. Rank had also suffered financially from a series of expensive flops, most notably Gabriel Pascal's *Caesar and Cleopatra* (1945). However, in the face of the American boycott he threw his company into an unprecedentedly ambitious programme of production, which was perhaps doomed to failure:[29]

> It was the familiar tale, in a slightly modified form, of the conflict between art and business. Rank discovered that productivity, in itself, was no guarantee of success. Criticized for so long for his policy of making high budget, prestige pictures, he was now similarly attacked for sponsoring mediocre, medium-budget pot-boilers. (Macnab 1993: 183)

By 1948 Rank was making massive losses, and as his debts rose, his influence over the creative side of his film empire steadily declined, to be replaced by that of John Davis, accountant and, according to many 'the pantomime villain of British film history' (Macnab 1993: 200).

Mills would probably have agreed with this description. Under Rank he had been invited to write his own contract, as a result of which he optimistically embarked on his production career. Under Davis the contract was cancelled and Mills, like most people in the film industry, felt the chill of recession. He had wanted to stretch himself creatively, but the relative failure of both *The History of Mr Polly* and *The Rocking Horse Winner*, combined with a couple of theatrical flops, left him prepared to appear in anything that would pay the rent. The 1950s would be a decade of genre films and comedy cycles epitomised by *Doctor in the House* and the first *Carry On* films. According to Geoffrey Macnab: '[A] different style of production emerged at Pinewood, one that in its regulation and efficiency, if not its inspiration, was as close as Britain ever got to a classical Hollywood cinema' (1993: 216). The crisis within the industry, and the uncertainties of the postwar period had resolved themselves into a desire for the known and familiar, but it was a familiarity inflected with a different and distinctly postwar flavour. Gritty disillusionment would vie with generic reinscriptions of the heroic fantasy and in the 1950s Mills, once the symbol of a national modernity, would become an emblem of the past. Fortunately, Everyman was a figure that could be recycled, and as the new decade progressed directors reached for Mills in a diversity of new capacities. Where once he had been an emblem of the nation as steady, plucky and reliable, now he embraced the new versions of national masculinity that were slowly beginning to emerge. As the 1950s progressed he would become variously angry, flawed, wronged and frustrated. He would lose his authority, become a relic of a bygone age, appear as oppressed, impotent and foolish. The nation was changing, and the body of Mills became a screen upon which the pain of transformation would be written.

NOTES

1. Dorothy Sheridan's Mass Observation anthology, *Wartime Women*, for example, describes scenes of celebration, but the predominant tone of the VE day reports is subdued and wary: 'There seems to be nothing but strife and confusion ahead when we should be seeing the bright skies of peace – and we are all feeling tired and hardly capable of coping with it' (Sheridan 1991: 236).

2. Hennessy stresses, however, that there was not a general and widespread perception of the collapse of empire in the immediate postwar period. That began to emerge after 1948 and only fully developed in the 1950s.

3. Robert Murphy's *Realism and Tinsel* (1989) cites *Waterloo Road* as the beginning of a trend that would go on to encompass such box-office successes as *They Made Me a Fugitive* (1947) and *Brighton Rock* (1947).

4. Michael Balcon, head of Ealing studios and the film's producer, offered a pertinent analysis of the film's lack of success in America: 'The American public has no interest in failure, even if it is heroic failure, and certainly they do not easily accept other people's legends' (1969: 174). After six years of war, and many more years of American films, it is likely that some of this feeling had rubbed off on British audiences.

5. Pathetic fallacy is particularly noticeable in relation to Magwitch. His return is symbolised by a violently stormy night, while the chill wind that whistles around the safehouse is suggestive of the spying eyes that would prevent his escape.

6. In this context, the casting of the 37-year-old Mills to play the 21-year-old Pip is singularly appropriate. Mills was sufficiently well-preserved to carry off the part, but in some scenes – such as the twenty-first birthday encounter in Jaggers's office – there is a certain dissonance between the physical appearance of the actor and the stage of the character's life enacted.

7. The phrase 'poetic realism' is Richard Winnington's and is quoted from John Ellis's fascinating survey of film criticism in the immediate postwar period (Ellis 1996: 71).

8. Indeed, in the case of *The Way to the Stars*, the magazine was out of line with a significant body of popular opinion. Readers of the *Daily Mail* voted the film the most popular of the war years (Aldgate and Richards 1994: 277).

9. *Picturegoer*'s first substantial article on Mills is not by any of the staff writers, but is rather a piece sent in by a serviceman, Lt G. Rowell (29 September 1945), who praises the versatility, accomplishment and consistency of Mills's performances and puts forward his claim 'to a higher place in the public esteem than some of our newly arrived stars'. Mills makes the cover of the magazine three times in the 1940s. Once, in 1943, for *We Dive at Dawn*, once for *Great Expectations* – in costume with his co-star Valerie Hobson (4 January 1947) – and finally, on his own (14 February 1948), in a photograph that cannot be linked to any specific film, and which would seem to suggest his increased status as a star towards the end of the decade.

10. Lean's film is littered with expressive objects. In a later table scene, the work is performed by Bernard Miles as Joe Gargery's ghastly formal hat literally rises up against him. In its anarchic progress around the room, it destroys the façade of politeness covering Pip's snobbish resentment of Joe. As he watches this spectacle,

Mills's face is hard, the lips thin and drawn, registering silent disgust and barely controlled anger – both of which are easily read by Joe.

11. In contrast to the older, wiser, almost melancholic character of Dickens's novel.

12. Perhaps the most famous example of James Mason's film sadism is his horsewhipping of Margaret Lockwood in *The Man in Grey*. Mills is spared such direct action, but his complicity is heightened by his initial conspicuous ignoring of Miss Havisham's screams.

13. The *Picturegoer* gold medal was awarded for the best performance by an actor and an actress in a film of the previous year. Although it presented itself as a reward for acting, it nonetheless operated as a gauge of popularity, and it undoubtedly raised the profile of its winners within the magazine.

14. Very few parts could have offered the opportunity for ensemble playing, comedy, vulnerability, Byronic masculinity, romance, aggression, action and mature reflection that *Great Expectations* provides.

15. Roland Huntford's 1979 biography provides an unflinching account of Scott's failings: his stubborn refusal to recognise the superiority of dogs in the Antarctic environment, his poor planning and fickle decision-making, the impossible distances left between stores on the return journey, the convoluted and restrictive instructions with which he bound the remaining members of the expedition. Most of these failings were recognised in 1948, but the filmmakers' determination to make a consensual picture that offended neither relatives nor survivors of the original expedition ensured that any acknowledgement of error was implicit rather than explicit. It is also the case that some failings, such as Scott's sentimental attachment to the ponies and dogs that led him to put animal welfare above the welfare of his men, can be actively rehabilitated as laudable manifestations of English character.

16. For the filmmakers, there must also have been something liberating (if also difficult and daunting) in the epic scale of the production. There were three overseas locations: Switzerland, Norway and Antarctica itself, to where Osmond Borradaile, one of the film's directors of photography, was dispatched to gather the remarkable, vivid Technicolor ice and sea sequences that still strike the viewer as awe-inspiring some fifty years later. To make something this visually expansive simply had not been possible during the war years.

17. Both Bowers and Oates travelled from India in the hope of convincing Scott to take them on the expedition.

18. In *The Battle for Britain* David Morgan and Mary Evans argue that while the welfare reforms of the period 'mitigated grosser inequalities and rationalised the fragmented provisions of the past', they nonetheless 'left the structures of inequality and their hierarchies of privilege largely untouched' (1993: 131–2).

19. Charles Frend's career to date had very much been grounded in the documentary approach. His directorial début, *The Big Blockade* (1942), was followed by such films as *The Foreman went to France* (1942) and *San Demetrio, London* (1943).

20. 'It was a good film, well-made and well-acted under appalling conditions. But I feel that if we'd been allowed to delve more deeply into the characters of the men themselves, it could have been a great one' (Mills 2001: 296).

21. The most obvious example is the eloquent pattern of paw-prints that decorates the snow around Amundsen's Polheim tent, reminding the spectator of Scott's reliance on motors rather than dogs. However, Wilson's speechlessness after Scott's announcement that he will take a fifth man on a journey provisioned for four is perhaps equally damning.

22. Alone amongst the critics C. A. Lejeune remarked upon the ambiguity in the film's presentation of Scott: 'I came away with the unfortunate impression of an obstinate, rather vainglorious man who grew pettish at the thought of competition . . . and who deliberately threw away the lives of men and animals in an expedition that he knew to be abortive.' Yet curiously her response to this perception is to desire a more confidently heroic narrative: 'Even if Scott had not been a greater man than this, the interests of a national legend demand that he should be shown as such' (*Observer*, 5 December 1948).

23. *Picturegoer*, for example, praised the quality of the adaptation, the camerawork, the colour and the quality of the acting, but was mildly outraged by what it felt was the film's failure to do justice to the full nobility of Oates's sacrifice (1 January 1949). Ironically, behind the scenes the American censor was threatening to prevent this 'suicide' being depicted at all (Balcon 1969: 174).

24. Graham Dawson observes that it has become increasingly difficult to tell the stories of Empire and to make sense of Britain's imperial past (1994: 154), and this observation perhaps sheds further light on the resilience of the Scott myth as a somehow respectable manifestation of an otherwise discredited ideal.

25. As Geraghty (2000: 21–37) and Spicer (2001: 55–8) have noted, the ambiguous forces of technology would become a key trope of the 1950s.

26. In *Between Men: English Literature and Male Homosocial Desire*, Sedgwick describes an erotic triangle comprising two active, competing members and a passive object of desire, arguing that: '[I]n any erotic rivalry, the bond that links the two rivals is as intense and potent as the bond that links either of the rivals to the beloved' (1985: 21).

27. There is a distinction to be drawn between the feminine, which is wholly antithetical to patriarchal structures, and homosexuality, which is not. As Eve Sedgwick observes, there is nothing to suggest that because 'most patriarchies structurally include homophobia, therefore patriarchy structurally *requires* homophobia' (1985: 4).

28. There is a degree of irony in Ackland's efforts to vindicate himself. When he tells the truth, nobody believes him, but once he begins to lie – fabricating a series of stories while on the run from the police – he becomes wholly plausible and convincing.

29. A useful survey of the crisis is provided by Peter Forster's 'J. Arthur Rank and the Shrinking Screen', in Sissons and French 1986.

Part III

Part III

5

Dead Men, Angry Men and Drunks: Post-traumatic stress and the 1950s

We used to think ourselves a nation of muddlers, of opportunists, of individualists, of lovers of the voluntary habit of action, of amateurs, *et id genus omne*. If we were once of that sort, are we still of that sort today? Are we not moving towards the planned life, the regimented state, a system of orders and regulations, and a general professional habit of action in which the old volunteer and amateur quality is destined to be engulfed? (Barker 1948: xii)

When conditions for the defence of patriarchy change, the bases for the dominance of a particular masculinity are eroded. New groups may challenge old solutions and construct a new hegemony. (Connell 1995: 77)

Social misfit – that's what I am. ('Mr Polly', in *The History of Mr Polly* 1949)

Although the following three chapters pursue a roughly chronological development from 1950 to 1970, they are also subject to temporal overlaps, and move between the films of two decades in a rather more fluid manner than was the case in Part I. This shift to a thematic rather than a strictly chronological approach emerges from the impossibility of imposing a straightforward scheme of development upon a period of rapid and radical change in terms of both gender and national self-image. Together the 1950s and 1960s comprise a period of national reinscription, and it is not possible to chart a linear progression through either Mills's films or the events of the decades. New genres and preoccupations emerged within the British film industry as patterns of production changed in response to falling cinema attendances and the gradual withdrawal of the major combines (Rank and ABPC) from large-scale filmmaking programmes.[1] As the decade progressed, competition from television had an increasing impact on patterns of cinema-going, while Rank and ABPC discovered there was more money to be made in exhibition than production. Nonetheless, the combines remained the most powerful force in film production, controlling the financing and distribution of much of the industry's output. However, their moves towards diversification created some space for change, and the end of the decade saw the growth of independent film production companies such as Allied Film Makers and Woodfall, who would be responsible for such influential films as *The League of Gentlemen* (1960) and *Saturday Night and Sunday Morning* (1960).

Although actors such as Richard Attenborough and Bryan Forbes would play major roles in independent production, Mills made no further movements in that direction after the relative box-office failure of *The History of Mr Polly* (1949) and *The Rocking Horse Winner* (1950). Instead he concentrated on acting, appearing in some twenty-one films between 1950 and 1959. These films did not work to construct a homogeneous screen persona of the type that Mills had acquired during the 1940s, but they did continue to draw on fundamental characteristics associated with the Everyman figure, complicating and developing the concept of national masculinity which he had come to embody over the previous two decades. From the 1950s onwards, then, four types of roles became associated with, or were offered to, Mills. After the heroism, albeit flawed, of *Great Expectations* and *Scott of the Antarctic*, Mills's roles drifted inexorably towards the mock heroic – a mode typified by his performance as Willie Mossop in *Hobson's Choice* (1954) – and the anti-heroic, exemplified by a series of roles featuring variously angry, flawed and displaced men. By the 1960s a third category was evolving – the symbol of impotent authority – which co-existed with a number of roles as a more benign father figure. Finally, Mills played the fool in a number of guises, most notably as Michael in David Lean's *Ryan's Daughter* (1970).

Yet in spite of the element of diversification suggested by this categorisation of Mills's roles, it is important to acknowledge that these changes co-existed with a profound continuity in the symbolic value represented by the actor. In the years after 1948, Mills's screen persona was subject to new pressures and humiliations, but his status as a national icon was nonetheless consolidated. Consequently, this chapter will begin by examining the trends emerging in the British cinema of the 1950s that would ensure that, almost irrespective of role, Mills would be perceived as standing for 'old fashioned British decency' (Richards 1997: 144). In large part this was the legacy of *Scott of the Antarctic*. In the aftermath of Captain Scott, the cultural status of Mills's screen persona had undergone a paradigm shift, and while he would continue to play a seemingly diverse range of roles, for many, including the critics, he would be perceived as performing a masculinity of repetition. In the flawed masculinities of the dead men, the angry men and the drunks can be seen the stoicism, understatement and 'decency' of heroic British failure, while the less complex heroes of the generic war films that emerged in the later half of the decade prompted the actor to reiterate the characteristic gestures of wartime crisis in a new context of national adventure.[2] Yet Mills's new status as an exemplary old-fashioned hero was also the product of a wider diversification in patterns of stardom. The war had, if nothing else, broadened the range of acceptable screen masculinities, and Mills's screen persona was now in competition with a range of new faces and new national embodiments.

Andrew Spicer links both Jack Hawkins and Kenneth More to versions of a robust postwar Britishness. Hawkins conveyed a paternal solidity, a gritty toughness that was leavened by a carefully modulated sensitivity. More, by contrast, is described by Spicer as a combination of the 'debonair' and the 'blokeish', the hyper-confident, but nonetheless acceptable, face of the middle classes (2001: 39). These new national figures were supplemented by actors such as Trevor Howard, Alec Guinness, Michael Redgrave, Jack Warner, Stanley Baker and Dirk Bogarde. Mills's screen persona was sufficiently elastic to compete with the flawed masculinities of Howard, the comic eccentricities of Guinness, the stolidity of Warner and the ebullience of More, but the models of masculinity embodied by Baker and Bogarde represented territories he could not occupy. He did not have Baker's looming physicality, self-evident toughness and dark, brooding intensity. Bogarde likewise was a far more romantic and sexually charismatic screen presence, although for much of the 1950s his potentially unsettling physicality was contained by the strait-jacket of Rank family values. Obviously no actor can be all men to all films, but the space that Mills had occupied in the 1940s, the Everyman persona that enabled his casting in roles from William Wilberforce to Shorty Blake, from Peter Penrose to Mr Polly and from Pip to Captain Scott, was no longer regarded as such a versatile territory. Rather Mills's screen persona became, as befits the era, a site of specialisation.[3] As the reviews of his films suggest, Mills was occupying familiar territory, but with subtle variations on the theme. The *Manchester Guardian*, for example, described his work in *The Long Memory* as a 'highly competent repetition of a familiar performance':

> Mr Mills, given the right sort of part, is one of the most heart-stirring players of the British screen. . . . So it is exasperating to find that in 'The Long Memory' Mr Mills is just repeating the sort of role to which he has been condemned (or has condemned himself) in film after film – that of the honest fellow on whom fate has played a dirty trick but who keeps a very stiff upper lip and triumphs in the virtuous end. (*Manchester Guardian*, 24 January 1953)

The question of who or what was responsible for Mills's transition from innovation to repetition is difficult to determine. *The History of Mr Polly* and *The Rocking Horse Winner*, two films in which, as producer, he had indisputable control over his casting, suggest both a desire for change and a resistance to the concept of a 'star persona'. Playing Polly gave him the opportunity to rewrite the Everyman figure as a hapless romantic dreamer, a frequently humiliated accidental hero who finds peace in a withdrawal from conventional society. By contrast, but still at odds with constructions of the star, in *The Rocking Horse Winner* he took on the supporting role of Barrett, the odd-job man who tries to befriend the lonely son of a seriously dysfunctional family. This is a self-effacing and effective performance that does nothing to detract from the central and more demanding roles taken by Valerie Hobson and the child actor John Howard Davies. However, as the previous chapter suggested, trends in cinema production worked against Mills's attempts to capitalise constructively upon his postwar stardom. It also seems likely that as time passed, the perception of his screen persona had concretised into a more clearly heroic and less subtly variable form. However, at a basic level, the standardisation of Mills's roles and performances was also the product of economic necessity. *The Long Memory*, like many of his films at this time, was made to pay the tax man (Mills 2001: 314). Through this combination of unpropitious factors, Mills mutated into the familiar under pressure – the norm pushed to the limit – an asexual, safe masculinity which could be cast in a variety of 'dangerous' roles in the secure knowledge that nothing bad would happen. In a retreat from the model of casting which had seen him play a traitor in *Cottage to Let*, Mills spent much of the 1950s as a reliable indicator of filmic conservatism. Irrespective of the superficial demands of plot and characterisation, his body came to symbolise an incorruptible core of British integrity: with Mills in the lead, society need have no fear of ex-convicts (*The Long Memory*, 1953), murderous fathers (*Mr Denning Drives North*, 1951) or even the IRA (*The Gentle Gunman*, 1952).

The retrenchment evident in the trajectory of Mills's career was symptomatic of British cinema as a whole. The paradoxical desire for both stability and change that had characterised the postwar period faded into a more clearly conservative comfort zone and, as Jeffrey Richards has noted, the cinema turned increasingly to the themes and genres of the 1930s (1997: 144). Describing the 1950s as a time in which 'more sheerly tedious and uninspired films were produced in Britain than at any other time' (p. 145), Richards evokes a decade of gender normativity, respectability and rehashed adventure narratives. Christine Geraghty, however, argues that British cinema in this period was the site of an ongoing struggle between the discourses of modernity and tradition, in which, almost invariably, tradition came out on top.[4] Across a wide variety of genres, from comedy to crime, British films worked to contain the symbols of progress within the structures of conformity. New influences were not necessarily unwelcome, but they seldom supplanted the old. Rather they were 'apprenticed' to familiar structures of authority, which were in turn reinvigorated by the influx of new blood. Geraghty observes, in relation to such films as *The Mouse that Roared* (1959) and *Doctor in the House* (1954):

> [M]ainstream comedies that lampooned the traditional classes and hierarchies also served to support them in the face of modernising threats to blow them away . . . these comedies have the curious quality of being both stultifying and rebellious and . . . when faced with a conflict between the traditional and the modern, they revert to the traditional in a way that blocks off the challenges and risks that comedy can present. (Geraghty 2000: 56)

This analysis of comedy is equally applicable to drama, and in Mills's case it has considerable resonances for the transformation of his screen persona in the aftermath of *Scott*.[5] Ironically, in the space of less than five years, the actor identified by Andrew Spicer as the most modern figure to emerge from Second World War British cinema had become the definitive symbol of tradition.[6]

The shift in the cultural value accorded to Mills's screen persona was paralleled by an equally regressive shift in the construction of the British war film. This regression is most immediately evident in the mutation of the wartime group and the resurgence of the individual hero. Geraghty observes a transition from 'a representative group of individuals with whom the audience can identify to an elite group whom the audience is invited to admire' (2000: 187). Within this group, the leader stands out as an isolated figure, moving gradually from the position of emotional complexity exhibited by Jack Hawkins's Captain Ericson in *The Cruel Sea* (1953) to the professional aloofness of Richard Todd's Guy Gibson in *The Dam Busters* (1955) (2000: 186–90). The greater focus on the single heroic figure confirms Richards's perception of a return to pre-war narrative patterns and the war film emerged as the adventure narrative for the new decade. In the words of Andrew Spicer: '[I]t was the cycle of war films, from around 1950 onwards, that replaced imperialism as the source for epic and inspiring stories about British male endeavour and the national character' (2001: 35). The generic war film thus embodies, to a lesser or greater extent, a concept which might be termed 'nostalgic virility', and Mills's contribution to this reassertion of national pride came in films such as *The Colditz Story* (1955), *Above Us the Waves* (1955) and *I Was Monty's Double* (1958).[7] Films such as these revisit the crises of wartime and rewrite them as adventures. They also repeatedly cite the British soldier, sailor or airman as supremely competent, tough, humorous and resourceful, and in so doing they make a significant statement about the nation. As the decade progressed and Britain's status as an imperial power was further undermined by humiliations such as the Suez Crisis, the nostalgic virility of the generic war film served to regenerate the nation through the quality of its masculinity. In a trope suggested as far back as 1935's *First Offence*, British soil is regarded as uniquely fertile: Britain produces remarkable men, and these men in turn make the nation remarkable, irrespective of its actual social, economic or political state.[8]

Nostalgic virility permeated a high percentage of war-themed pictures made during the 1950s, but not all of Mills's service pictures conformed to this pattern. Indeed, the decade was bracketed by two films that presented a significant challenge to these narratives of reassurance: *Morning Departure* (1950) and *Ice Cold in Alex* (1958). For all the courage displayed by the protagonists of these films, their narratives can offer only ambiguous closure and a provisional statement of national character. The problems that emerge from the later film, *Ice Cold in Alex*, are indicative of tensions in the construction of a national heroic figure that would intensify in the 1960s, and which will be the subject of a later discussion. *Morning Departure*, by contrast, is problematised by its proximity to the 1940s. Like *Scott of the Antarctic* this is a film concerned with cultural mourning, and like *Scott*, it adds weight to this process through the deployment – and destruction – of the national figure of Mills.

A BAD DAY AT THE OFFICE: *MORNING DEPARTURE*

'You, Sir? Not stay in the navy? You'll never leave the sea.'

Able Seaman Higgins's prophetic words, spoken with incredulity to Mills's Lieutenant Commander Armstrong, unwittingly embody the central irony of Roy Baker's *Morning Departure*. The process of transition from war to peace, including the hero's choice between the heterosexual space of domesticity and the homosocial bond of service life, are rendered redundant by death. When the submarine *Trojan* is sunk by a left-over mine on a peacetime training exercise, the anxieties and hopes of postwar reconstruction are painfully overwritten by a narrative of loss. The men die, we are told, because of 'bad luck and bad weather', and irrespective of the criticisms of the historical record, Captain Scott could have said much the same of his Polar party.

That *Morning Departure* should on its release primarily be interpreted as a memorial was the inevitable outcome of its being completed shortly before the loss of the submarine *Truculent*, in which sixty-four men died. Mills records that the extreme proximity between fiction and reality almost resulted in the film being withdrawn, but that the decision to release it was vindicated by the positive response it elicited from the relatives of the *Truculent*'s dead (2001: 306–8). The critical reponse to the film was exceptional, and as was the case with *Scott*, much of the praise was couched in explicitly national terms. The *Manchester Guardian* suggested that the film displayed a 'national idiom of courage' (25 February 1950), while C. A. Lejeune of the *Observer* argued that there must be an inexplicable 'racial attachment' that explains the way that 'a story of ships and the men who serve in them will stir an Englishman' (26 February 1950).[9] Mills's performance was also highly praised. Dilys Powell in the *Sunday Times* described it as 'one of the subtly understated performances which have made his reputation: you can feel the tensions beneath the surface behaviour, but the behaviour itself is controlled, business-like and even' (26 February 1950). There was, however, one aspect of the film that gave rise to minor criticisms, namely the on-shore preface comprising snapshots of the crew's personal lives. Those critics who commented on the opening were generally relieved when this domestic dimension was over and attention could be focused on the serious business of male bonding beneath the sea. Yet the prefatory material is far from superfluous. Indeed, it is these opening sequences that give substance to the 'tensions beneath the surface' identified by Powell in the performance of Mills. While the four men trapped in the submarine all gradually come to the realisation that they will die, this fate is not inevitable from the outset of the film. Consequently much of the dialogue and interaction operates within a temporary time bubble, a 'space between' that becomes a locus for reflection upon the pressing issues facing men at the time of the film's production. Not surprisingly, *Morning Departure*'s concern with contemporary class and gender tensions was overshadowed by the events that accompanied its release, but these issues are nonetheless embedded within the film, and are fundamental to its status as a postwar narrative.

Although very much a 'service' picture, *Morning Departure* precedes the cycle of war films that seek to reinscribe national virility through the repetition of past glories. Rather it is a transitional film that is permeated with the anxieties of postwar reconstruction, and those critics who commented on the inappropriate opening were perhaps responding to the disjuncture between the worlds negotiated by the film. *Morning Departure* touches on a considerable range of potentially painful topics, from demobilisation to the war neurosis implicit in the first officer's loss of self-confidence following a previous submarine disaster. Consequently, although the tropes of wartime group heroism are revisited and reworked, the film cannot be contained within this framework. The concerns mobilised by the preface pervade the narrative and suggest that the film is motivated by the same heterosexualising imperative that fuelled *The Way to the Stars*. The film is also indelibly marked by the conflict between tradition and modernity identified by Geraghty as characteristic of the 1950s. The core tensions of *Morning Departure* are those of class and gender, and the film negotiates these conflicts through a series of visual and narrative threads that connect the hermetic environment of the sunken submarine with the wider world beyond.

The film's transitional status, on the borderline between a militarised and a demobilised society, between war and postwar, public service and private repopulation, is evident from the outset: this is a war film that begins in the home. After a brief glimpse of a battleship, the camera cuts to the typical bedroom location of the companionate 1950s couple. Husband and wife lie asleep in their twin divan beds, and awake to the cry of their firstborn child. Mills's performance here is one of light comedy. His hair is ruffled in sleep, with exaggerated movements he attempts to get up without waking his wife. She wakes nonetheless and their conversation continues in the unchallenging vein established by Mills's body language. Approaching each other with casual affection, they joke about their roles as wife and submarine commander in an exchange that establishes a key trope of the film: the increasingly permeable boundary separating the domestic space of home from the working space of the navy. In response to his wife's offer of breakfast, Armstrong responds, 'Rules for gallant submarine commanders: be able to do everything that your men can do and that includes frying eggs. I'll cook my own.'

In the light of what is to follow this scene could come from a different film, most probably a domestic comedy entitled *The Navy Lark* or *All at Sea* [Fig. 5.1]. However, the vision of domestic bliss is short-lived. In the very next scene a palpable tension is evident as Armstrong's wife Helen (Helen Cherry) asks him to leave the navy. 'Surely you've had enough of submarines,' she exclaims in a speech that is effectively an order to give up childish things. The male space of war is here rewritten as a phase, or even an adventure, to be transcended and replaced by the serious business of managing a vacuum-cleaner factory. He is reluctant to give up the homosocial community of the submarine. She wants to have a home, to 'belong somewhere'. The demand that women choose rooted domesticity over flux and change is typical of postwar narratives, as is the need for men to relearn the rules of peace. *Morning Departure*, however, is unusual in the amount of time it gives to debating this choice, and in the ambiguity with which it frames its conclusions.

The debate begins with Helen Armstrong's ultimatum, presented as her husband shaves in front of the bathroom mirror. As the dialogue between the couple progresses, the camera remains fixed on Mills's reflection. Her tone is serious, while he attempts to avoid the issue by maintaining the bantering tone of the opening sequence; but however light his voice, the subtle hesitations and breaks in his shaving process indicate the unwelcome impact of his wife's request. Armstrong's reluctance to confront the future is thus suggested through the classical trope of the mirror's indirection, while the doubling implicit in the hero's reflection indicates that leaving the navy will involve a

Fig. 5.1 All at sea: Mills and Helen Cherry in *Morning Departure* (1950). British Film Institute/London Features International

fundamental reinscription of identity – a metaphor extended by allowing Mills to complete the scene in a half-shaved state. However, while the male is only in the process of being retrained for peace, the film rather comically suggests that the navy has already been domesticated. The structure of a submarine commander's day is now no different from an office worker's and, in a departure that is the absolute antithesis of the wartime navy, Armstrong leaves the house promising to be home for tea.

Morning Departure undoubtedly depicts a fundamentally different navy from that of the war years. There is something faintly shambolic about the officers who sit slouched in the depot ship's office, an impression heightened by a later scene in which Armstrong's professional composure is undermined by a crewman's escaping pigeon. Although reference is made to wartime heroics, the more pressing point of interest amongst the officers is whether a baby-sitter can be found for the weekly social get-together. The emphasis on the ordinary and the everyday, combined with the disconsolate hint of 'peacetime fatigue', transforms warriors into bureaucrats and blurs the previously sacrosanct boundaries between homosocial and heterosexual space. It is not until the *Trojan* is safely beneath the waves that Mills will metamorphose into an infinitely less mannered, but equally dignified, version of Noël Coward's Captain Kinross from *In Which We Serve*. This connection was made by some reviewers at the time of release and it bears repeating for the insight it gives into Mills's performance of authority. The patrician element of Coward's performance is avoided, locating Armstrong in closer proximity to both his officers and his men. In part such a proximity is an inevitable consequence of a submarine drama: as we are repeatedly reminded in *Morning Departure*, submariners are a breed apart. But the performance also bears the hallmark of wartime shifts in the representation of authority: the element of consensus is implicit in Mills's more approachable figure. Yet what remains of Coward is an emphasis on the duty of leadership. Armstrong must be both the group leader and a man apart, and it is only in Mills's quiet gestures of exhaustion and despair that the burden of responsibility can be expressed. *In Which We Serve* was variously cited as a benchmark naval drama (C. A. Lejeune), a problematic forebear (William Whitebait) and, in the case of Noël Coward's performance, an example to be avoided (Joan Lester). However, while the earlier film maintained strict boundaries between its scenes of civilian life and its celebration of masculine courage, in *Morning Departure* the boundaries are altogether more blurred. The chief engineer, like Captain Scott escaping to sea, 'always feels better' once they are under the water, and Armstrong shares this relief at escaping from shorebound difficulties. But although the submarine is presented as a means of reclaiming masculine space, the dilemma proposed by his wife's demand for roots follows Armstrong to the bottom of the sea and forms the substance of key dialogues both with his friend, Lieutenant Manson (Nigel Patrick), and with his subordinates, Stoker Snipe (Richard Attenborough) and A. B. Higgins (James Hayter).[10]

There are numerous ways in which the film suggests both the invasion of the workspace by the domestic and the extent to which the space is itself already domesticated. The snatches of dialogue overheard as the submarine prepares for departure are predominantly concerned with plans for the evening on shore, while Higgins literally brings the domestic on board when he is left holding Nobby Clarke's homing pigeon. Clarke has abandoned his pet for a more pressing emergency – his wife is giving birth to their first child. Appropriately, it is Clarke's urgent response to this domestic call that will save his life. Yet plot and dialogue are not the only channels of domestic infiltration. The *mise-en-scène* also works to emphasise the overlap and when Armstrong and Manson must decide which of the surviving men will be the first to escape, Armstrong reaches for the packed lunch conveniently provided by Helen [Fig. 5.2]. The formal space of the wardroom is rewritten through the casual dining of the two men, who in their concentrated list-making resemble nothing so much as schoolboys picking teams.

Fig. 5.2 Homosocial spaces: Mills and Nigel Patrick safe beneath the sea in *Morning Departure* (1950). British Film Institute/London Features International

However, it is Higgins, the ship's cook, who is fundamental to the homosocial domestication of the submarine space. As the second party of men prepare to make their escape, he circulates with a plate of sardines, claiming that, like a well-to-do household, the submarine could not function without its cook. After beginning the film in the clearly demarcated space of lower-class comic relief, Hayter's Higgins evolves into something of a maternal figure: staunch, uncomplicated and unflappable. This feminisation of the working classes can be read as a regression to patterns of class representation that predominated before the Second World War, and its resurgence in the context of *Morning Departure* complements the parallel re-emergence of a distinct officer hero. While the war had gradually seen a diminution of class differences through the structure of the group hero, the generic war film of the later 1950s increasingly returned to the valorisation of officers and gentlemen. *Morning Departure* might be seen as a hybrid class construction, operating on the cusp between wartime community and postwar reaction: the plot demands the breakdown of class barriers, with the surviving men bound together in the wardroom, but the *mise-en-scène* repeatedly undermines this communal ideal. When Armstrong makes the democratic gesture of inviting the men into the wardroom, his irritation at their conversation and manners makes Snipe and Higgins deeply uncomfortable. Later, the continued presence of firm class boundaries is evident in the negotiation of the personal in the men's conversation. When Higgins proposes a post-rescue celebration at the 'Red Lion', he is surprised and delighted to discover Armstrong's familiarity with the same pub. So delighted in fact that he suggests the captain should bring his wife. The pause that follows clearly indicates Higgins's anxiety at having over-stepped the mark by invoking the sacrosanct figure of the middle-class woman. Armstrong reassures him that his wife would 'love' such a party, but it is clear from the exchange that only authorised transgressions will be permitted in what is a top-down process of democratisation. This class dynamic is succinctly summarised by the exchange that accompanies the first break with tradition – Armstrong's dispensing of drinks in the wardroom. Higgins's cheery cry of 'Drinking in the wardroom, eating in the wardroom. Blimey! It's almost worth getting sunk', is met with something of a rebuff as Armstrong simply tells him to 'stop saying "blimey"'. It is also worth noting that, given the rare opportunity to imbibe the captain's brandy, Higgins requests a glass of port. Again this associates him with the feminine, as does the unexpected tact and discretion he reveals in his sympathetic dealings with the vulnerable stoker Snipe.[11]

Snipe, played by Richard Attenborough in a reprise of his performance in *In Which We Serve*, is a claustrophobic coward, set apart from the other men, the film implies, by his bondage to the worthless good-time girl who is his wife. He panics at the prospect of remaining in the submarine, but redeems himself by overcoming his fears and making the mystical transformation from boy to man. Armstrong is instrumental in recognising that Snipe is capable of this transition, and thus it is that by the end of the film a homosocial family dynamic has emerged, comprising Armstrong as the paternal head, Higgins as the horoscope-reading, port-drinking domestic goddess, and Snipe as the son who, having resolved his semi-Oedipal crisis and emerged into a suitable state of symbolic father-worship, will never grow to maturity. The older brother and first son of the family, Lieutenant Manson, dies before the other men. It is in caring for Manson that Snipe builds on his initial sacrificial gesture (giving up the chance of escape) and proves himself a worthy inheritor of the mantle of stoic English masculinity so elegantly displayed by Armstrong.

The film thus constructs a homosocial version of the idealised patriarchal family dynamic, but this masculine community is both literally and figuratively doomed. The sea, however, will bring a relatively quick death compared to the emasculatory dwindling represented by the spectre of the vacuum-cleaner factory. In a revealing dialogue between the two remaining officers, Armstrong and Manson, Mills's performance is left to speak the volumes that his words evade:

Armstrong: 'I'm not going to be an admiral. I shan't even get a brass hat.'
Manson: 'Of course you will. Sometimes I wonder which you love most – Helen or the sea?'
Armstrong: 'Well, to tell you the honest truth, I wasn't quite sure myself. But I'm sure now. I'm getting out of the service.'
Manson: 'Helen?'
Armstrong: 'Oh, yes. She's right, of course. She wants a home, somewhere permanent where she can grow roots, family roots.'
Manson: 'A house in the country with a garden . . .'
Armstrong: 'And a rich father-in-law to pay for it all. Why not? I've had twelve years at sea. I enjoyed it.'
Manson: 'Perhaps he'll give you a little model yacht to play with as well?'
Armstrong: 'He might even do that.'

Throughout the exchange Mills speaks in a monotone, his subdued tone suggesting resignation rather than enthusiasm. His movements are restrained and predominantly focused on the process of rolling poker dice, which both he and Patrick use as expressive objects to convey the difficulty of their discussion. Significantly he speaks of what Helen wants: he does not associate himself with the desire for home and roots.[12] For all their apparent togetherness in the opening sequence of the film, there is an uncomfortable dissonance in the relationship between Armstrong and his wife. His disappointment at giving up his career persists in spite of his assertions to the contrary, and the constraint represented by enclosure within the home is compounded by the emasculatory force of her father's presence. The father will 'pay for it all', and will give him a new toy. In this formulation the demobilised male is infantilised; deprived not only of his heroic status as warrior, but also of his basic breadwinning function within the family. Thus the film undermines the promise of the prototypical nuclear family with which it began and constructs instead a nostalgic homosocial version of the same. As the film closes on a final tableau in which Mills's paterfamilias reads aloud from the scriptures, flanked by his wife and son, the spectator is left with an elegiac memorial to a masculinity that was becoming surplus to requirements.

As was evident from Roy Baker's earlier, but equally claustrophobic drama, *The October Man*, structures of authority, and by extension, masculinity, were coming under pressure in this period. *Morning Departure* emphasises this pressure not through the questioning of Armstrong's professional authority, but through the displacement of value from that sphere of competence. What

Armstrong is good at is no longer of use to society. The clarity of purpose that directed the soldier hero of the early 1940s has been replaced by a loss of role, and with it an increasingly fragile sense of identity. In an analysis that equally evokes Mills's performance in *The October Man*, Marcia Landy comments:

> In general, the films of the 1950s, even when they attempt to resolve social unrest, cannot conceal the underlying tensions centering around the precariousness of authority. John Mills's portrayal in *The Long Memory* (1953) of a man trying desperately to preserve his sanity and adjust to the exigencies of middle-class work and social relations is representative of many male portrayals of the time. (1991: 48)[13]

In *Morning Departure*, the hero has no future. In both *The October Man* and *The Long Memory* society refuses to believe, or believe in, the hero, creating self-doubt that verges on self-destructiveness. However, there is no doubt that Robert Hamer's vision in *The Long Memory* is bleaker and more bitter than *The October Man*. The desolate landscapes, the absence of redeemable characters, and in particular the untrustworthiness of women, combine to suggest there is nothing in this modern world for the man who has served his time. In the case of *The Long Memory* that time is a prison sentence unjustly dispensed to an innocent man, but there is little to distinguish the figure of the newly released convict with his brown-paper parcel and ill-fitting suit from the still resonant figure of the demobbed soldier. The returning hero is literally and metaphorically homeless, and it is notable that Philip Davidson does not even attempt to reintegrate himself into the pretty but corrupt civilisation of suburban streets, but chooses instead to settle on a decrepit houseboat set against a desolate landscape of mud-flats.

Philip Davidson was one of Mills's first 'angry' roles, and his lack of practice is at times rather painfully evident.[14] Nonetheless, the film is significant in its suggestion that there is something to be angry about, and in its indictment of the complacent amnesia of postwar culture. But for all the evident faults of this brave new world, the narrative ultimately pulls its punches rather than driving home its doubts about the emerging affluent society. Davidson receives sympathetic treatment from both the journalist, Craig, and the policeman, Lowther, suggesting that there are still good men to be found and, as an ethics of masculine solidarity is reasserted, the wider problems of an unjust society are displaced onto a convenient female scapegoat. The film presents a typical madonna/whore opposition, and within this streamlined logic, Davidson's original betrayal by Faye (Elizabeth Sellars) is overwritten by the redemptive actions of Elsa (Eva Bergh). With the right woman to support him, Davidson abandons his demand for revenge. 'When you come to the point,' he announces, while standing over his nemesis, Boyd (John Chandos), 'revenge isn't worth it. You plan it and plan it and then when you start it makes you feel as filthy as the other person.' Mills seems much comfier occupying this moral high ground than in his earlier depictions of bitterness and resentment.[15] In plot terms the angry man has been neutralised by the unconditional love of a woman who knows her place, while performatively, he is rendered safe by Mills's residual relationship to the consensual heroes of the Second World War. Although the film does not go so far as to incorporate Davidson within the society that has betrayed him, his return to the houseboat with Elsa is a clear indication that the odd couple will cause no further disturbance to the social order.

In *The Long Memory*, then, anger is easily defused. A masculinity that had been devitalised by public injustice is restored by the private authority of heterosexual desire. Such a transition would be increasingly difficult to achieve as the decade progressed, and the doubts underpinning both national and masculine identities became impossible to avoid. In this context, the decade itself appears fractured, divided between the initial consolidation of relatively familiar modes of masculinity and the reintegration of men into the family structure, and the later anticipation of generational conflicts that would characterise the 1960s. As a reflection of this transition John Hill's study, *Sex, Class and Realism*, focuses not on the 1950s in their entirety, but on what is arguably a more homogeneous period: the years 1956 to 1963. The logic behind this division is both political and cultural. Although Hill does not claim that the angry young man was a direct product of the 1956 Suez crisis, he does suggest that this 'symbolic castration' of the nation created an arena within which such a figure could thrive (1986: 25). The success of writers such as John Osborne and Kingsley Amis, argues Hill, is indicative of 'a more generalised cultural anxiety around the question of male identity' (1986: 25).[16] National failure – the loss of a still cherished self-perception of Britain as an imperial force and a significant international player – was as firmly linked to constructions of masculinity as national success had been, and the blow to British political pride was culturally refracted in the search for a suitable scapegoat onto which the weight of masculine frustration could be displaced.

At the front of the queue for this dubious honour was the working woman, an easy target who could be blamed for supplanting men from their rightful economic role and for failing in her primary duty as the nurturer of the nation's young.[17] That such a perception of women's work bore little relation to a reality of poorly paid, low-status, part-time employment was immaterial. The 'liberated' woman was an emasculatory force, especially when her liberation was further encoded in sexual display. Hill observes that the fundamental fear underpinning the rhetoric of the angry young men was a horror of effeminacy (1986: 25), a quality associated not only with women, but also with a particular, upper-class masculinity and, of course, with the homosexual other, regarded in this period as a fundamental threat to the imperilled virility of the national psyche. Lynne Segal's *Slow Motion: Changing Masculinities, Changing Men* confirms the extent to which 'unmanliness' was regarded as a site of national subversion, quoting the 1951 findings of B. Seebohm Rowntree and G. R. Lavers who argued that 'sexual excesses are both a symptom of national weakness and a powerful secondary cause of it' (Segal 1990: 17). Whether it was manifested in a male or a female body, sexual excess could mean only one thing: a surfeit of femininity, and while the effeminate male was often regarded as a figure of fun, women were increasingly presented as voracious animals, whose primary goal was to weaken men with sexual desire before ensnaring them in the trap of domesticity.

As the changing sexual politics of the period attest, the impact of the angry young man on the cultural landscape of post-Suez Britain can scarcely be understated. However, the attention paid to this phenomenon has tended to obscure the ongoing resentments and frustrations of his close relative, the angry older man. This is not to deny the fundamental importance of youth, the teenager and the delinquent, but rather to suggest that the focus on one generation of male anger has tended to obscure the fact that men were angry across a much wider spectrum of possibilities. Hill argues that not least of the young men's anger emerged from their recognition that the new world of welfare-state Britain was still the old world of class-conscious deference to a seemingly impregnable conservative élite.[18] This realisation was equally painful for the war generation, as is evident from John Guillermin's 1957 thriller, *Town on Trial*. Fast-paced and unusual in its approach to the much revered institution of the British police force, the film uses genre form to expose the new postwar Britain as a culture of complacency and class hypocrisy.

No More Mr Nice Guy: *Town on Trial*

[T]he 'problem of youth' really has its roots in the anxieties of the parent culture: its concerns with the social changes wrought by 'affluence', the advent of mass culture and, more particularly, the changing role of the family and proliferation of 'perverse sexualities' (Hill 1986: 16)

By 1957, Mills had become altogether better at being angry, and in *Town on Trial* he does so with a power and conviction that makes him almost nasty. The critical response to Mills's transformation was positive. *The Times* described him as 'exhilarating' (28 January 1957), while Isabel Quigly in *The Spectator* was pleased to note that 'for once' Mills was 'far from cosy' (1 February 1957). What distressed the critics, however, was the film's 'peculiar transatlantic slant'. 'Are there really country clubs like this in Subtopia?' asked Derek Granger, 'And does

Dorking, say, possess this smug American small-town pride?' (*Financial Times*, 28 January 1957). Isabel Quigly was more blunt: '[T]his portrait of life in an English town is about as authentic as the Piltdown Man.' It is difficult to see why a film so clearly working within genre parameters should have incited such a response, and it seems likely that the demand for realism – emerging in particular from the more highbrow critics – disguises both a renewed fear of the Americanisation of British culture, and a range of anxieties about the changing shape of British society.[19] Here, as in many of its themes and performances, *Town on Trial* negotiates a boundary. It is recognisably generic, and yet sufficiently close to a realist representation of some of the emerging aspects of the new Britain as to make for uncomfortable viewing. Peopled with characters who are still negotiating their relationship to the wartime past, *Town on Trial* is intimately concerned with the conflict between youth and a more or less 'respectable' older generation. The town of Oakley Park is put on trial for its values and its complicity in the murder of an attractive young woman, and the traditional English 'virtues' of respectability and privacy emerge as vices when viewed through the defamiliarising perspective of the hardboiled detective outsider.

Superintendent Mike Halloran, played by Mills, is an Anglicised version of the classical American detective. The hardboiled private eye, as exemplified by Raymond Chandler's Philip Marlowe, is a blue-collar figure whose investigations are motivated by an intensely personal moral code. Seeking an often unpalatable truth, the detective is caught between the affluent class of his leisured employers, and a police force which resents his interference. Both police and employers are frequently revealed to be at best corrupt and at worst wholeheartedly criminal. However, while the concept of police corruption remained unthinkable within British cinema, there was little space for the assertive masculinity of the private investigator.[20] *Town on Trial* thus attempts to construct an Anglo-American hybrid which will provide the best of both worlds. Halloran is an incorruptible and dedicated police officer, but in every other respect he exhibits the behaviour and attitudes of the American hardboiled detective.[21] Having worked his way up through the ranks, he has no time for the leisured classes, and he refuses to respect the class-based assertions of authority with which he is confronted in his investigation. He makes little effort to be 'polite', and his interrogation technique is both verbally and physically aggressive. The assertive pseudo-American masculinity that characterises the role of Halloran is initially conveyed through Mills's voice. The film opens with a sharply cut, ambitious sequence in which we see only fragments of the players involved. A handcuffed criminal is brought into a police station: the camera focuses on hands, feet, suits, car parts and office furniture, but at no point are we allowed to see the faces of either the criminal or the detectives. A voice, recognisable as that of Mills, but defamiliarised by a flat London accent and an almost American intonation, begins to read the prisoner's statement to a typist. The detective's voice is measured, forceful and devoid of emotion, and as he continues to read the camera makes a disorientating shift to the point of view of the actions being described, giving the spectator a murderer's-eye view of the events that will bring Halloran to the town of Oakley Park.

What the camera records is the murder of Molly Stevens, a good-time girl who is effectively punished for her pursuit of pleasure. The solving of this crime is the ostensible purpose of the narrative, but as the title makes explicit, there is more at stake than the identification of a single criminal scapegoat. Although she is killed within the first ten minutes of the film, Molly Stevens (Magda Miller) presents a problem through her capacity to disrupt the regulatory codes of both class and gender behaviour. Her excessive sexuality, encoded in platinum blonde hair and a glamorous, figure-hugging tennis outfit, gives her access to a domain beyond her class position: namely, membership of Oakley Park Country Club. In what seems to be a confirmation of the fears of those who oppose the breakdown of class boundaries, her presence contaminates those around her. Fiona Dixon (Elizabeth Seal), daughter of the town's prospective mayor, listens to her parents' disapproval before observing: 'I wish men would look at me like that.' Fiona embodies a different model of transgression: teenage rebellion. Her crime is to cross the class boundary in the opposite direction, seeking escape from middle-class conformity. She drinks pints, she dances shamelessly, she 'likes' Molly Stevens, and she will be duly punished by becoming the murderer's second victim.[22] Thus, through the reliable genre convention of killing sexually attractive women, *Town on Trial* displaces the anxiety surrounding class mutability and the blurring of traditional boundaries. But while preserving their 'integrity' is the motor that drives the community under investigation, a different outlook emerges from the perspective of the detective outsider. The murder of the transgressive woman is symptomatic of a deeper malaise. Molly Stevens is only part of the country-club set because of the weakness of its phoney, hypocritical secretary, Mark Roper (Derek Farr). Roper's inadequacy as a man is evident from his faked war record and his hopeless philandering. He is dominated by his desires and this lack of moral fibre encourages him to admit the disreputable serpent Molly into Oakley Park's bourgeois Garden of Eden. But Roper's weakness is not the only example of attenuated masculinity in the town, as is revealed by Halloran's initial interview of a second suspect, Peter Crowley (Alec McCowan).

The most immediate indication of Crowley's inadequate masculinity is his over-protective mother. Crowley still lives at home, and as Halloran questions him, it is his mother who replies. As the scene progresses, mother and son rehearse what is clearly a familiar argument about the unworthiness of Molly. Halloran stands silent throughout, letting the hysterical discourse wash over him, before asking his single, pertinent question. The contrast is typical of generic constructions of 'tough' masculinity. Tough guys say only what is necessary – they are men of few words, and for the most part they assert themselves through an active, almost threatening silence. Talking is for women, and for effeminate or inadequate men. Crowley, we are told by the town's somewhat shady doctor, is a sick man. He is also the film's killer, but the film attributes his pathology to as yet undiagnosed schizophrenia rather than to dissonant masculinity. This illness is convenient, as in terms of motivation, the film is notably incoherent. Without this diagnosis, Crowley might be read as a lower-middle-class youth who is so distressed by female excess that he feels obliged to kill two women. Although not depicted as overly religious, he cites the Bible as a legitimising authority for his actions, and he runs to the sanctuary of the church when exposure seems inevitable. In *Town on Trial*, youthful rebellion leads to madness or death, and it meets with little in the way of sympathy from the detective, who having chased his suspect up the church steeple, exacts his confession by describing Crowley not as a madman, but as a disaffected youth:

> Is this the only way you can draw attention to yourself? Is this your way of showing the world that they don't understand you? Because that's what you're trying to do, isn't it? You're saying, 'Listen to me. I've got a problem. Everybody's got to listen.' Isn't that it? Well, whatever your problem is, son, you can solve it very easily, right now. But you're afraid, aren't you? You don't want to die, do you?

This is a somewhat sensational approach to the spectre of the delinquent. Little effort is made to explain either Peter or Fiona, although the *mise-en-scène* makes it evident that behind the façade of respectability, both are the products of seriously dysfunctional families. Crowley lacks a father, while Fiona's has no qualms about hitting her when she fails to conform to his standards of behaviour. But although the narrative is short on explanation, it is nonetheless disturbing in its assertion that delinquency resides at the heart of the middle classes. Those who believe themselves fit to police the behaviour and the parenting of the working classes, are here revealed as almost criminally inadequate.

The town, then, is a dysfunctional entity, and the threat it poses to the detective and his 'authentic' values is evident in Halloran's failure to break Crowley in the interrogation room. As he shouts repeatedly at his silent suspect, it is Halloran who verges on the hysterical, and Crowley who begins to look tough. The angry older man cannot penetrate the mindset of the new generation, nor can he rid himself of the resentment he feels against those who have survived the war unscathed. In *Town on Trial* the detective hero is still negotiating his relationship with the war which killed his wife and child. Halloran's post-traumatic state emerges from his own perceived impotence: at the time of their deaths he was busy arresting a drunk. Elizabeth Fenner (Barbara Bates), the film's love interest, successfully diagnoses a case of emasculation: 'Maybe that's your grudge? You wanted to hit back at someone and couldn't.' In Guillermin's 'subtopia' even the detective's masculinity is precarious and provisional. Fortunately, such a crisis is easily accommodated by the sadomasochistic formula of the thriller, a genre that demands the hero must be beaten before emerging victorious. Redemption, typically, is achieved through action, and the ludicrous rooftop peril sequence that ends the film provides Halloran with the chance to reassert a masculinity undermined by the war and newly threatened by Crowley's inexplicability. Visually, he is aided in this process by Guillermin's direction. Shot from above as he tries to 'talk down' Crowley, Mills's forehead is lined with creases and his eyebrows raised in points. Ironically, and some twenty years too late, his face finally achieves something of Cagney's demonic leer, his newly craggy features suggesting aggression, vulnerability and a not inconsiderable threat.[23]

The unexpected hint of Cagney in the photographing of Mills is indicative of the extent to which the film is a triumph of style over substance. Irrespective of the incoherences of the plot, John Guillermin succeeds, where many had failed, in exacting menace from the fundamentally benign form of Mills. The film is constructed around a series of set-piece interrogations, linked by screeching police cars and the odd romantic interlude. Each interrogation is choreographed with care, counterposing medium shots indicating the relationship of the actors to the space with almost lurid close-ups of the principals' faces. The scenes follow a pattern. A low-key opening creates a false sense of security, which is followed by movement as Mills circles his suspect. Scenting weakness, he literally moves in for the kill, stepping into uncomfortably close proximity to his prey before turning on his heel and departing. Mills's invasion of the other actors' space is aggressive and fundamentally un-English, and it makes manifest the transgression of boundaries that structure the film. Disturbingly, Guillermin uses the same choreography for the visual organisation of the film's love story. Halloran is attracted to nurse Elizabeth Fenner. His seduction technique, however, is difficult to distinguish from his menacing interrogations, as Mills repeats the pattern of moving into intimate space to press home a verbal advantage. Proximity, in this visual schema, exposes the truth – be it of desire or of criminality [Fig. 5.3].

In *Town on Trial*, then, Guillermin extracts from Mills a performance that disrupts the parameters of his customary Englishness. Mike Halloran's working-class masculinity, set as it is within the conventions of genre, achieves the self-expression of anger in part through the abandonment of the structuring forms of appropriately English behaviour. The characteristics of formality, politeness, good humour and emotional repression so crucial to perceptions of the national character are displaced by the increasingly international language

Fig. 5.3 No respecter of boundaries: Mills gets close to Barbara Bates in *Town on Trial* (1957). Columbia/The Kobal Collection

of toughness. Generic displacement facilitates the articulation of long-held class resentments and postwar anxieties. However, as the 1950s drew to a close, this element of disguise became superfluous. The cracks in the façade of English masculinity were becoming increasingly evident, even to the extent of invading British cinema's pre-eminent form, the war film.

In her influential study *Gender Trouble* (1990), Judith Butler argues that there is nothing 'natural' about gender, rather it is a compulsory performance that we are compelled to re-cite. Constant attention must be paid to ensure that gender roles are adequately performed, as society has little tolerance for those who transgress the boundaries of heteronormative behaviour. However, Butler also observes that because gender is performative, and must constantly be re-presented, gaps and inconsistencies will inevitably emerge which might destabilise the imprisoning concepts. Repetition of gender norms can only ensure an approximation, not an exact replica. In the context of such an understanding of gender, the question arises, how many times would Mills be compelled to re-cite the norms of his performance of heroic English masculinity before the inconsistencies underpinning this cultural production became evident? At what point would the ritual performance of the characteristic tropes of English masculinity slide from the invisibility of convention to the self-conscious visibility of parody? At what point would the performance of understatement and emotional restraint become so excessive as to draw attention to its constructed rather than its natural status? Throughout the 1950s Mills appeared in a range of 'nostalgic virility' films, presenting a range of military heroes whose construction repeated the middle- and working-class masculinities that had made him the Everyman of the 1940s. These films worked hard to preserve the illusion of a coherent and stable masculinity. Any doubts were reserved for the more disenchanted landscapes of Mills's (and others') civilian roles. But the process of repetition was far from straightforward and, as Andrew Spicer has observed, postwar heroes 'had to work harder': 'Refighting the Second World War did not fully compensate for [the] loss of empire and gradually the officer hero was exposed as an anachronism or a neurotic' (Spicer 2001: 201).

By 1957, there was considerably less cultural investment in the preservation of consensus masculinity and in J. Lee Thompson's *Ice Cold in Alex* the doubt that had already permeated crime films and domestic dramas finally invaded the territory of the English soldier hero.

'PRETTY WELL POOPED OUT': *ICE COLD IN ALEX*

I think if it had been another straightforward hero, he wouldn't have wanted to do it. The man is at the end of his tether, and I think there must have been lots of people watching the film who knew what that was like. (Sylvia Syms, 'A Very British War Movie', Channel 4, 28 August 1999)

Ice Cold in Alex represents a paradigm shift in Mills's relationship to a national masculinity. Unlike *Morning Departure*, it is not a case of the same performance having a different cultural value. In this film Mills is permitted, indeed encouraged, actively to deconstruct his previous screen persona. The film was directed by J. Lee Thompson, a figure described by Steve Chibnall as having a 'policy of transforming star personas' (2000: 199), and in *Ice Cold in Alex* he found an ideal vehicle for the rewriting of Mills. The film's narrative is well-suited to the reconfiguration of heroic masculinity, set as it is in the context of defeat.[24] As the British army withdraws from Tobruk, a group of disparate characters, divided by class, gender and nationality, are left to struggle across the desert in a dilapidated ambulance in the hope of reaching safety in Alexandria. The journey is riven with dangers, and the four must work together if they are to have any chance of survival. Mills plays the neurotic Captain Anson, nominally the leader of the party, but dependent throughout upon the physical strength and mental nurturance provided by the other principal characters, Sergeant Major Tom Pugh (Harry Andrews), Nursing Sister Diana Murdoch (Sylvia Syms), and the mysterious South African Captain van der Poel (Anthony Quayle). As the narrative progresses through a breathtaking series of perilous encounters, van der Poel is revealed to be a German spy, but in an unprecedented development for a British war film, he ends the story not only alive, but vindicated as an honourable man who has played his part in the struggle against the 'greater enemy' of the desert.

Although the film is constructed as an ensemble piece, the publicity material and cinema trailer clearly designate Mills as the 'star' of the picture – indeed, ABPC brought him in to boost the profile and potential appeal of the film, necessitating substantial changes to the script and narrative. Chibnall records that Christopher Landon's novel, from which the film was adapted, focuses not on Anson, but on Pugh. The casting of Mills consequently involved not only a change of protagonist, but also a significant transformation of the erotic patterns within the novel:

> John Mills' star status demanded that Anson be the film's main protagonist and the principal recipient of Diana's affections. Even though Mills was more than twice the age of Sylvia Syms and much the puniest of the male cast, his claim to be the romantic lead pressed itself well above that of a craggy middle-aged supporting actor like Andrews. (Chibnall 2000: 187)[25]

There is a certain irony in these developments, given Mills's singularly unspectacular track record as a romantic lead, but it is nonetheless a significant indication of the extent to which, at the age of 49, Mills continued to be regarded as both a leading man and a box-office draw. Whether he could still be termed a star, is, perhaps, more difficult to determine. If a star is an actor deemed capable of carrying a film, then Mills undoubtedly remained in this category. However, if the term is reserved for those actors around whom there is a significant extra-filmic discourse, then the evidence of *Picturegoer* magazine suggests that the term had ceased to apply. By 1957, when *Ice Cold in Alex* went into production, Mills had largely disappeared from the pages of the fading but still significant flagship of British fan culture.

Over the course of the decade *Picturegoer* had come to focus predominantly on Hollywood cinema and the lives of its stars, but it remained ever hopeful about the prospect of discovering new British talent. To this end there was no shortage of coverage for those British actors deemed to have the elusive extra dimension required to be a 'star'. Bright new things, such as David McCallum, were exposed to the glare of publicity, while features explored the fluctuating status of actors such as Stanley Baker, Kenneth More and Trevor Howard. One actor, however, stands out as typifying the image desired by *Picturegoer* and its readers: Dirk Bogarde. Winning the magazine's annual award in both 1958 and 1959, Bogarde embodied an ideal of British stardom in the late 1950s, much as James Mason and Stewart Granger had done ten years previously. Not only was he the subject of articles and fan mail, he was also presented as writing personally for the magazine. Pieces regularly appeared under his name, fostering a perception of intimacy and reinforcing the relationship between the ordinary and the extraordinary so central to the workings of stardom.

Even in the late 1940s, at the height of his popular stardom, Mills could not have been described as a *Picturegoer* favourite. The reasons for this are not easy to determine. Certainly there is little evidence of any effort on his part to engage with or manipulate the discourses of stardom and fame, and his stable family life could arguably have worked against his construction as a figure of romantic fantasy. However, a more likely reason for *Picturegoer's* lack of interest would seem to be his Everyman persona and his predominant association with war films and thrillers. *Picturegoer's* preferences always lay with actors who could be constructed in a romantic mode: the gentlemanly Gregory Peck, the Byronic Marlon Brando or the 'saturnine' Trevor Howard (Babington 2001: 141).[26] Regular Hollywood correspondent Donovan Pedelty, writing about British stars, turned to the reliable figure of Bogarde to explain the phenomenon:

> Dirk Bogarde is box office for essentially one reason. He looks romantic. His attitude suggests there is no hope of happiness in it. He *provokes* us into *wanting* that contradictory prediction to turn out to be wrong. (*Picturegoer*, 27 July 1957)

The screen John Mills, by contrast, was fundamentally unromantic, as *Picturegoer* was keen to stress in an article on Sylvia Syms, who was, as far as the magazine was concerned, the 'star' of *Ice Cold in Alex*. Her screen romance with 'a scruffy, unshaven and unwashed John Mills' wrote Margaret Hinxman, was 'certainly not the picture of romantic screen conventionality' (29 March 1958). Mills was so implicated in the conventions of an English masculinity incapable of articulating desire that, were it not for the paradoxes presented by his physique, it would be more appropriate to describe him as an action hero than a leading man.[27] In this context, *Ice Cold in Alex* is a remarkable film. Not only does Lee Thompson work to transform the 'boy's own' image of his star through the deconstruction of his stiff-upper-lip persona, but he also reconstructs the dishevelled hero as a romantic lead. Admittedly, Anson is a significantly flawed and wounded lover, but by reintroducing desire, however problematic, into the masculinity embodied by Mills, *Ice Cold in Alex* began a sexual reawakening singularly appropriate to the age.

However, the transformation of Mills's 'star' persona is initially most powerfully conveyed in the casting of the three male roles. Set alongside the much larger figures of Quayle and Andrews, he appears small, almost scrawny, and distinctly vulnerable [Fig. 5.4]. The exposure of Mills's smallness, little emphasised in his other leading roles of the 1950s, is compounded by costume. Like the other male characters he spends the film in shorts, but while Anthony Quayle is given an almost distressingly tight pair, Mills sports an excessively baggy outfit, from which his legs emerge as spindly sticks. A similar contrast is achieved in the gravedigging scene where all three men expose their torsos, and Quayle is framed as a monumental figure standing astride the puny figure of Mills [Fig. 5.5]. His customary appearance is further destabilised by the unusual step of dying his hair blond, which defamiliarises his features and has a surprisingly disturbing visual effect. But the alterations to Mills's appearance are only a part of the radical deconstruction of his long-standing screen persona. Before the desert adventure has begun, an opening sequence not only exposes Anson as an exhausted, shell-shocked alcoholic, it also suggests there is an element of moral cowardice in his make-up.[28] These scenes set the pattern for the first half of the film as Lee Thompson shoots his trembling, slurring hero in a variety of undignified poses.[29] Anson's attempts at insouciance only drive the point further home: the façade of English masculinity is collapsing. The protective shell of duty and conformity has cracked, and the terrifying 'other' of emotional excess is demanding expression.

In his analysis of Charlie Chaplin's Monsieur Verdoux, James Naremore suggests that the ambiguous, murdering Verdoux could be read as the 'unconscious' of the friendly and familiar tramp. Much the same could be said of Mills's Captain Anson who acts as the uncomfortable double of the actor's countless

Fig. 5.4 Not measuring up: Captain Anson has one for the road in *Ice Cold in Alex* (1958). British Film Institute/Canal+ Image UK Ltd

upright, courageous heroes of the 1940s and 1950s. Anson, like Davidson and Halloran before him, speaks something of the anger, resentment, pain and confusion that must be repressed in order to be an Englishman. In *Town on Trial* such an articulation was facilitated through the conventions of genre. In *Ice Cold in Alex* it is only possible because Anson is a drunk: his wounded masculinity facilitates the expression of a vulnerability that had hitherto been both politically and culturally unacceptable. He is, in his own words, 'pretty well pooped out', no longer in command of himself or others, and the film is as much about his struggle to regain his self-control and, by extension, his masculinity, as it is about the journey across the desert. Nonetheless, the film is also an adventure, and it demands that the audience care about the fate of its characters. Consequently, after the initial shocking exposure of Anson's weaknesses, the spectator is comforted by a scene that works to legitimise his 'failure'. Pugh tells Murdoch about Anson's capture by the Germans and the selfless, driven behaviour that preceded it, before discreetly asking her not to offer the captain a drink. Here, as elsewhere in the film, Pugh and Diana Murdoch act as concerned parents, carefully mothering their wayward child.

Fig. 5.5 Hegemonic masculinity? Mills and Anthony Quayle in *Ice Cold in Alex* (1958). British Film Institute/Canal+ Image UK Ltd

Anson thus presents a paradox, and a new development for the English soldier hero. As a British officer, he is, in theory, the embodiment of hegemonic masculinity, the authorised upholder of patriarchal authority. Yet *Ice Cold in Alex* simultaneously positions Anson as either a childish or a feminised figure: an embodiment of weakness, dependency and unreliability, and the antithesis of the patriarchal ideal. It is, however, in the nature of hegemonic structures that, in terms of his authority, this does not really matter. As R.W. Connell observes, 'it is the successful claim to authority, more than direct violence, that is the mark of hegemony': Anson can depend upon the support structures central to the maintenance of patriarchy to ensure that his weakness is tolerated. In other words, he can depend upon women and the working classes, or in this case, the non-commissioned lower orders, to keep his authority intact. Throughout the film, Pugh works to protect Anson, and when the spectator might begin to doubt that the captain could maintain a shred of dignity, Pugh can be relied upon to reinstate him with a reassuring 'Sir'. Each time Mills's drunken weakling is interpellated as such, his authority is restored, no matter how wide the disjuncture between his physical presence and his symbolic status. Diana's role is similar. She excuses his reckless behaviour that caused the Germans to fire upon the ambulance, saying simply, 'You couldn't help it', and even after his most significant tantrum, when he has subjected her to both verbal and physical abuse, she makes a remarkable effort to soothe the fractious child. This scene is typical of patriarchal gender relations. Emasculated by his hysterical outburst, Anson sits alone while the other two men work to crank the ambulance up a hill. Diana restores his masculinity through the expression of female helplessness: 'I've no idea what they're doing. They tried to explain to me, but I'm hopeless at that sort of thing.' Obliged to explain the mechanics of the operation, Anson is reinstated as the possessor of knowledge and phallic power. The return of his masculine authority is then symbolised by Syms ceremonially placing the compass he had discarded back around Mills's neck.

This is a pivotal moment in the film, the point at which, through the complete breakdown represented by his regression to childhood, Anson is finally laid bare. His unreasonable demands, his attempt to fight van der Poel and his incipient tears shatter the façade of masculinity. However, as Christine Geraghty has observed, the 1950s war film can be read as 'a safe space in which problems around masculinity can be resolved effectively' (2000: 192) and, having exposed the vulnerable state of repressed English masculinity, *Ice Cold in Alex* quickly works to recuperate its errant captain. Paradoxically, the disgraceful loss of masculine control is equally a moment of therapeutic release. That Anson is in recovery is evident from the next of the film's series of tense encounters. When Diana lets go of the cranking handle and the ambulance rolls back down the hill, undoing hours of back-breaking labour, silence falls. A palpable tension builds as Diana, Tom and van der Poel walk down the hill towards Anson who is silently punching the side of the ambulance. The audience is led to anticipate another explosion. Instead, in a brief but highly significant speech, Mills's performance indicates that English masculinity is rapidly being rebuilt. In a casual tone he greets the others: 'My fault . . . I should have had somebody on the brake. [To Diana] That's your job on the next trip. . . . [To the group] Well. Let's take a little exercise, shall we?' Anson has taken responsibility, he has protected rather than exposed the vulnerable Diana, he has made light of a difficult situation and he has regained his capacity for euphemistic understatement. He is, once again, the archetypal Englishman. Through this juxtaposition of crises, the film works to stabilise that which it had exposed as radically unstable, and the horrors suggested by the failure of masculine performance are overwritten by the 'happy ending' of Anson's renewed self-control.

The narrative progression which has seen Anson's masculinity restored through courage, catharsis and the regaining of self-restraint, is a journey symbolised in part by his relationship to alcohol. He begins the film dependent upon whisky: the beverage of choice for the hard-drinking male. This is the substance that is holding the masculine shell in place. When the whisky is lost he reaches his lowest ebb, bribed by the promise of gin into allowing van der Poel to join the party. The German has read his weakness and exploits it mercilessly. Gin – 'mother's ruin' and the archetypal drink of the slatternly woman – is a symbol of Anson's feminisation. The ice-cold lager that awaits him in Alex, by contrast, is a man's drink, a drink taken in public rather than in private and a symbol of homosocial bonding. The beer is both symbol of salvation and object of desire, and it is no coincidence that there is a far greater erotic charge to Mills's encounter with the lightly perspiring glass of lager than there is in his seduction by Sylvia Syms.

The erotics of the film are significant, not least because of the media interest generated when the censor demanded that the love scene between Mills and Syms be cut. Not only was the scene in which the actors make love amongst the sand-dunes deemed too risky, it was also, as I suggested earlier, seen as a radical departure for Mills.[30] However, between the actions of the censor and the context of the film, the love scene that emerges is at best ambiguous. Away from the ambulance, Mills lies back, while Syms takes the dominant position, seated above him, before leaning over him first to stroke and then to kiss his face. Throughout the scene Mills's face is immobile and he speaks in a monotone about his relationship to Paul Crosbie and the mythical Ariadne who awaits him – or Crosbie – in Alex. He is the passive object of seduction rather than the seducer, and the cutting of the scene at the point of their eventual kiss ensures that this is the final representation of Anson as a lover. The scene as it appears in the film, however, is substantially different even from the cinema trailer, examination of which is instructive in terms of the negotiation of erotic power between the principals. In the trailer the action continues beyond the point of Anson's submission. There is a sharp cut and we see Mills on top of Syms, asserting his control of the encounter, after which Syms is left to utter a cliché of female dependency: 'In a few days you'll have forgotten we ever met.' Obviously what appears in the film is the result of compromises between director and censor, and the contents of the trailer cannot be seen as a definitive indication of the director's intent. It is nonetheless significant that the censor's demand for 'decency' does not so much work to protect the audience from the spectacle of Syms's cleavage, as to expose them to the more disturbing vision of the British hero's impotent passivity.

Irrespective of the love scene, though, it should also be noted how unusual it was for a woman to have a substantial role in a war film, and the presence of Syms is a key indicator of how far *Ice Cold in Alex* strayed from the generic template. Yet her presence is an absolutely necessary one: without a woman in the group, the intimacy that forms between the male characters would be a far more disturbing force. That Syms fulfils this purpose is evident in how little emphasis the film places on her status as an object of desire. Although the group comprises three men and a woman, there is not even the suggestion of erotic conflict. Sister Murdoch quickly settles into an affectionate sibling relationship with Pugh, and evinces both a dislike and a distrust of van der Poel, who, after a token opening flirt, does not seem that interested himself. Anson is similarly uninterested in pursuing Diana. It is she who variously seduces or mothers him. It is rather the case that, as with more traditional war stories, the emotional force of the film emerges from the negotiation of the relationship between the three men. Steve Chibnall suggests that:

> If *Ice Cold in Alex* carries any propaganda message, it is not about the tyranny of Nazism or the benefits of heroic sacrifice, but about the ways in which the common confrontation of adversity can promote understanding and forge affectionate relationships between individuals. (Chibnall 2000: 193)

Yet this ultimately triumphant narrative of cooperation should not obscure the more conflictual narrative of man-making that is a fundamental part of the journey undertaken in particular by Anson and van der Poel. From the moment of their first encounter, luridly framed by Lee Thompson to emphasise the physical contrast between the two actors, the captains are in competition for the status of the group's alpha male.

Superficially it might seem as if there could be no contest. Anthony Quayle far 'outweighs' John Mills, his screen presence emblematic of an ideal, almost monumental masculinity characterised by effortless strength and an absence of fear. He is a 'big' man, and at this level his status is assured. But hegemonic masculinity is not determined by physicality alone, and his character's potential to challenge Anson's leadership is compromised by his status as a foreigner. The film resonates with incidents that reinforce traditional conceptions of national identity and which play to the British sympathy for the underdog. The crossing of the minefield is one such encounter. Van der Poel insists on accompanying Anson, arguing that 'a Springbok can go where any bloody Englishman can', but as the two men mark out safe passage for the ambulance, it is noticeable that Quayle is more interested in watching Mills than the track. Contrasting shots of the two men's legs reveal the confident, firm-booted steps of Quayle, while Mills takes tentative steps in lightweight English desert boots and full-length schoolboy socks. When Anson looks up, he sees van der Poel laughing at him, thinking him a coward for his caution. Not surprisingly, van der Poel's stereotypical German arrogance must be punished. Thinking he has stepped on a mine, he must be rescued by Anson who, after painstaking excavation, offers him a tin can as a 'souvenir'. Throwing the offending object away in disgust, van der Poel replies, 'You have a funny sense of humour, Captain' – a line which, within the clichés of the Second World War, should surely have exposed him as a German. Watching this encounter, Pugh is left to comment, 'That should take him down a peg.' The English are here resurgent, Anson's authority reinforced by his possession of knowledge and expertise, and his exhibition of the 'English' virtues of humour, modesty and grace under pressure.

Throughout the film the two men compete for the status conferred by knowledge, control and strength, but the more they compete, the more a homosocial bond is forged between them. In mirrored sequences they comment on each other's bravery. Notably, in each case praise is only possible while the object of admiration is unconscious. Pulling van der Poel from under the ambulance after he has taken the weight of the vehicle on his back, Anson comments, 'That's the most wonderful bloody effort you'll ever see.' A few scenes later, the compliment is repaid when, after collapsing with exhaustion, Anson is scooped up and tended by a surprisingly gentle van der Poel. The emergence of the homosocial bond – the inarticulable love between men that is culturally more powerful than the recreational matter of heterosexual desire – is finally consolidated after Anson's redemptive performance in the ambulance-cranking disaster. As Anson puts his hand on the handle and braces himself to begin again, Quayle covers his hand and the two men exchange a look. Mills steps away and lets the big man take the strain. The need for competition has passed in a moment of mutual admiration that acknowledges the masculine virtues of strength and self-control.

Mills's performance in *Ice Cold in Alex* is one of radical contrasts, and although generally well received, it was described by Harold Conway as 'theatrical' (*Daily Sketch*, 27 June 1958), and by Fred Majdalany as 'excessively hysterical' (*Daily Mail*, 27 June 1958). A more appropriate pathologising description might be 'bipolar', as Lee Thompson encourages his actor to move from static features and a dull monotonous delivery to a phenomenal explosion of pent-up frustration and rage, in which Mills shakes, screams and appears on the verge of tears. In between these two extremes, he alternates between relaxed moments of humour and a frantic, desperate energy directed at the process of reaching Alex and drinking that longed-for ice-cold beer. Although Majdalany was almost alone in his complaint, the accusation sheds interesting light on the parameters of male performance in the late 1950s. Steve Chibnall's analysis of Lee Thompson's directorial habits suggests that the element of excess that he coaxes from Mills should come as no surprise. Discussing the director's previous film, *Woman in a Dressing Gown* (1957), he compares Lee Thompson's style to that of Douglas Sirk and Nicholas Ray, whose contemporary melodramas were reinscribing the emotive conventions of Hollywood cinema. Sirk's cinema practice sought to mediate the lush sentimentality more typical of Hollywood through a range of alienating camera techniques, and distancing features would be counterpointed against intense emotionality in an effort to expose 'the hidden problems of the American bourgeois family' (Chibnall 2000: 148). Lee Thompson likewise worked to juxtapose distance and intensity, but in *Woman in a Dressing Gown* his deployment of excess divided the critics, particularly in their response to the performance of Yvonne Mitchell as the film's female protagonist, Amy. Lee Thompson encouraged the actress to go 'over the top', exploiting the full range of emotional possibilities presented by her character's predicament, and Chibnall implies that the critics who resisted Mitchell were reacting against a perceived theatricality in her work at a time when more low-key, naturalistic modes of performance were becoming fashionable (2000: 156).

Yet for male actors schooled in the tradition of performing British masculinities, low-key was the cinematic norm. For them any naturalism had to encode an increase in intensity and a far wider range of highs and lows.[31] As Mills's performance in *Ice Cold in Alex* suggests, it was finally becoming possible for the representation of English masculinity to move away from stylised restraint and to give voice to previously repressed emotional states. The transformation of performance styles, performers and subjects for performance that emerged in the wake of the British new wave effected a fundamental change in the portrayal of screen masculinities. R.W. Connell stresses that hegemony is 'a historically mobile relation', arguing that once the conditions that legitimised the dominance of a particular mode of masculinity begin to change, '[n]ew groups may challenge old solutions and construct a new hegemony' (1995: 77). As the 1950s drew to a close, the national masculinity embodied by Mills, while still recognisably English, could no longer be seen as hegemonic. And while this in one respect reflects the wider status of the nation, itself in decline internationally, it is also indicative of the extent to which the idea of a representative 'national' masculinity was fragmenting. In the films that immediately followed *Ice Cold in Alex*, Mills remained a figure of authority,[32] but the exposure exacted by Lee Thompson was the shape of things to come, and set the scene for the altogether more complex and disturbing roles he would be offered in the 1960s. It is also notable that audiences were being encouraged to shift their identification from the centre to the margins. In *Tiger Bay* (1959), for example, the point of view is that of a lonely but deceitful child and the murderer she befriends, rather than Mills's upstanding policeman.

As Mills passed the age of 50, he continued to be cast in Everyman-inflected roles, but the status of the little guy had changed. In part this was due to the expanding parameters of masculine performance in the years since the Second World War.[33] The working classes and their narratives had been liberated from the function of comic relief, while the complacent middle classes were facing a newly uncertain future in the face of political and social change. Increasingly Mills's dramatic roles would focus on masculinity under pressure, examining the emotions repressed by the structures of a class-conscious, heteronormative society. Mills had always been a 'homosocial' actor, more at home in the masculine group than in the romantic encounter, but as a new decade opened, the increased possibilities of cinematic expression resulted in a significant shift. In the 1960s, the unspoken emotions of three decades would finally find expression in what might best be described as the queering of the English Everyman.

NOTES

1. Harper and Porter (2003) offer a comprehensive analysis of the changes that beset the industry in the 1950s, while more succinct accounts are provided by Hill (1986) and Street (1997).
2. From *We Dive at Dawn* (1943) to *Above Us the Waves* (1955), Mills's periscope technique remains a benchmark for the performance of tension and the corporeal representation of the inarticulable pressures of command.
3. As Geraghty (2000) and Spicer (2001) have argued, the 'expert' emerged as a key figure in postwar cinema. This significantly classless figure could be manifest in any profession from the policeman to the scientist, but a degree of ambiguity about the 'modern' ensured that this symbol of a new age was as likely to appear as a bumbling bureaucrat or a mad scientist as an authoritative and dignified professional.
4. Geraghty's record of cultural struggle is endorsed by Harper and Porter. Arguing against the perception of the period as 'dull', they suggest that, 'the 1950s was essentially a period of transition for the British film industry, and such periods are usually marked by a struggle between old-fashioned, "residual" artistic forms and those newer, "emergent" types which confer status upon their consumers' (2003: 1). For Harper and Porter, the tension between the residual and the emergent permeates the industry at every level from the politics of funding, to the dynamics of technological innovation, to the fluctuations of audience response.
5. Indeed, Geraghty concludes her enjoyable study of the decade by drawing a parallel between the British war film and the popular comedies of the period. Both, she argues, are ultimately reactionary in outlook, 'safe spaces in which the demands of modern citizenship can be resiliently shrugged off' (2000: 195).
6. Even in films such as *Hobson's Choice* (1954) and *Town on Trial* (1957) when he might be read as representative of an emergent, newly powerful, working class, Mills does not stand for modernity. Rather he becomes a conduit through which 'true' values are preserved or restored after their abuse by the careless and irresponsible governing classes.
7. Michael Balcon's epic production *Dunkirk* (1958) could arguably be included in this group, but is perhaps more accurately described as a hybrid form combining the reassertion of national virility typical of the 1950s war film with the assertion of community values that characterised the 1940s. The film makes room for three

'heroes', played by Bernard Lee, Richard Attenborough and John Mills, but while this evokes the group hero of wartime, beyond these figures the other soldiers and civilians, especially the members of Mills's makeshift company, are largely indistinguishable. The film's status is also complicated by its attempt to engage with the wider picture of political responsibility through the character of Lee's journalist.

8. Prisoner-of-war dramas were particularly productive ground for such constructions in their implicit, and ironically imperial, suggestion that England is made wherever there are Englishmen. This is evident from one of the earliest POW films, *The Captive Heart* (1946), which shows the bleak prison camp gradually transformed into a facsimile England, with vegetable plots, games and activities. By turning the alien environment into a home from home, the men's English identities are reinforced and valorised, facilitating their survival and inhibiting any potential dilution of the link between masculine and national strength. Later films, such as *The Wooden Horse* (1950) and *The Colditz Story* (1955) pay less attention to the domestic re-creation of home, building 'England' instead through the assertion of a public-school boisterousness that positions the Germans as teachers to be ridiculed and outwitted.

9. Only Margaret Hinxman in *Time and Tide* dissented from the general view, arguing that: 'though the film strives after and intermittently achieves the severe realism which its subject deserves, it has not sufficient faith in itself to allow many of its characters to be anything but conventional types' (4 March 1950).

10. This masculine space, however, is a limited one. Displaced from its customary centrality, it is claustrophobic, isolated from 'real life' and narrowly defined.

11. It could also be argued that Higgins's request for port reveals an acute awareness of the conventions of the territory he is about to enter and a self-conscious refusal to have his experience of this 'pleasure' circumscribed by the expectations of others.

12. Although in many respects Armstrong's reluctance to embrace a concept of home is archetypally masculine, it is not entirely typical of the configuration of English masculinity. Paradoxically the English man desires freedom from the domestic, while nonetheless cherishing a significant concept of the home. That this concept is more dearly beloved in theory than in practice, however, is suggested by the resistance encoded in such factors as pubs, allotments and the refusal to be involved in any domestic activity.

13. I wonder whether, in fact, Landy *is* thinking of *The October Man* here.

14. Mills's performance was not particularly well received. Fred Majdalany, writing in *Time and Tide*, encapsulated the problem when he described the actor as 'Pinewood's head prefect'. No amount of grime and scowling could erase the traces of the Everyman persona from his still remarkably smooth and untroubling face.

15. However, as Davidson punctuates this speech by repeatedly hitting the semi-conscious Boyd, the character might be seen to be having his cake and eating it too.

16. The rise to cinematic prominence of the angry young man was itself a short-lived phase. Harper and Porter conclude that by the 1960s, 'modernity in British cinema was characterized by a certain brutality and technological fetishism.

Arthur Seaton's successor as the epochal British film hero turned out to be James Bond' (2003: 272).

17. Psychological discourses of the family proliferated in this period, and considerable pressure was put upon women to accept their maternal destiny. John Bowlby's enormously influential *Childcare and the Growth of Love*, published in 1953, introduced the concept of 'maternal deprivation', which 'was used to explain every conceivable personal and social problem, from educational failure and mental breakdown to delinquency, divorce, promiscuity and general social unrest' (Segal 1990: 10). However, as films such as *Cosh Boy* (1953) suggest, women could not win. Here it is the overprotective mother who is held responsible for the delinquency of her son.

18. It is an irony also noted by Hill that many of the angries and their characters ended up by joining or accepting this establishment élite.

19. The demand for realism was fairly clearly drawn along populist and highbrow lines. The *Telegraph* called the film 'un-English and implausible', while Dilys Powell suggested it had 'taken out denaturalisation papers' (*Sunday Times*, 27 January 1957). William Whitebait in the *New Statesman* simply asserted that such people and such places did not exist (9 January 1957). Only C. A. Lejeune was unperturbed, calling it 'one of the crispest little thrillers we have seen for some time' (*Observer*, 27 January 57).

20. While the American PI was masculinised by his position as a class outsider, his British equivalent was usually regarded as seedy and impoverished – a somewhat pathetic figure, as illustrated by the character of Albert Parkis (also played by Mills) in *The End of the Affair* (1955).

21. The dominant representation of the police, certainly in the first half of the decade, was as kindly and paternal, as exemplified by Jack Warner in *The Blue Lamp* (1950). Although some rough edges crept in as the decade progressed, officers remained dedicated and professional throughout (Spicer 2001: 51–3).

22. For the critic Campbell Dixon, the film itself crossed a boundary in its depiction of Fiona's sexuality, prompting him to describe Elizabeth Seal's dancing as 'deserving of any rebuke just short of murder' (*Daily Telegraph*, 26 January 1957).

23. Cagney's mobile and contradictory features enabled him simultaneously to convey menace, charm and vulnerability. See Chapter 2 for an account of the relationship between Cagney's screen persona and that of Mills.

24. Although it should of course be noted that the British are particularly good at reconfiguring defeat as a victory for the national character, as is seen in the mythologisation of the Scott story and Dunkirk.

25. The implications of the changes made in adapting Landon's novel are further explored by Chibnall, who observes that in changing the heterosexual love plot, the film also diffuses the book's suggestion of Pugh's homosexual desire for Anson (pp. 196–7).

26. Geoffrey Macnab draws a significant distinction between the screen persona of Howard and those of his British contemporaries, arguing that: '[H]e worked better with – and seemed more interested in – women than they ever did . . . there was

always a sensual spark and an erotic quality (albeit often understated) to his characters' relationships' (Macnab 2001: 141).

27. The sexual reticence of the Englishman was integral to Mills's Everyman persona,
with the result that it is difficult to see even his embodiment of nation as a particularly virile one. The swashbuckling, Masonesque sensuality demonstrated in
Great Expectations consequently has to be seen as a temporary aberration, a case of
demob hysteria prompted by the unrepeatable combination of Lean's grotesque
vision and Mills's escape from acting in uniform.

28. He cannot face telling his 'friend' Captain Crosbie that he will be left behind to
face the German siege, and asks his CO to break the bad news instead.

29. In perhaps the most surreal of these establishing shots, Anson's CO cheerily gives
orders from his bathtub, unperturbed by the bombardment overhead. The
camera cuts from the CO's energetic scrubbing to a mouselike Mills, shrunk
to the size of the beer bottle which the director has interposed between
actor and camera. This technique is typical of Lee Thompson's symbolic use of
mise-en-scène.

30. The *Daily Express* ran an article headlined: 'Yes! This *is* John Mills!' accompanied
by one of the film's censored shots. Mills was quoted as being 'unrepentant', claiming: 'It's a sheer relief to act as if I'm in love with the girl for a change, after so
many years of giving a polite peck between battles' (23 April 1958).

31. This, of course, raises the question of whether the cinematic representation of masculinity was a representation of existing masculinities, or whether it was itself an
element in the construction of Englishness. Obviously screen masculinities drew
on culturally validated qualities, but many of these could be dated back to the consolidation of a 'British' national cinema during the Second World War. These features had long since shed their subtlety and hardened into stereotypical heroic
representations.

32. For example, Major Harvey in *I Was Monty's Double* (1958) and Superintendent
Graham in *Tiger Bay* (1959).

33. This is in marked contrast to the parameters of female performance which had
been radically foreclosed. Potential roles for women now seemed limited to some
combination of conspicuous consumption, domesticity, or betrayal.

6

The Spectre of Impotence:
Fathers, lovers and defeated authority

More than any other postwar decade the 1960s was a period of randomness and cultural volatility in which planning and measured prediction
became largely untenable, with seismic shifts in generational relationships, aesthetic sensibilities and the loci of creative energy. (Chibnall
2000: 329)

[T]ensions between men are rarely free of sexual undercurrents. (Medhurst
1993: 99)

'Ridicule's always the finish. You know that?' (Kennaway 1988: 58)

At what point does the ageing war hero become an impotent figure of defeated
authority? Quite possibly at the point when the prescriptive pressure of performing hegemonic masculinity becomes too demanding, and the hard shell
of self-control, restraint and toughness finally cracks to reveal the vulnerable
body beneath. For traditional British masculinities at the end of the 1950s, such
a rupture had been on the cards for a while. Concluding their monumental
survey of the period, Sue Harper and Vincent Porter suggest that the 1950s
produced 'an *anxious* cinema, which worried away at the new social and sexual
boundaries'. This was a cinema that was 'uneven, questioning, full of speaking
absences, and shot through with new insights about the body and its discontents' (2003: 272–3). The gradual emergence of 'the body and its discontents'
from behind a set of long-held and powerful cultural imperatives focused
around coolness, calmness, repression and restraint had been all too painfully
evident in the raw vulnerability of Mills's performance in *Ice Cold in Alex*, and
the impossibility of continuing to live up to the expectations of phallic

masculinity would become one of the central tropes of his work in the 1960s. In films such as *Summer of the Seventeenth Doll* (1960) and *Tunes of Glory* (1960) Mills would build on the innovatory fragility of Captain Anson to give some of his most impressive screen performances, becoming in the process the embodiment of a residual hegemonic masculinity struggling to cope with the demands of a changing society.

Yet it was not only Mills's roles that underwent a transformation, the culture of cinema-going and the ethos of film production in Britain were also experiencing far-reaching and fundamental changes. Between the late 1940s and 1960 the cinema industry had seen annual admissions decline by two-thirds, from 1.6 billion to 515 million (Harper and Porter 2003: 244). This decline in attendance was paralleled by a significant demographic shift as family audiences stayed home with their TV sets and the cinema became the domain of a newly economically empowered youth market. Harper and Porter summarise the transition by comparing *The Blue Lamp*, the most popular film of 1950, with its counterpart in 1960, *Saturday Night and Sunday Morning* (2003: 249); but what this transformation in taste really presaged was the breakdown of any consistent idea of audience consensus and the final fragmentation of the concept of a large-scale national cinema.

Steve Chibnall's description of the 1960s as 'a period of randomness and cultural volatility' (2000: 329) is borne out by the extreme diversity of film production in the decade. The New Wave's socially conscious realism co-existed with the lurid imaginative excesses of Hammer horror and the growing comic phenomenon of the *Carry On* films. As the decade progressed, pop musicals such as *The Young Ones* (1961) and *A Hard Day's Night* (1964) appeared alongside 'Swinging London' films typified by *Alfie* (1966) and *Georgy Girl* (1966). There was also a rich vein of historical costume pictures that emerged in the wake of the flamboyant, energetic and erotic *Tom Jones* (1963). And, running throughout the decade, from his first memorable appearance in *Dr No* (1962) to the more downbeat *On Her Majesty's Secret Service* (1969), there was James Bond.[1] Andrew Spicer argues that Bond is a 'complicating factor' within the dominant trends of masculine representation in the 1960s. Drawing on the screen personae of Michael Caine (Harry Palmer in *The Ipcress File* (1965) and the eponymous *Alfie*), Albert Finney (Arthur Seaton in *Saturday Night and Sunday Morning* and *Tom Jones*) and Tom Courtney (*The Loneliness of the Long Distance Runner* (1962)), Spicer concludes that: 'The most interesting, charismatic and glamorous male figures were now oppositional, at odds with the state and preoccupied with personal gratifications' (2001: 203). Commander James Bond stands in obvious contrast to these assertive outsiders, but the decision to cast Sean Connery in the role made the character an accessible fantasy figure for a new generation. In Spicer's words:

Connery's rugged masculinity, and . . . Edinburgh burr made the screen Bond classless rather than patrician. . . . It was this paradoxical rugged elegance, insouciant but aggressively macho, that allowed Connery to project Bond's transitional status, incarnating both the unwavering patriotism of the traditional British gentleman hero and the guiltless sexual philandering of the international playboy who embodied the 'swinging' sixties. (Spicer 2001: 75)

Connery as Bond was a remarkably multifaced model of masculinity – Byronic, hedonistic, populist, powerful, authoritative, innovative and traditional – a fantasy that could appeal to almost everyone, but in no conceivable way an Everyman. Everyman, at least in the formulation so successfully embodied by Mills, was dead; and, as the actor gravitated towards roles associated with flawed and ageing masculinity, no new version emerged to take his place. The new stars of British cinema – Connery, Caine, Finney, the Beatles – were characterised by an oppositional energy and an unquestioned, unrepressed sexuality.[2] Although disempowered and disenfranchised masculinities still found narrative expression on screen, there was no place for the man who stoically accepted his position, and who sublimated his desires into an ethic of duty. By 1960, the characteristics embodied by Mills's traditional screen persona had become the stuff of crisis and ridicule, and in no film is this transition more powerfully evoked than in Ronald Neame's *Tunes of Glory* (1960).[3]

'SOME SPRY WEE GENT': *TUNES OF GLORY*

The film's fascination is to watch Sir Alec and Mr Mills, marvellously matched, turning in performances which only preservable celluloid will prevent from becoming legendary. (Paul Dehn, *Daily Herald*, 2 December 1960)

Tunes of Glory was a tightly scripted melodrama, adapted by James Kennaway from his critically acclaimed novel of 1956. The film was as well received as the book had been, and minor quibbles regarding the plausibility of plot and motivation were overridden by the fulsome praise that greeted the performances of Alec Guinness and John Mills in the leading roles. The plaudits were such that both men were nominated for the Best Actor Award at the Venice Film Festival and although Mills's role as the repressed and cerebral Basil Barrow initially seems to be much less spectacular than Guinness's vibrant, violent and intensely physical Jock Sinclair, it was Mills who won the award for a *tour de force* performance of great subtlety and power.[4] The film is a narrative of competing masculinities built around the story of two men's struggle to control a Highland battalion that, for very different reasons, means everything to them. Behind the clash between the principals, however, lie the same tensions that characterised Kennaway's succinct, claustrophic novel: conflicts of class, education and nation colour every encounter between the two men, and these differences are exacerbated by the uncertain status of a peacetime army. The regiment is not without purpose, but it is residual: to the men within it, it represents the security of structure, order, history, and a glorious past comprised of dangerous, but perhaps simpler, times. It looks backwards to a form of man–making that is no longer socially acceptable. As the critic Isabel Quigly came close to suggesting at the time of the film's release, if war is supposed to make men out of boys, it might well be the case than peace makes boys out of men:

> [T]he whole situation, the passions aroused, the lengths gone to, the schoolboyish atmosphere – hysterical, claustrophobic, faintly homosexual – all confirm what one feels must be true about the regular army, the most absolutely unproductive institution ever thought up to keep grown men busy. (Isabel Quigly, *Spectator*, 9 December 1960)

Tunes of Glory, then, depicts the once secure homosocial environment of the services as a hothouse of competing vanities, within which men, devoid of a shared purpose, regress from a belief in community to a more atavistic individualism.

Within the distinctly shaky community of the battalion, a crisis is reached when Colonel Barrow, a man with impeccable class credentials, is appointed over the head of the ranker colonel Jock Sinclair, who has commanded the battalion since the war. Yet these two characters do not represent a simple binary opposition between war and peace, past and future; indeed, in its depiction of the ultimate breakdown of both men, the film asks whether either of them was adequate to face the challenges of modernity. Nonetheless, at first sight, Barrow and Sinclair could not be further apart as models of masculinity. As a well-educated member of the upper-middle classes, Barrow is, theoretically, the hegemonic ideal, but he can neither communicate with the men around him, nor express the pain of the traumatic war experiences he has suffered. Sinclair, by contrast, is the archetypal 'man's man'. Having risen through the ranks, he too is a misfit. His behaviour towards his men oscillates between extremes of paternalism, bullying and sentimentality, but he is totally at home within the violently homosocial environment he has created within the officers' mess. Seemingly the dominant force from the outset, he is not immune from the pressures created by Barrow's appointment and the clear statement this represents regarding his illegitimate class position. Although a man of many words in the language of homosocial banter, when events begin to take their toll on him, his first impulse is to speak with his fists. Over the course of the film, both men disgrace themselves in public. At a cocktail party for the county, Barrow throws a public tantrum when Jock and his 'cronies' show him up, while Jock breaks every rule in the book by 'bashing a corporal' who has had the temerity to get involved with his daughter. These irruptions of repressed anger and frustration represent a crisis point for both men. The film ends with Barrow's suicide and Sinclair's slide into madness as he plans a magnificent martial funeral for the man whose authority he had worked so hard to undermine. As Jock is led away distraught, the battalion is left to a new generation of men, exemplified by the smoothly machiavellian Major Charlie Scott, played by Dennis Price, in a performance at times uncomfortably reminiscent of his elegant mass murderer, Louis Mazzini.[5]

The conflict between masculine types is further complicated by the discourse of nation. The setting is Scottish and, although his family has links to the regiment, Barrow looks and sounds English. Sinclair, by contrast, is 'authentically' Scottish, his national identity written on his body through his speech, his sentiments and his excessive behaviour. But where once the concept of the group hero could have accommodated differences of region and nation, in *Tunes of Glory* the mess is divided between those who follow Jock as an emblem of nation as well as a soldier hero, and those who side with the 'civilising' influence of Barrow. Kennaway's scenario here revisits the Enlightenment conflict between civic Lowland rationalism and tribal Highland superstition. Barrow's Scottishness comes via Eton, Oxford and Sandhurst, Jock's via Barlinnie prison and the heat of battle. Clearly the two are incompatible, and Barrow's arrival is perceived by Jock's camp as an attempt by a centralising power to impose a specifically English authority upon the non-conforming self-expression of the Highlanders. This tension is evident in Jock's repeated insistence upon diminishing and Anglicising Barrow as 'the spry wee gent', and in Barrow's determination to turn the officers' intensely physical Highland dancing into the ordered, contained patterns of civilised English behaviour. Yet although Barrow arrives bearing the weight of English hegemonic authority, he is soon made painfully aware of the conditional nature of such power. The class outsider (Sinclair) has become the dominant force and Barrow, technically the man in power, fails to be 'man enough' to re-establish the colonial imperative. Barrow becomes a symbol of superseded authority, forced – like the nation he represents – into ignominious withdrawal.

In the conflict between the colonels, then, *Tunes of Glory* mobilises multiple ideological conflicts and, visually, both the *mise-en-scène* and the performances work to heighten the contrast between these central figures. While Mills as Barrow is repeatedly placed on the margins, framed in doorways, seated away from the crowd or excluded from the group, Guinness is always centre stage and, except when listening to his beloved pipe music, in a state of constant movement. In contrast to the still, restrained body language of Mills, Guinness makes expansive gestures to the room, pulls faces on parade, slaps any back within reach, embraces his men, fondles his women and dances with an exuberant, violent fervour in an atavistic display of male splendour. Script and editing also work to establish the contrast through an early montage sequence in which the new colonel is introduced to the camp and its routines. Jock's motivational ability is set against Barrow's precision in a series of brief encounters typified by their reaction to an anonymous passing soldier: Jock declares the man to have been the best heavyweight in the battalion until wounded in the war; Barrow simply replies, 'Someone should tell him to put his hat on straight.'

The contrast in attitudes and behaviour is equally evident in the appearance of the two men. Considerable effort has been put into ageing Mills, and his appearance is radically different even from such recent military outings as *Ice Cold in Alex*, *Dunkirk* (1958), and *I Was Monty's Double*. His hair is grey, his face noticeably thinner and he sports a pencil moustache. He is every inch the dapper military gent, but the transformation also evokes a sense of constriction, of a man being tightly held in.[6] There is a tautness to his face and body, allied to an extreme economy of movement, and these characteristics are exacerbated by juxtaposition against nearly all the other actors. Alec Guinness, vibrant in what C. A. Lejeune described as the 'determined marmalade' of an outrageous ginger wig (*Observer*, 4 December 1960); Gordon Jackson, relaxed and diffident in his role as adjutant and peacemaker; Dennis Price, louche and aristocratic, his hair slick, black and certain: all these figures inhabit their bodies with a comfort and ease that exposes the formal rigidity of Mills. Even the smaller roles, such as that of the quartermaster Dusty Millar (Paul Whitsun-Jones), are filled with actors whose size, colouring or body language work to emphasise the muted quality of Basil Barrow. From the moment of Mills's first entrance, when he must enter the room dominated by Guinness's bacchanalian dancing, there is a contrast in the leads between presence and absence. As he advances into the room, Mills's small stature, grey hair and houndstooth check jacket are set against Jock's red face, even redder hair and gleaming brass buttons [Fig. 6.1]. Yet the contrast between the two men cannot simply be categorised in black and white terms – Kennaway's narrative persistently refuses to let our sympathies lie with one side or the other – rather, the visual construction of the film highlights the possibility that Barrow is, from the outset, a spectral figure. The character's almost supernatural absent presence is suggested both by the final haunting of Jock, whose madness takes the form of an obsession with the ghost of Barrow, and by the brutal words with which Charlie Scott delivers the death blow to his colonel. Referring to Barrow's decision to give Jock a second chance, Scott's tone is light and utterly dismissive:

Scott: 'It sounds as though it's a popular idea anyway, Colonel.'
Barrow: 'Do you really think I made it for my popularity?' . . .

Fig. 6.1 Residual masculinities: Mills and Alec Guinness in *Tunes of Glory* (1960).
United Artists/The Kobal Collection

Scott: 'My dear colonel, we didn't know *you'd* made any decision.'
Barrow: 'You must have heard the matter's not to go to Brigade?'
Scott: 'Yes, we heard that, but we thought that was *Jock's* decision.
           Why my dear fellow, we didn't even realise you were there.'

In a role that demands both self-effacement and hysterical self-expression, Mills's performance is a masterpiece of understatement, built through the subtle use of hands and eyes within a body that is otherwise largely still. The most extravagant gesture that he uses to indicate the inner torment of Barrow is when these two key body parts are brought together: the onset of crisis is signified by moving hand to temple in a vain attempt to stem the twitch of his eye. Significantly, even in his hysterical outburst at the cocktail party when he screams at Jock to 'stop the dancing', Mills maintains the character's military bearing. Although he is almost jumping up and down with rage, his arms never leave his side. Yet the white-knuckled clenching of his fists and the slight inward turn of his toes are enough to suggest the tantrum of a spoilt child, and in so doing transform the performance from authority to impotence. He can control neither himself nor the men he is supposed to command; a failure emphasised by his return to self-awareness. A small shake of the head, an intake of breath, the gesture of hand to temple, and the re-emergence, albeit hesistantly, of his civilised voice. Barrow's body has betrayed him. It has failed to contain the inappropriate emotions of fear, rage and jealousy, and the archetypal Englishman has been 'undone' by the revelation of the terrified schoolboy within. In later moments of crisis, Mills's performance draws on this initial breakdown to suggest the ever-present possibility of the return of the repressed. Through his grip on a glass and the repeated scrunching of a napkin, the earlier clenched fists are suggested, while a hint of hyperventilation suggests the rising pressure within. Compared with Alec Guinness, Mills has few speeches with which to work, but he succeeds in speaking volumes through eyes and hands alone. In this he is assisted by Ronald Neame's direction, which is sparing in its use of full frontal shots. We often see Mills react through a stiffening of his back or a slump of his shoulders, with the result that when his face is exposed, it is painful in its intensity. His final close-up of the film sees him turned to stone by the words of Charlie Scott (quoted above) while two discreet tears trickle down the taut, inexpressive mask. After this it is left to his body to encode despair as he walks slowly up the stairs to his death.

In a thoughtful profile of the actor published in 1962, Ian Johnson argues that Mills's performance in *Tunes of Glory* was:

> in essentials . . . precisely the same as the one he gave in *Ice Cold in Alex* . . . in both films a critical point is reached: an incredibly skilful performance, this, of tight-lipped angry repression, commencing with a trembling lip and near tears, and gradually boiling over to a nervous flashpoint, a shattering paroxysm of neurotic rage. Held in close-up in both films, this is an extremely harrowing performance to watch. (*Films and Filming*, June 1962)

To a certain extent, Johnson is right. In the two films Mills is performing the same crisis of masculinity, and the same breakdown of a particular mode of national self-perception. Yet in other respects the performances are significantly different. Anson the drunk sweats, shakes and screams as an indication of the impossible pressures of masculine performance. Barrow's breakdown is conveyed in the minutiae of a rebelling body: twitches, clenches and almost imperceptible tears. In part this is a reflection of different directorial styles: J. Lee Thompson's visual extravagance can be juxtaposed against the slightly stagey realism of Ronald Neame. But the films are also marked by the difference between 1957 and 1961. *Ice Cold in Alex* exposed the vulnerability of the nonetheless redeemable English soldier hero; *Tunes of Glory* exposes his fundamental inadequacy – and in so doing becomes a far more pessimistic film. In *Tunes of Glory* there can be no happy ending, no recuperation and no way back from the loss of authority. There are no Diana Murdochs or Sergeant Major

Pughs to interpellate the colonel and reinstate him in his hegemonic position. Indeed, perhaps one of the most sinister aspects of the film is the way in which it drives home the point that both the pre-war gentlemanly masculinity of Barrow and the wartime heroism of Jock are ill-suited to the demands of a peacetime army that is not about history (as Barrow would believe) nor about war (as Jock thinks), but about appearances; something that perhaps only Charlie Scott fully understands. Barrow's cocktail party for the county initially suggests that he is aware of the need to sell the 'idea of the battalion', to reintegrate it into a social body no longer convinced of its relevance or tolerant of its foibles. His failure to court-marshal Jock, however, indicates both weakness and sentiment. Manipulated by Sinclair into believing that he can save a 'brother officer', he operates within a code of honour instead of understanding how his change of mind will *look* both to the men of the battalion and the wider community.

Ultimately, then, the division between modes of masculinity lies less between Jock and Barrow, who both exhibit extreme volatility of temperament and backward looking mindsets, than between these two wounded men and Charlie Scott.[7] Scott is the character whose voice never rises, and whose tone never changes from a suave, elegant casualness, even when he is betraying his friend or effectively killing his commanding officer with his gratuitously brutal honesty. Charlie Scott, the 'smooth old stoat', is the shape of the future, and Neame neatly positions Dennis Price at the end of each key encounter between the two military dinosaurs: watching, waiting, playing the long game.

In *Tunes of Glory*, then, the man who survives is the man who is free from 'unreal loyalties' and who knows how to look out for himself. The group is redundant, no longer able to offer salvation, comfort or the possibility of redemption, and the individual is no longer an alienated figure (as was so often the case in the 1950s), but rather a free agent making the most of what society has to offer. The emergence of this newly confident individual was an integral part of the fundamental changes taking place in British society as the 1960s gathered momentum. This was an increasingly affluent Britain, with an emergent consumer society; it was a Britain marked by the 'end of Victorianism' (Marwick 2003) in which long held orthodoxies of sexual and cultural practice were being challenged; it was a Britain characterised by new diversity and new divisions, as youth cultures, immigrant populations and the working classes all assumed a greater visibility within the body politic. These forces were integral to the breakdown in consensus that divided cinema audiences into interest groups, but they also contributed powerfully to the development of a 'social problem' cinema that sought to make a liberal intervention into the debates and anxieties circulating within British society.

As the previous chapter suggested, the cinema had – directly or indirectly – long been concerned with social problems. Throughout the 1950s, from *Cosh*

Boy (1953) to *Violent Playground* (1957), films had attempted to engage with the disturbing emergence of a new youth culture, but as the decade drew to a close, the incidence of realist narratives tackling topical social concerns underwent a significant increase, diversifying into such 'problems' as prostitution, adultery, education policy, homosexuality and miscegenation.[8] Although seemingly structured around liberal debate, the films also operated as narratives of reassurance, raising problems in order to resolve them, a structural tension that leads John Hill to associate the trend with a desire for the preservation of consensus through the reintegration of 'troubling elements' into the community (1986: 124–5). The narrative structure of the social problem film can equally be seen, in Harper and Porter's terms, as residual – a mode of filmmaking that depended upon realist conventions and practices that emerged in the 1940s and dominated the popular cinema of the 1950s. In a review of 1961, David Robinson dubbed the style 'Rank realism' in a sharp acknowledgement of the ideological constraints that ultimately circumscribed filmic attempts to represent reality (*Financial Times*, 23 June 1961). These, then, were conventional films that attempted to negotiate new topics by locating them within the safe and the familiar, and – even in 1961 – what could be more safe and familiar than the screen persona of John Mills?

Tunes of Glory suggested that Mills's screen persona was gradually mutating, permitting the actor to be cast in weaker, more ambiguous roles. But although age was beginning to undermine the heroic imperative which had shadowed his every performance in the 1950s, he remained an actor predominantly associated with all that was laudable about a particular mode of British masculinity. This masculinity, forged in wartime and calcified in the 1950s, had been under pressure for some time and seemed to have little appeal to the new generation of filmgoers – but in spite of its increasingly residual status, it continued to speak to values cherished by, amongst others, the Rank Organisation. Consequently, when Mills was called upon to lend his reassuring presence to Roy Baker's *Flame in the Streets* (1961), the publicists at Rank worked to resurrect the fading spirit of Everyman:

> There is no doubt that John Mills is one of the most versatile actors of the British screen today, equally at home playing the colonel of a leading regiment or a humble cockney Sergeant. There is a quality of sincerity, an accurate observation of human nature in his acting, which makes each performance convincing. (Pressbook for *Flame in the Streets*, BFI collections)

This description encodes a subtle but significant shift in Mills's screen persona. His status has changed from star to actor, from embodiment to performance. He no longer *is* the English Everyman, but he can perform a version of anyman. For its central character, *Flame in the Streets* required an actor who could plausibly and sympathetically convey the visceral fears that shaped British racism in the aftermath of a decade of immigration. Unlike many social problem films that relied upon a middle-class discourse of male rationality to diffuse the emotive territory of the 'problem' or give credence to a particular ideological position, *Flame in the Streets* is firmly located within a working-class context. However, in its apparent resistance to the lure of a conventional authority figure, it loads a considerable weight of signification onto the body of the emblematic working-class man. The film attempts to locate both its discourse of rationality and its deep-rooted fears within the same national body, and in so doing gives rise to what is probably Mills's final performance as a consensual English Everyman.

Everyman's Last Stand? *Flame in the Streets*

'I feel sorry for you. You people are sad . . . Maybe it's the weather – could be the weather – people all muffled up, with tight lips, no smiling.'('Peter Lincoln' in *Flame in the Streets*)

Based on Ted Willis's television play, *Hot Summer Night, Flame in the Streets* emerged just three years after the 1958 Notting Hill riots had raised the tempo of debate regarding both new immigration and the status of those immigrants already settled in Britain. Arthur Marwick describes the paradoxical responses of theoretical tolerance and practical hostility that characterised the nation's attempts to assimilate the new:

> British sentiments, quite simply, were confused. There had been a marked absence of a constructive lead from policy-makers. Deep grass-roots hostility to immigrants, and, above all, to further immigration went along with popular support for some kind of legislation against racial discrimination. (Marwick 2003: 134)

In this context of confusion, the film draws on Mills's capacity to embody an archetypally decent Britishness, and the honest working-class hero of the war years is here translated into a trade union official. Just as Mills in the 1940s was able to symbolise the wartime spirit of class cooperation, so in 1960 he is able to do his bit for race relations, and his character, Jacko Palmer, is a man utterly committed, in theory at least, to the principle that all men are equal. However, while Jacko fights forcefully and eloquently for the rights of a black worker within his factory, he finds it harder to assimilate difference when his daughter announces her intention to marry a Jamaican teacher.[9] The film's attempt to deal with this transition from the political to the personal is complicated by its revelation of a domestic crisis. After twenty-four years as part of the 'fixtures', Jacko's wife Nell (Brenda de Banzie) finally gives vent to her frustrations. That these emerge in the form of a violent diatribe against inter-racial relations is one more shock for the complacent, 'politically correct' Jacko. As the film progresses, class difference, generational misunderstanding and gender are all implicated in the instability of the supposedly secure family unit, opening up for scrutiny a range of 'problems' considerably in excess of the film's superficial preoccupation with race relations.

Flame in the Streets has received a fair amount of critical attention, but most commentators agree that its political impact is diffused by the displacement of dysfunction from the public to the private (Hill 1986; Murphy 1992; Young 1996). It is difficult to disagree with this conclusion, but it must nonetheless be acknowledged that the domestic scenario is structurally important, providing some small element of narrative consolation to set against the irresolvable tensions of the wider world. The 'public' narrative focuses on the character of Gabe Gomez (Earl Cameron). Popular in the community, married to a white woman and promoted to chargehand, he is designed as an exemplary figure, but sadly this does not prevent his sacrifice to the gods of melodrama. The public story concludes with the unpleasantly traditional punishment of a black man with ideas above his station, and Gomez is last seen being carried off in an ambulance after having been thrown on the communal 5th November bonfire. Gomez's fate is the result of racial tensions that have been brewing throughout the film and which finally erupt into a riot instigated by a group of disaffected 'Teds'. Both Young and Hill cite this as an incidence of the construction of 'folk devils' within the narrative – the pathologising of individuals or groups in order to displace responsibility from wider social structures. 'In order for a solution to be reached,' argues Hill, 'the dilemma has to be displaced onto other issues and into a form with which the characters can cope' (1986: 102); in the case of *Flame in the Streets*, this form takes the shape of the deviance of white working-class youth.[10] But although the 'Teds' are constructed as scapegoats, there is nothing very reassuring about the conclusion of the riot. The police intervene, but the Teds are mobile and multiple, and it is only Gomez who receives any obvious punishment. Given the intractability of the 'problem' raised by *Flame in the Streets*'s public debate, its parallel private narrative seeks a more definitive closure. A reduction of the problem to the micro level of the family is the film's attempt to find a positive outcome to set against the bleak vision of social discord. Nonetheless, the private sphere also has its folk devil, in the figure of the hysterical, irrational middle-aged woman, but she is relatively easily contained through an appeal to maternal love and the promise of a little more husbandly affection. The film concludes with a tableau. Jacko and Nell stand in the doorway of their living room, preparing to talk to their prospective son-in-law, the black schoolteacher Peter Lincoln (Johnny

Sekka), who stands in stiff and formal symmetry next to their daughter Kathie. Its closure is compromised and provisional, but in comparison to the fate of Gomez, it could be termed Rank optimism.

As the demonisation of Nell suggests, *Flame in the Streets* is deeply implicated in the inherently sexist gender landscape of the 1950s. The male communities of work and union have a far higher priority than the feminised space of home, and all the laudable aims of Jacko Palmer have been achieved at the expense of his long-suffering wife. Nonetheless, the family remains an important site of signification within the film. Lola Young draws attention to the fundamental link between family and nation, arguing that in the cinema of the late 1950s, the 'stoical English family, consolidated during World War II, was seemingly under attack' (1996: 92). Young links this perception to the legacy of British colonialism, which traded in family metaphors to become both paternal authority and nurturing motherland:

> Thus the figure of the family may be seen as analogous with the predicament of a Britain without the 'Great': a country which was losing its identity as the custodian of its colonial subjects/children as they struggled for independence from oppressive/parental rule. (1996: 92)

The postcolonial context puts a different perspective on the ideology underpinning the film's domestic conclusion. By accepting, however provisionally, that Peter Lincoln will become part of the English family, an attempt is made to broaden the parameters of nation. The outsider is accepted in order to maintain the status quo. Assimilation, particularly in the case of such a nice, well-educated boy as Peter, is seen as the safest way to neutralise a potentially hostile force. So far, so tidy; but, while it is inevitably the case that the 'selection of some "problems" rather than others for attention in the cinema is rarely ideologically innocent' (Hill 1986: 126), it is equally the case that any given social problem film is likely to expose problems in excess of those it ostensibly addresses. Thus it is with *Flame in the Streets*, which in its attempt to promote a rational liberal consensus on the problem of racial prejudice, in fact does just as much to expose the precariousness of established concepts of Britain and the national character.

From the perspective of Peter Lincoln, there is nothing very desirable about the prospect of assimilation. He is an eloquent, albeit mild, critic of British life and attitudes, and he is also the figure who does most to expose the redundancy of the Everyman figure. In a powerful encounter between 'father' and 'son', Jacko Palmer is made to confront the very 'British' nature of his racial prejudice.[11] It is a scene which forces the spectator to reconsider the value placed upon qualities supposedly fundamental to the national character, and it suggests once again the generational divide that throws into question the possibility of a representative national masculinity. Crucially, the scene also acts as a salutary reminder that the national masculinity embodied by Mills is, and always has been, without thought or question, a white masculinity. Whiteness is such an absolute norm in representations of mid-twentieth-century Englishness that it literally cannot be seen, and is extremely difficult to analyse. In Richard Dyer's words:

> The subject seems to fall apart in your hands as soon as you begin. Any instance of white representation is always immediately something more specific – *Brief Encounter* is not about white people, it is about English middle-class people; *The Godfather* is not about white people, it is about Italian American people; but *The Color Purple* is about black people, before it is about poor, southern US people. (Dyer 2002: 128)

Jacko's meeting with Peter works to shift the direction of the gaze away from the 'problem' of colour and onto the meanings of a specifically English whiteness. Whiteness is thrown into relief, made tangible and thus rendered available for criticism and challenge.

The scene takes place in the shabby surroundings of Peter's tenement room and it represents a verbal battle for signifying authority. In the first half of the film, Jacko Palmer is a vibrant, buoyant figure. He is boisterous, loud, energetic and oblivious. He knows he is right and has neither the time nor the ability to listen to anybody. James Breen in the *Observer* neatly summarised the performance: 'John Mills, always happier as a cockney spark than as a gent, gives Jacko the thrust of an amiable, noisy terrier' (25 June 1961). By the time he arrives in Peter's room, however, the terrier is far less amiable, if just as noisy. Jacko has an unusual command of rhetoric for an English Everyman, but this verbal facility can be excused as it is always deployed in the good cause of the group (the union) and is entirely lacking in introspection. When he confronts Peter, however, eloquence gives way to a blunt assertiveness. The rudeness of his approach is cloaked in the spurious claim of the 'national' virtue of plain speaking. 'Right, now let's get this clear,' begins Jacko; 'I'm going to ask you a straight question,' he continues, without ever quite coming to the point. Under the guise of setting things straight, a more traditional masculine inarticulacy is reasserting itself. Finally he succeeds in hitting his mark, which is nothing less than an appeal to what was once the English Everyman's *raison d'être*: the creed of duty and self-sacrifice. Drawing on an already outmoded ideal Jacko asks Peter: 'Do you love her enough to give her up?', and in so doing exposes the 'virtue' of self-denial as simply another mechanism of repression. Duty and self-sacrifice, called upon here, are exposed as emotional blackmail. Jacko's next strategy is an appeal to reason: the British virtue of common sense. The odds are stacked against a mixed marriage succeeding, he claims, conveniently forgetting the Englishman's traditional sympathy for the underdog.

Plain speaking, duty, self-sacrifice, common sense: the characteristic features of English national masculinity are deployed in Jacko's opening volley. They are returned with interest in Peter's reply which succinctly anatomises and exposes the other side of Englishness, beginning with the hypocrisy that disguises itself as English reserve:

> Jacko: '. . . Now I'm just giving you facts – and don't throw the colour bar at me, I've fought that one all my life.'
>
> Peter: 'Oh, yes, I know, some of your best friends are spades.'
>
> Jacko: 'Now look here. I didn't mention that word.'
>
> Peter: 'Why do you talk to me like this? Do you think I'm a fool – an ignorant man? Why do you talk to me like this? There's the door, you say. Find yourself a black girl, you say. Why do you talk to me like this? Only one reason – this [holds up his hand] – this skin. Click, click – words out like bullets – don't say anything you black bastard, we don't want you in this family. Get out . . . You know in other countries they have better ways. There they tell you, 'Keep out nigger', 'Walk in the gutter, nigger' – signs up all the time. But here, there's no sign, but we can tell. You smile at us never with the eyes, only with the mouth.'

Jacko is unable to answer Peter's accusations, either here or elsewhere in the film [Fig. 6.2]. As the scene progresses, Jacko is made to confront his own hypocrisy, and Mills's terrier deflates into a more hangdog creation. His head drops, his hand wipes anxiously across the mouth that has failed him, and for once he is unable to find words. Yet, ultimately, the film evades acknowledgement of the gulf it has exposed, working instead to heal the wound through a resurrection of community. The damage done to national self-perceptions by Peter's painfully accurate denunciation is rapidly overwritten by action as the film cuts to the chaos of the riot. This dramatic apocalypse acts – as war once did – to disguise social and political divisions, and it is Peter and Jacko together who drag the burning body of Gabe from the fire.

Yet although Dyer cautions against overlooking the normative power of whiteness, it is impossible to ignore the extent to which the conclusion of the film is also profoundly complicated by class. Lola Young has described Peter Lincoln as a modern 'noble savage', and contrasts the extreme blackness of the actor Johnny Sekka against the extreme whiteness of Sylvia Syms. But, in every respect except the visual, Peter is positioned as white. Although Jacko may have begun the film as the embodiment of male rationality, by the end of the narrative the mantle has been passed to Peter, who assumes the voice of

Fig. 6.2 Englishness exposed: Mills and Johnny Sekka in *Flame in the Streets* (1961).
British Film Institute/London Features International

authority that is central to the social problem film. In Sekka's performance,
Peter does not sound like an immigrant. His patterns of speech are almost
wholly Anglicised, and his manners, bearing and education complicate his relationship to Mills's self-taught working man. The encounter between these two
unsettles the traditional colonial binarism, categorised by Dyer as linking
whiteness to 'order, rationality, rigidity' and blackness to 'disorder, irrationality and looseness' (2002: 130). Such a disruption occurs because of Jacko's
working–class status. He is not the hegemonic male figure who can bring order
and rationality to bear on a crisis situation, rather he is the autodidact who has
taught himself liberalism, but whose ability to apply this knowledge collapses
under the pressure of the emotive irrationality 'typical' of his class. Consequently, as neither character can be regarded as wholly authoritative, neither
can act definitively to resolve the crisis of inter-racial desire. An impasse is
reached, and the film resolves it through its abrupt, but not wholly unexpected,
transition from rationality to riot.

I suggested above that Everyman's capacity for self-sacrifice and duty was,
in the changing climate of the 1960s, more likely to be perceived as a nasty

case of repression. This generational shift in attitudes is integral to the decline of the Everyman figure, and indicates the nostalgia underpinning the character of Jacko. Although he remains a serious figure within the film, it is also the case that he is socially and politically impotent. *Flame in the Streets* thus works in conjunction with *Tunes of Glory* to suggest that, across the spectrum of class possibilities, a particular mode of English masculinity was being rendered redundant, not least because of its inability to articulate or understand desire. Ian Johnson observes of Mills that he 'is not a romantic actor and usually makes even the most passionate scene seem uninteresting' (*Films and Filming*, June 1962) – but it is equally the case that the parts played by Mills, and the Englishness he was required to embody, were singularly devoid of passion. To desire another is to lose control of the self, and such a loss of control has traditionally been perceived as fundamentally un-English.[12] By the beginning of the 1960s, however, the absent sexuality of the Englishman was gradually being exposed to scrutiny: Captain Anson, needing a mother more than a lover; Colonel Barrow, devoid of female company and unable to express himself amongst men; Jacko Palmer, described by his wife as making love to her as if he 'were taking a quick drink'. And alongside these case studies in masculine inadequacy can be set the figure of Barney, the self-deluding great lover in Leslie Norman's *Summer of the Seventeenth Doll* (1961).

Summer of the Seventeenth Doll continues the diversification in Mills's screen roles by casting him as an Australian cane cutter, but it also highlights his increasingly 'queer' status, as directors began to use his vulnerable face and slight body to suggest an unstable relationship to masculine norms. Cast alongside Ernest Borgnine's Roo – a big man 'going to seed' – Mills seems smaller and scrawnier even than he did as Captain Anson. His insignificance is further emphasised by the narrative diegesis: his role is not one of authority, but of subordination. The question that dominates this film is, in a sense, the same one that motivated his films of the 1930s; namely, what makes a man? But, while Mills's early forays into filmmaking focused on the process of becoming a man, *Summer of the Seventeenth Doll* presents the dilemma of decline. Focusing on a community of workers amongst whom physical and sexual prowess are pre-eminently the defining criteria of masculinity, the film develops into an evolutionary tale in which a particular mode of masculinity is threatened with extinction through age and inability to adapt. The film offers two narrative trajectories. The first is a conflict over the role of 'alpha male', a competition from which Mills, as the small and, arguably, parasitic Barney, is both physically and temperamentally excluded. He can only attempt to mediate between the once powerful Roo and his successor, Dowd (Vincent Ball). The second trajectory follows the struggle to construct a normative model of heterosexuality from a non-conforming matrix of desire. As part of the film's concern with age and change, Borgnine's

Roo seeks to regularise his relationship with his long-term girlfriend, Olive (Anne Baxter). Barney, however, remains wholly committed to preserving the status quo that divides an exclusively homosocial work community from a holiday world peopled by recreational women. The reasons for this are evident in Olive's observation that: 'If Barney had been a woman, I wouldn't have got a look-in.' However, her diagnosis is only partially correct. It is Barney, rather than Roo, who is dependent upon the illegitimate, inarticulable love that connects the two men, and within the logic of the film, Barney's weakness is encoded in his inability to transcend the immaturity of his homosexual desire.

Mills's performance as Barney is an impressive one, and indeed confirms that not only is he, in Johnson's terms, an 'unromantic' actor, but also that his best work emerges from a homosocial context. Mills excels at conveying the inarticulable subtleties of relationships between men, and while nearly all his films could be categorised as homosocial in their emphasis on the male group, many of the best also demonstrate an intangible libidinal charge more appropriately described as homoerotic. In a definition that admirably conveys the sensibility of films such as *Forever England* and *The Way to the Stars*, Richard Dyer suggests that homoeroticism 'tends to stress libidinal attraction without sexual expression, sometimes even at the level of imagination and feeling'. It is, he continues, a term that conveys 'a sense of male pleasure in the physical presence of men' (2002: 3). This subtext of desire had been integral to cinematic representations of British masculinity for over twenty years, but like so much else in British culture and society, it could not continue unchallenged in the changing atmosphere of the 1960s. The gradual relaxation of some aspects of censorship (Harper and Porter 2003: 241) had paved the way for the more sexually explicit cinema of the New Wave, while screen representations of homosexuality increased in the aftermath of the 1957 Wolfenden Report's recommendation that homosexual acts be decriminalised.[13] Sexuality and desire were no longer absent presences in the performance of British masculinity, even if the articulation of desire was largely to be found in the bodies of angry young men and the 'problems' of realist cinema. For Mills, however, it was more often the case that he was called upon to represent the crisis of traditional masculinity in a changing environment, and he continued to be cast in apparently conservative roles, replicating the modes of masculinity with which he had so long been associated. But, as the previous chapter suggested, the repetition of gender norms is an inherently unstable process. Although a heteronormative society depends upon the repeated citation of appropriately 'masculine' and 'feminine' behaviour, the impossibility of ever fully conforming to the ideal means that representations will always contain within them the possibility of otherness, and from this 'failure' emerges the potential for criticism and change. *Tunes of Glory* capitalised upon this potential in its exposure of the contradictions and frailties of traditional masculine performance. *The Singer Not the Song*, by contrast, sought to repeat reliable tropes of narrative and masculine performance, only to find them signifying something quite other in the final cut. Critically slated upon its release, Roy Baker's 1961 pot-boiler about the conflict between a Catholic priest and a Mexican bandit, set the traditional English masculinity of Mills against the self-conscious modernity of Dirk Bogarde. The result was a dissonant clash of acting styles that worked to expose the archetypally repressed Englishman as a powerless and absurd figure, unable to identify, let alone articulate his desires.[14]

MEN IN BLACK: *THE SINGER NOT THE SONG*

'It must be heartbreaking to fall in love with a man you can never have.' ('Anacleto Comachi' in *The Singer Not the Song*)

Harper and Porter observe that realism was the 'dominant discourse of 1950s art direction and production design' (2003: 203), and this discourse was not significantly challenged until the advent of the New Wave, whose filmmakers 'inaugurated a new type of shooting, in which the visual codes were carefully uncoordinated and the old relationships between performance and visual style were shaken loose' (p. 216). A distinction thus emerges at the end of the decade between a residual 'high' realism and an emergent social realism that fragmented the visual and narrative certainties of British cinema. It is, however, impossible to place *The Singer Not the Song* within this otherwise useful distinction: the film persistently evades the categorical tropes of late 1950s and early 1960s filmmaking by achieving the rare distinction of being neither realist nor innovative. Rather, the film harks back to the spectacle and narrative of Gainsborough melodrama, but without the brevity, or the *joie de vivre*, that characterised the earlier films. The film's ambitions are undermined by a tonal uncertainty that emerges from the radical variety of acting styles on display, and this probably contributed to its poor critical reception. While Mills performs in his standard realist mode, Bogarde's performance is, to quote Stephen Bourne, 'as camp as Christmas' (1996: 152). Male character actors in the supporting roles roar and tremble like fugitives from the Victorian stage, the Mexican housekeeper sounds like a member of the Women's Institute, and the female lead, platinum blonde Frenchwoman Mylene Demongeot, is so visually inappropriate for her Mexican role that she seems to have wandered in from a different film.

The film's problems were not eased by its somewhat chequered production history. The director, Roy Baker, had doubts from the start, but recalls in his autobiography that Rank's John Davis saw *The Singer Not the Song* as an ideal vehicle for their contract star, Dirk Bogarde (Baker 2000: 110). According to

Baker, Mills was the choice of Earl St John, head of production at Pinewood. But however the casting came about, it was not fortuitous. Accounts of the film's production by Baker and Mills both acknowledge Bogarde's animosity towards his co-star, while Bogarde simply observes that the film 'wasn't much fun' (1979: 232). The exact cause of Bogarde's hostility is impossible to determine, but it undoubtedly contributed to the somewhat peculiar on-screen dynamic between the two performers.[15] With a disgruntled star and censorship problems emerging from the Catholic Church and the Spanish authorities, Baker opted to focus on the design of his production: 'I resolved to do all I could to make the thing look good' (p. 112), and in many respects he succeeded, opting for the extreme contrast of two men in black fighting for supremacy against a stylised white landscape. Mills is cast in his customary role – the tough, dutiful, authoritative and celibate war hero – only this time his soldier is a servant of God rather than the British army. But although Mills replicates his service persona, visually and structurally the film is closer to a Western, a parallel established in the opening sequence when Father Keogh, the hero/stranger/lawman, walks through the terrorised town. The film's other man in black is Anacleto the bandit, an anti-clerical cat lover, who finds himself strangely fascinated by the virtues of the new priest, and determines to establish whether Keogh is 'an exceptional man' of whom the Church is unworthy, or whether it is the Church that has made him so. Keogh in turn becomes obsessed with the idea that he can redeem Anacleto, and bring him back into the body of the Church. The ideological struggle between Bogarde's camp Mephistophelean bandit and Mills's manly but pious priest is complicated by the presence of Locha, the daughter of the local landowner, who inexplicably falls in love with the priest and thus conveniently gives heterosexual legitimacy to an otherwise wholly homoerotic plot.

As I suggested above, French actress Mylene Demongeot looks completely out of place as Locha. While it might be argued that her blondeness functions as a symbol of purity within Baker's black and white landscape, in effect it works largely to emphasise her superfluity. Against the whiteness of the landscape the eye is drawn to the dramatic blackness of Mills's cassock and the glossy sheen of Bogarde's leather trousers (which made a greater impact on the critics than almost any other aspect of the film). In his desire to make his film look good, Baker opens up a space of camp possibility, within which everything from the costumes to the close-ups work to expose the absurdity of the heterosexual love plot. The crucial encounters within the film take place between the two men. Baker makes intense use of close-ups, with Mills largely shot square on and in full light, while Bogarde is seen in profile or with half his face in shadow. The symbolism is obvious, as are the implications of the bandit's costume changes. Anacleto dresses all in black, except when he takes shelter and religious instruction from Keogh, during which time he adopts a range of pastel waist-coats and shirts that suggest the possibility of his redemption through the love of a good man. Richard Dyer suggests that camp can be defined as 'a way of prising the form of something away from its content, of revelling in the style while dismissing the content as trivial' (2002: 52) and this is helpful in thinking about the tensions within the film. While Mills appears to take the moral and religious dilemmas of Father Keogh completely seriously, Bogarde quite liter-ally performs with one eye-brow raised. He looks ravishing in his black outfit, accessorised with hat, silver-topped cane and white cat, and this 'excess', along with the knowingness of his gaze, determines that the content of the film is not so much rendered trivial as made fluid. We cannot be sure what Anacleto wants or why, we only know that he is in command of a situation that Keogh simply does not understand.

It is Keogh's obliviousness that most clearly links him to the soldier heroes and Everymen of previous decades. Mills's priest is a man of action who has repressed all knowledge of the body. In one sense this makes him a nostalgic figure, mobil-ising myths of an earlier, more innocent time, but it is also the case that this very unworldliness makes him an object of desire. Keogh is a source of fascination for both Anacleto and Locha because he symbolises an unblemished masculine ideal. He is a pure man, a symbol of truth who cannot lie or dissemble, an unobtain-able object of desire. This characterisation speaks to the classical binary division between an ideal masculine realm of the mind and a pragmatic, debased bodily dimension associated with the feminine. Female sexuality is the serpent that will eventually tempt and corrupt the purity of the male bond. In a patriarchal tradition that privileges the word over the body, it is significant that the rela-tionship between Keogh and Anacleto is cemented when the priest gives the bandit his word. And just as the giving of the word brings the two men together, it is the breaking of the word that ultimately divides them, and symbolises Keogh's fall from grace. But before this betrayal takes place, the relationship between the two men takes the form of a prelapsarian idyll in which Anacleto challenges Keogh to save his soul: 'I've never liked your Church, or your God, but if they satisfy a man like you, why shouldn't they satisfy me?'

Keogh's resemblance to an earlier mode of hero is significant, but unlike earlier narratives, *The Singer Not the Song* offers no rewards for repression, and the priest is made to suffer for his inability to read either his own body or the bodies of those around him. Keogh, like any good spiritually-minded man, fails to notice Locha's desire until Anacleto tells him about it, and he fails to notice his own desire until Anacleto tells him that he is in love with the girl. Anacleto's interpellation of Keogh into an economy of heterosexual desire comes as something of a surprise – not least because until this point Keogh's actions have suggested that all his emotional energy is actually focused on Anacleto.

The encounter that 'confirms' this heterosexuality might thus be described, in Alexander Doty's terms, as a 'queer moment'. Doty argues that 'basically heterocentrist texts can contain queer elements, and basically heterosexual, straight–identifying people can experience queer moments' (1995: 72). In the case of *The Singer Not the Song* a queer moment occurs, somewhat ironically, when one character forcibly imposes heterosexual desires onto an otherwise homoerotic framework. Taken to see the kidnapped Locha, Keogh demands to speak to her alone. Anacleto refuses his request and remains in the room with the couple, not just as a voyeur, but as an agent who speaks for the largely silent priest. Not only does Father Keogh have to be told who he desires, he also needs help to speak the language of heterosexuality:

> Locha: [To Keogh] 'Would you have been ready to be my lover, or perhaps to marry me and stop being a priest?'
> Anacleto: 'Unlikely, but not impossible. He didn't know it, but the good father's feelings for you were the same as yours for him.'
> Locha: [To Keogh] 'What's he saying?'
> Anacleto: 'I'm saying that he's in love with you.'
> Locha: [Drawing away from Keogh] 'Is it true? If it is true, say so, say it.'
> Keogh: 'Yes Locha. I love you. In my conceit I didn't realise . . . didn't know that this could happen to me.'

Keogh's eventual reply is spoken in a dead and emotionless tone. It is a repetition of Anacleto's words rather than an expression of his own desires, and it operates as a form of mimicry. It is a mode of repetition that fails to replicate fully the norms of heterosexuality, and in its failure it defamiliarises that which it seeks to copy, and exposes the constructedness of the heterosexual matrix. Feminist theorist Luce Irigaray argues that women must work to expose the construction of femininity through an excessive inhabitation of oppressive feminine 'norms' – 'so as to make "visible" by an effect of playful repetition, what was supposed to remain invisible' (1985: 76). There is nothing playful about *The Singer Not the Song*, but litotes can defamiliarise as effectively as hyperbole, and Keogh's passionless performance of heterosexual desire operates to expose the extent of its artifice. The only passion that Keogh has revealed is for the possession of Anacleto's soul, and as the film approaches its end, it is Anacleto he pursues, not Locha. The torrid climax of the film, in which the two men finally embrace in death is another 'queer moment' in which the bodies of Bogarde and Mills tell a story quite other to the ostensible conclusion of the narrative [Fig. 6.3].

Over the course of the film, then, a figure that began as an archetypal Millsian homosocial hero is transformed into a passive love object whose

Fig. 6.3 Together at last: Mills and Dirk Bogarde experience a queer moment in *The Singer Not the Song* (1961). British Film Institute/London Features International

repressed emotions have been painfully revealed, whose authority has been undermined, and whose 'word' has been broken. Rather than representing a set of values or a national ideal, Keogh has been valued for his body in and of itself. He has been reduced from the song to the singer, and he dies a deluded lover, fooled by Anacleto into thinking he still stands for something.[16]

The Singer Not the Song and *Summer of the Seventeenth Doll* together comprise a significant reinscription of Mills's national masculinity. That which was once the norm is exposed as dissonant, unsettling and queer. Yet the ability of these films to undermine archetypal modes of Englishness remains limited, not least because the impact of their queer narratives is diluted by 'foreign' locations and characters. The particularity of Mills's English masculinity is overlaid by the distancing factors of Barney's Australian lifestyle and Keogh's Irish Catholicism. It would be left instead to the Boulting brothers, established critics and chroniclers of the state of the nation, finally to bring the critique home, and to queer the English Everyman on his own territory.

'THERE'S NOTHING ODD OR QUEER ABOUT ME': *THE FAMILY WAY*

'No good ever comes of these challenges between father and son' ('Lucy Fitton' in *The Family Way*)

By 1966 the independent producers John and Roy Boulting were firmly established as cynical observers of British society. Although their early careers were characterised by the wartime idealism of *Pastor Hall* (1940) and *Thunder Rock* (1942), by the mid-1950s their disillusionment with the postwar world had become evident. This disenchantment found its most successful expression in a series of satires ridiculing the sacred cows of British self-perception, beginning in 1956 with *Private's Progress*. This debunking of the army was followed by films attacking, amongst other things, the law (*Brothers in Law*, 1957), the church (*Heavens Above!*, 1963) and the honest working man (*I'm All Right Jack*, 1959). Although the critics were ambivalent about the change of direction in the Boultings' filmmaking, the public warmed to the brothers' assault on the establishment and its institutions:

> *Private's Progress* depicted that 'other war' fought by malingerers and opportunists, the dark underbelly of 'our finest hour', rather than the national myth. Its huge popularity showed that the Boultings' anarchic world of fools and knaves was recognised and enjoyed by a mass public. (Spicer 2000: 72)

Andrew Spicer also argues that the Boultings' work is characterised by a focus on the 'male misfit', and *The Family Way* (1966) is no exception to this rule. In other respects, however, the film is a notable departure from the brothers' often ruthless exposure of human greed and frailty. Based on Bill Naughton's stage play *All In Good Time*, *The Family Way* is a sympathetic and moving depiction of the inarticulable emotions that shape two generations of a Northern working-class family. Focusing in particular on the relationship between father and son, the film exposes the painful consequences of the failure to meet the demands of masculine performance.

The Family Way could be summarised as a working-class Oedipal comedy of manners. Arthur (Hywel Bennett), the favoured son of Lucy (Marjorie Rhodes), is oppressed by his aggressively masculine father Ezra (John Mills), but hopes to escape the conflict and assert his own masculinity through marriage to Jenny (Hayley Mills). However, although Jenny represents a legitimate object of desire in place of the forbidden mother, the marriage does not resolve the Oedipal conflict between father and son. The problem is compounded by Arthur's inability to consummate his marriage: a failure in large part attributable to the strain of still living in his father's house. The constant interruption of the nervous newly-weds is an ongoing source of comedy within the film, but Arthur's inability to perform becomes a more serious matter when word leaks out regarding the fact that the marriage 'hasn't taken on yet'. Various more or less comic remedies are attempted, from Arthur's visit to the Marriage Guidance Council to Jenny's consultation with her rabbit-breeding physiotherapist Uncle Fred. The situation is finally resolved, however, through an emblematic act of violence (displaced onto Arthur's unpleasant employer), which acts as such a powerful assertion of the son's masculinity that his potency is regained. Up until this point, the introverted Arthur Fitton has been a serious and sympathetic version of Spicer's 'male misfit', but the twist in the narrative, and the particular achievement of the film, lies not in the depiction of Arthur's self-assertion, but in the parallel breakdown of his father. As the film progresses, Ezra Fitton is revealed to be both 'odd and queer' and an infinitely less secure example of the dominant working-class male paradigm than he originally appeared.

Mills's Ezra Fitton unites much that has already been discussed. He is the deceived husband, the bemused father, the deluded patriarch, the mourning lover. He exhibits an oppressive adherence to patriarchal concepts of masculinity, and these beliefs set him wholly at odds with his bookish son. But the film moves beyond this opposition to expose the contradictions underpinning heteropatriarchal masculinities, and it works persistently to complicate the boundaries demarcating dominant and subordinate gender roles. For all his bluster, the vulnerability of ageing patriarch Ezra is evident from the start, largely thanks to a powerful performance from Mills that won substantial critical acclaim. *Time* described it as 'a brilliant full-length portrait of a proletarian father who tries to reach his children but who cannot touch them without giving hurt' (14 July 1967), Penelope Gilliat in the *Observer* called it 'beautifully substantial' (18 December 1966), Anne Pacey in *The Sun* opted for 'memorably moving' (19 December 1966), and Ian Christie settled on 'one of the best performances of his life' (*Daily Express*, 19 December 1966). In some respects the role can be regarded as summative in that it enables Mills to draw on the full range of his acting skills developed over the previous thirty years. Considerable impact is achieved through body language alone. Mills juxtaposes moments of extreme stillness, for example, sitting upright and rapt before an episode of *Coronation Street*, with passages of restless movement and with the thoughtful and unobtrusive manipulation of such expressive objects as a pipe and a plate of shepherd's pie. And at all points he stands as Ezra Fitton would stand: legs slightly apart, rocking back on his heels, ready to confront the inexplicable forces of the modern world. His North-country accent is secure throughout, and his voice moves persuasively from drunken volume, to the gentle poetry of memory, to the hesitancy of inarticulable emotion. His face is similarly flexible. The majority of Mills's earlier heroic roles gave little scope for him to exercise the elasticity of his face, but comedies such as *The History of Mr Polly* offered some indication of his ability to distort and transform his features. For Ezra Fitton, Mills's hair is thin and oiled into an unflattering central parting. His delicate upper lip is obliterated by an enormous moustache under which his chin variously recedes or juts forward aggressively. Massive crow's feet disrupt the relative smoothness of his cheeks and scrunch his face into a grimace of pain or the pleasure of a smile. Bushy eyebrows complement the moustache and above them, three entrenched furrows and a strong vertical line work to indicate the depth of the character's confusion.

The importance of Mills's ability to express complex emotions through the face and body of the inarticulate Ezra is evident from the outset. On the evening of Arthur's wedding, father and son compete at arm-wrestling, in a scene that encapsulates the central drama of the film. Ezra is drunk and raucous, his mood swinging from sentimentality to aggression. Having already clashed with Arthur on several occasions during the day, his challenge to the group for someone to fight him at 'the elbow game' is that of an insecure and somewhat bewildered man who needs to reconfirm his status. No volunteers are forthcoming until Arthur is teased into agreement by his even more aggressive employer Joe Thompson (Barry Foster). Ezra's over-investment in the contest is immediately evident in an attempt to get an unfair advantage by crushing Arthur's hand. He is made to 'play fair', but the shot/reverse shot sequence that follows exposes just how much is at stake in the father-son competition. As Ezra gains the early advantage, his excitement is evident in the hint of a smile, the impish wrinkles around his eyes and the forward jut of his chin. When the camera cuts to Bennett's smooth unlined face the contrast between the two men could not be greater. Bennett's concentration is intense, but his focus is on his hand, or the table, and not his father. Mills, by contrast, stares fixedly at his opponent. Briefly the camera pulls back to show the wider group, shouting their support, but returns to the principals as Arthur begins to prevail.

The cut to Mills is shocking: his face is beetroot red and covered in a sheen of sweat, the ease and confidence that characterised the opening of the bout has vanished. Arthur, by contrast, is enjoying a sense of imminent victory, which encourages him finally to look at his father. Mills by now is puce, his features distorted, pain evident in narrowed eyes and gritted teeth. He looks on the verge of tears: broken, vulnerable, exposed. But as his eyes meet Bennett's they do not simply convey the shocking realisation of his own vulnerability, they also convey a mute appeal born of fear. Intentionally or otherwise, Arthur is manipulated by his father's fear: he eases back and Ezra prevails [Fig. 6.4]. Arthur receives no gratitude for his willingness to shore up the crumbling patriarchal edifice of his father – rather, Ezra is harsh and bullying in victory. He cannot afford to be otherwise within the terms of a hegemonic masculinity that will not tolerate the display of weakness.

Both father and son have undergone an epiphany in the process of the contest, and the scene as a whole works to suggest that the father's power in this film is purely symbolic. Ezra is a largely marginalised figure within the

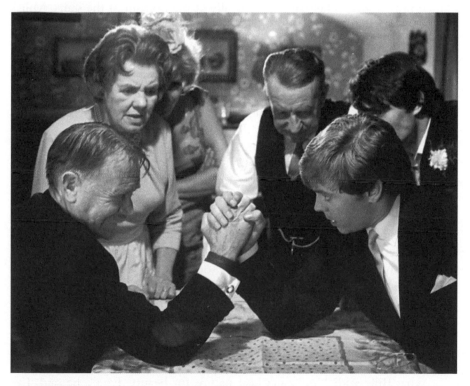

Fig. 6.4 Seeing through patriarchy: The 'elbow game' in *The Family Way* (1966).
Canal+Image UK Ltd

domestic day-to-day structure of the family, but he retains a symbolic power that is harder to confront than the reality of an ill-educated gas worker. His relationship with his son is further complicated by love. Ezra undoubtedly cares for the son he does not understand and with whom he cannot communicate, and when the guests have left, Lucy takes him to task for his behaviour:

> Lucy: 'Did you have to beat the lad like that in front of Jenny and every-
>   body?'
> Ezra: 'It was only a game.'
> Lucy: 'Would you have liked it if your father had licked you in front of
>   everybody and on your wedding night?'
> Ezra: 'Stop picking me up, Lucy. What counts is what a man feels inside.'
> Lucy: 'How do we know what you feel?'

There is no answer to Lucy's final question, for indeed she has made explicit the central problem of Ezra's masculinity: it leaves him with no language through which to express affection or concern for his son, let alone articulate his own emotions. Aware of what he has done, he attempts to apologise. Filmed from above as he stands pathetically at the bottom of the stairs, Mills's mute appeal is that of a disgraced dog seeking forgiveness. Eventually he finds words through indirection: 'I forgot to say goodnight,' he shouts up at Jenny, who understands his intentions and throws him a rose. Within the gender landscape of *The Family Way*, it is women who must translate that which men cannot express.[17]

Ezra is thus paradoxically both a symbol of power and an object of comic derision. More unexpectedly, he is also a queer subject.[18] This is a man who sees nothing odd about having taken his best friend Billy along on his honeymoon, and who speaks almost poetically in his elegiac recollection of their early-morning walks together. Billy Stringfellow is the structuring absence of the film, and the explanation behind the yearning appeal that complicates Mills's gaze in the arm-wrestling scene. It is Billy whom Ezra sees across the table at the moment of his imminent defeat, and Billy's name that encodes repressed desire within the film, his absent presence haunting every scene. On the subject of Billy, Ezra is a different man, suddenly blessed with a vivid capacity for speech:

> 'That first morning, standing at the edge of the sea. I remember a little, frothy wriggle of tide rolling right over our new brown leather, then off again, like water off a duck's back. Then the sun came out and our boots were covered in little drops of water, all glistening away. D'you know what Billy said? "You can't beat nature for beauty, Ezra", he said. I've never forgot it. [Pause] That were the best moment of my honeymoon.'

This, like most of his poetic or melancholic outbursts, is confined to the privacy of the domestic space. As Ezra looks up at the stars, his only audience is Lucy, herself somewhat queered by her implication in the erotic triangle of husband, lover and wife. But when the power of Billy's memory evades the safe containment of the domestic, the dangers of failing to conform to the masculine myth become evident.

Anthony Easthope observes that: 'Although men are always both masculine and feminine, the myth [of masculinity] demands that they should be masculine all the way through' (1992: 19). There is no room in dominant heteropatriarchal conceptions of masculinity for such concepts as uncertainty, ambivalence, fluidity or multiplicity, and the demonstration of such qualities invites the punishment of ridicule. Consequently, when Jenny's parents visit the Fittons to tell them of their son's failure, Ezra's responses are typically and appropriately masculine: 'What a disgrace . . . if a thing like this got out, I'd never live it down . . . that bloody son of yours has shamed me.' Lucy, by contrast, protects her son by exposing the secret of her 'honeymoon for three'. Yet Lucy's attempt to 'out' her husband and force him into an acknowledgement of his own 'otherness' is complicated by Ezra's failure to understand the problem represented by his relationship with Billy. There is incomprehension and incredulity in Mills's voice as he explains: 'But I'd never taken a holiday without him – that was the lad I was born next to. Did you expect me to leave him alone during holiday week just because I'd got wed to you?' Ezra's memory of his bond with Billy is almost pre-social, evoking in its recollection of early childhood the idealised space of the maternal dyad, when desires and drives were not subject to the regulation of paternal law. The relationship stands outside the normative parameters of compulsory heterosexuality, but Ezra either cannot or will not see it that way. Ezra thus inhabits the contradictory space of the homoerotic. His evident 'pleasure in the physical presence of men' (Dyer 2002: 3) co-exists with his conformity to the codes of heteropatriarchal masculinity, a contradiction that enables him to criticise his son for behaviour no more 'queer' than his own. Within a patriarchal society, the masculine myth operates to regulate male behaviour at both social and psychic levels. Ezra's repeated assertion that Billy was 'the best mate a man ever had' is his attempt to endow his relationship with heterosexual legitimacy through a process of self-interpellation, but the individual subject can never fully appropriate the process of social categorisation, and Ezra's attempts are destined for failure. His non-conformity is betrayed by his excessive behaviour: to speak of emotion is to be tainted by the feminine, and the fluency Ezra finds in his memories of Billy mark him out as other. Irrespective of his self-perception, at both intra- and extradiegetic levels, Ezra is read as queer. The comments of the unsympathetic Liz Piper (Avril Angers) make clear his uncertain hold on masculine authority: 'Well! They say that to understand the children, you have to know the parents . . . Young Arthur, he stands out in that family like a sore thumb.' Her implication here is that Arthur is not Ezra's son – but whether Ezra is criticised for transgressive desire or heterosexual inadequacy, he has failed to live up to the prescriptions of heteropatriarchal masculinity.

Having exposed the precariousness of the hard man's identity, however, the film concludes not with a valorisation of a more cerebral new masculinity, but with a reinvigorated version of tradition. The climax of *The Family Way* charts Arthur's self-assertion through that most archetypal of man-making narrative trajectories: fighting followed by sex. Indeed, the confrontation with Joe Thompson reveals that, in contrast to his mild-mannered appearance, Arthur is in fact the epitome of the masculine ideal. The 'tough guy' of legend has always been a man of few words, a man who keeps his own council but acts, swiftly and decisively, when the situation demands. Arthur answers Joe's offensive words with action, making Joe's hyperbolic verbal aggression look like a hysterical assertion of troubled masculinity. He talks too much and is revealed as empty, lacking the substance evident in Arthur's silent strength. The revelation of Arthur's toughness should not, however, come as a shock. Throughout the film, he has exhibited archetypally masculine traits that counterbalance his love of Beethoven and books. 'He's not the kind to say anything,' observes Lucy of her son, indicating that he, like his father, suffers from emotional inarticulacy. Similarly, his response to the discovery that everyone knows the secret of his impotence ironically mirrors that of Ezra: 'I'm nobody and nothing, but at least I've always been able to hold my head up in this neighbourhood . . . You've made me a bloody laughing stock.' Anger, then, makes Arthur a new man, and enables him to resolve the Oedipal conflict in a gesture of reconciliation. Egged on by Lucy, he asks Ezra's advice for the first time. It is a happy ending: Ezra will buy the newly-weds a house, and the stability of the patriarchal succession will be ensured. However, at the very moment of the ageing father's symbolic reinstatement, the structural absence of Billy Stringfellow is reasserted to ensure that Ezra remains on the margins of the dominant paradigm. Once more recognising Billy in Arthur, Ezra finally acknowledges the full extent of his loss. Mourning for the loss of the lover reincarnated in his son, he simultaneously faces both the heterosexual betrayal of his wife and the homosexual betrayal of his friend. Under such intense pressure, the façade of masculinity finally cracks and Ezra breaks down in tears – a sight that horrifies his younger son, Geoffrey (Murray Head). There is no script through which to convey these revelations: rather, Mills works with his face and body to convey physically that which his character could not possibly express. From a rueful half-smile, his face seems quite literally to fall. His brow furrows, his bottom lip is chewed. His shoulders slump and his walk has the distracted manner of shock. When Lucy comes to embrace him, he grasps her hand urgently in a gesture that 'speaks' the truth of his need and his pain. [Fig. 6.5]

The Family Way is thus both comedy and tragedy, and in its 'queering' of the older generation, it clears the path for the new modes of British masculinity then emerging. These new masculinities were louder than their predecessors, shaped by the confidence of the new culture of consumption and its celebration of the individual, but the increase in volume should not mask a fundamental continuity in the construct of masculinity itself. These tensions between continuity and change are at the heart of *The Family Way*, and the subtext of the film encodes the subtle transfer of power from father to son, and from old to new. That these two masculinities are largely indistinguishable is perhaps the crowning irony of both the film and the gender politics of postwar Britain.

The 1960s, then, was a decade of deceptive shifts in the filmic presentation of masculinity. Duty and self-sacrifice were no longer pre-eminent in the hierarchy of man-making qualities, but English masculinity remained as dependent as ever upon toughness, self-sufficiency and emotional inarticulacy. What it meant to be a man had been repackaged rather than revolutionised, and this compromise has significant implications for the relationship between masculinity and national identity. Between the mid-1930s and the early 1960s, John Mills had been the most flexible screen exemplar of a historically specific

Fig. 6.5 Everyman breaks down: *The Family Way* (1966). Canal+Image UK Ltd

mode of national masculinity. However, the lack of an obvious successor as the embodiment of the English Everyman would seem to suggest that Mills had, quite simply, been the right man, in the right place, at the right time. In the context of both war and 'postwar', his ordinary appeal and ability to embody an imperative of duty took precedence over more hyperbolic constructions of the hero, but inevitably, as austerity gave way to affluence, the masculine ideal was reconfigured to meet new desires and expectations. As R.W. Connell reminds us: 'Hegemonic masculinity can be defined as the configuration of gender practice which embodies the culturally accepted answer to the problem of the legitimacy of patriarchy' (1995: 77). For the 1960s, the culturally accept-able answers were not Commander Armstrong or Shorty Blake, but James Bond and Harry Palmer. Yet beneath the surface changes that rendered Millsian masculinity redundant lie continuities that cannot be ignored. The masculinity of duty is equally a masculinity of endurance, which in turn is the keynote of the tough guy. The imperative 'not to let the side down' demands that the team member be as self-sufficient as the individual. The banter of the 1940s is equally the wise-cracking, disrespectful tough-talk of the new gener-ation: neither mode of speech permits a direct address to the emotions, and neither will tolerate the over-stepping of the intangible boundary separating the homosocial from the homosexual. What is not quite so clear, and will be discussed in the final chapter, is whether these characteristic modes of mas-culinity can any longer be seen as specifically English, or whether the change in the manner of their manifestation represents a dilution of national specificity, and the end of a viable cinematic construction of the 'English' hero.

Notes

1. At first sight there seems little to connect the high production values and glossy surface of the Bond films with the grainy realist texture of the New Wave, but as Sarah Street observes: 'Bond's globetrotting and proven success with women reveals another, fantasy aspect of the social realist films' masculine nightmare of being trapped in the provinces with a wife and family' (1997: 87).

2. The power of such new cinema icons is evident from Robert Shails's account of Michael Caine as a 'working-class hero'. Shail argues that over the course of the 1960s, 'Caine's heroes reflect an ideological system in the process of being inverted. The oppositional ideology of the working-class "rebel" has actually become nor-mative. Caine becomes a "hero" for an alternative system of dominant values' (2004: 73).

3. It is worth noting that the extra-filmic dimension of Mills's screen persona had also undergone something of a shift since the success, in 1959, of J. Lee Thompson's *Tiger Bay*. In the film Mills plays a dogged policeman investigating a murder to

which the only witness is an uncooperative young girl. The girl was played by Hayley Mills in a screen début almost universally hailed as remarkable, and both reviews and publicity for the film foregrounded Mills's status as a doting father and family man.

4. This role also won him *Films and Filming*'s award for the best male performance of 1961.

5. Price played Louis Mazzini in Ealing's 1949 comedy *Kind Hearts and Coronets*. Mazzini, a lower-middle-class shop assistant sets about the business of murdering the entire D'Ascoyne family (all played by Alec Guinness) in order to inherit a dukedom.

6. We learn that Barrow was held prisoner by the Japanese, a biographical detail that gives substance to his incipient hysteria, and Mills's newly stretched, thin face appropriately suggests the character's past suffering.

7. The similarities between the two men are easily overlooked on account of the structure of the film and the nature of the performances. Guinness works with both body and voice to display Jock's volatility. Mills's variations are predominantly vocal. Everything about his personification of Barrow is designed to react against the corporeal immensity of Guinness's Jock Sinclair, and the physical antithesis between the two men distracts from the fact that while Barrow lives for a long outmoded prewar ideal, Jock harks back to a by now equally redundant myth of wartime.

8. For example, *The Flesh is Weak* (1957), *Woman in a Dressing Gown* (1957), *Spare the Rod* (1961), *Victim* (1961) and *Sapphire* (1959).

9. Mills's daughter is played by Sylvia Syms who, only three years earlier, had played his lover in *Ice Cold in Alex*. Such patterns of casting are, of course, far from uncommon in both British and Hollywood cinema, where men are permitted much greater longevity in terms of their desirability.

10. Lola Young observes:

> A major flaw of the liberal discourse of social realism of this period is the attempt to explain away racism by locating it in individuals who are often already pathologized Others, such as working class youth or sexually frustrated women. The individual act, thought and attitude are emphasized, whilst institutional and state endorsement of racial inequality is ignored. (1996: 109)

11. Throughout this scene, Jacko repeatedly addresses Peter as 'son' in a dissonant and patronising attempt to suggest some degree of male kinship in their discussion of Kathie's future.

12. Indeed, as John Hill argues, the threat posed by such uncontrollable drives was a key anxiety underpinning the social problem cinema. Middle-class morality, like whiteness, was assumed as a default position:

> [I]t is this assumption of a sexual norm and corresponding concern with regulation that is probably true of all the problem movies. Although the ostensive problem may be juvenile delinquency or race relations, the implicit 'problem' is often that of sexual excess. (1986: 124)

13. Vito Russo claims that Britain was distinctly 'less agitated' than America when it came to the cinematic representation of homosexuality. In the Hollywood of the 1960s, 'Lesbians and gay men were pathological, predatory and dangerous; villains and fools, but never heroes' (1987: 127, 122).

14. Given the stylised unreality of the film and the elusive quality of Mills's accent, it hardly seems to matter that, technically, the priest is an Irishman.

15. Mills attributes the problem to a casual remark made on set (2000: 415), but Baker records that Bogarde's objections to Mills started long before filming began. Baker observes: 'What Dirk had against Johnnie he never explained. As far as I know, they had never played together' (2000: 111). In fact they had previously appeared together in *The Gentle Gunman* (1953), an ill-conceived account of a reformed IRA man's (Mills) attempt to rescue his brother (Bogarde) from involvement in paramilitary activities. John Coldstream's recent biography of Bogarde provides new information about the on-set disagreements before concluding that: 'The fundamental problem was that Dirk refused to countenance his character falling in love convincingly with one played by John Mills' (2004: 256).

16 In allowing the dying Keogh to believe he is contrite, Anacleto performs a small act of kindness that is, of course, the moment of his redemption.

17. Indirection is a characteristic mode of communication across all classes of English masculinity. Basil Barrow, for example, makes use of the same strategy when he wants to thank Jimmy Cairns for listening, without actually acknowledging his need. Suddenly observing that Cairns has no coat, he uses practical concern to cover the chasm opened up by his confession of weakness.

18. Richard Dyer distinguishes between the concept of the queer as a 'historically bounded notion' of perverse embodiment, valid up until the Stonewall riots of 1969, and an analytic concept he distinguishes through the capital letter Queer:

> Queer Theory is especially interested in manifestations of male-male sexual attraction where you wouldn't expect to find it, where it's been diverted or repressed or else obliquely expressed or unknowingly sublimated . . . In some versions, homosexuality is discovered to be so pervasive as to constitute a defining element of all sexuality, of the very notion of sexuality – that's what's Queer. (2002: 4)

This definition underpins much of my use of the term 'queer' in this chapter, but outside the context of Dyer's historical discussion, the capital letter seems superfluous. Although replete with 'manifestations of male-male sexual attraction', Mills's career does not include direct representation of Dyer's 'historically bounded' queer.

7

Playing the Fool:
Comedy and the end of Everyman

The history of audience taste in the 1950s is a complex one . . . The boundaries of the old taste communities had become blurred, and it was unusually difficult to predict which films would please the new audiences. This was because the audiences *themselves* were in flux, unsure about their own place in the new, supposedly classless world of consumption and pleasure. (Harper and Porter 2003: 264)

A work that is identified in any way as comic automatically predisposes its audience to enter a state of liminality where the everyday is turned upside down and where cause and effect can be triumphed over and manipulated. Comedy thus can be partially described as a playful realm of consecrated freedom. (Horton 1991: 5)

'Underlying causality' – a figure of speech that alludes to the social contradictions that a given society can provisionally subdue in order to constitute itself as such. (Kristeva 1986: 153)

Comedy, argues Freud, facilitates the expression of fears and anxieties otherwise inarticulable within the constraints of society. In *Jokes and their Relation to the Unconscious*, he suggests that comic forms are a means of overcoming repression: jokes have the capacity to '*evade restrictions and open sources of pleasure that have become inaccessible*', while also encouraging audiences into a position of sympathy 'without any very close investigation' (1960: 103). Comedy thus creates a potentially subversive space, a 'liminal' territory in which 'the rules and regulations of a society are briefly suspended' (Horton 1991: 5). Historically the genre has been understood to operate along two contrasting paradigms, one concerned with comedy as a corrective whose ultimate aim is the restoration of a healthy social order, the other, more subversively, inclined towards a carnivalesque inversion of norms. Yet even the more conservative construction of the genre depends upon a temporary disruption of the status quo. Traditional romance comedies typically end with the symbolic restoration of order through marriage, but the value of this ceremony is predicated upon the destabilising topsy-turveydom that has preceded it. Whether comedy is regarded as anarchic or corrective, it depends upon an articulation of otherness and disorder, producing a transitional space within which the unthinkable can be thought. Formally, comedy requires transgression, and for this reason the comic film becomes one of the few sites within mainstream cinema where transgressive masculinities can be manifest without punitive consequences.

As the previous chapters have suggested, the dramatic narratives of postwar British cinema repeatedly imply that failure to conform to dominant models of masculinity is a serious matter, liable to end in the punishments of ridicule or death. From comedy, however, a very different scenario emerges. In *Typical Men* Andrew Spicer catalogues comic types as 'alternative masculinities', suggesting that the Fool and the Rogue might represent legitimate opposition to the demands of hegemonic masculinity:

> As 'unofficial selves' both Fools and Rogues occupy a liminal, licensed space on the margins of society for 'unacceptable' masculine traits, which can include deviousness and incompetence. Their ideological function varies, but they can be empowering for subordinated groups as their resourcefulness, ingenuity and resilience often expose the arbitrariness of social systems. (2001: 19)

Within the limited and fantastical space of the film text it becomes possible for the underdog, the little man, the fool and the rogue to triumph over forces more powerful than themselves, and to do so through the performance of a masculinity that is categorically opposed to the hegemonic ideal. Mills, it should be noted, did not appear in postwar cinema as a rogue[1], but he did make several significant appearances as little men and fools, and three brief examples from these performances indicate the transgressive potential of comic masculinities. In David Lean's *Hobson's Choice* (1954) Willie Mossop, the illiterate, oppressed boothand, achieves success through submitting himself to the indignity of an inverted Pygmalion experience: he ends the film as a businessman who has been 'made' by his wife. In *The Baby and the Battleship* (Jay Lewis 1956), the dim-witted sailor 'Puncher' Roberts escapes the punitive force of the navy by revealing undreamed-of depths of maternal talent. Having broken every rule in the book, his exemplary care of the eponymous baby enables him to mother his way out of trouble. But perhaps most disruptive of all is the triumph of Alfred

Polly, H. G. Wells's lazy, incompetent, cowardly, day-dreaming fantasist and 'social misfit'. In *The History of Mr Polly* (Anthony Pélissier 1949) this antithesis of the English masculine ideal escapes the torments of adult masculinity to end his days rewarded with an idyllic life fishing at the Potwell Inn.

Comedy, then, is a form that facilitates the disruption of gender norms, both through the stereotypical inversions of the henpecked husband and the shrewish wife, and through more subtle manipulations of conventional gender roles. But what can the transgressions of comedy and Mills's intermittent performances in comic roles tell us about the changing shape of English masculinity? As the previous chapter suggested, by 1970 the concept of 'English' masculinity had fragmented. Regionally specific forms (the cockney, the working-class northerner, the cheeky Liverpudlian) had replaced nationally representative figures, and screen versions of Englishness were increasingly restricted to the parodic or ironic forms of the toff, the eccentric and the fool. This transition had been gathering momentum since the early 1950s, and the collapse of the Everyman hero into a parodic or ridiculous 'other' was preceded by the regeneration of two key comic types whose anarchic qualities had seen them fade from view during the community-minded war years. As Andrew Spicer observes:

> After their significant decline during the war, the re-emergence of Fools and Rogues was a striking feature of post-war British cinema. The Fool, as a bumbling Everyman, exposes the arbitrariness of social regulations and masculine norms that were becoming either irrelevant or unattainable . . . By contrast, the Rogue is best placed to adjust to rapidly changing social conditions and 'get away with it' against various regulations, restrictions and authoritarian institutions, notably the army and the health service, and lauds quick-witted opportunistic individualism at various social levels. (2001: 102)

While actors such as Terry-Thomas, Richard Attenborough and George Cole became part of a cross-class gallery of English rogues, fools were perhaps most memorably embodied by Ian Carmichael and Norman Wisdom. Carmichael's performances for the Boulting brothers in films such as *Private's Progress* (1956), *Brothers in Law* (1957) and *I'm All Right Jack* (1959) rendered ridiculous such notable 'English' virtues as honesty and fair play, while Wisdom's construction of the hapless little-man hero made him, in Spicer's words, 'a *contemporary* comic Everyman' (2001: 104). Spicer's description is significant. The concept of the Everyman requires the displacement of hierarchies of class and privilege, and is in consequence an ideal wartime icon. But it is not clear that such a figure can long survive the transition to peace. However much the wartime consensus might have demanded a brave new world, the restoration of postwar 'normality' brought, first and foremost, the return of the jaded but still powerful etiquette of the old. In her account of the 1950s, Christine Geraghty argues that 'class continues to be . . . a strong and powerful signifier in films of the period, despite the modern political, sociological and educational discourses that were proclaiming its rapid demise' (2000: 68), and it was the initial resilience of this hierarchical framework that ensured the displacement of the modern Everyman from heroic centrality to comic marginality. In the postwar world it became increasingly impossible for the contemporary Everyman to be anything other than comic, because only from the fool's privileged position of social illiteracy could the fast reforming boundaries of society be disrupted.[2] In a hybrid decade of radical impulse and reactionary practice, misunderstanding the rules became the most 'acceptable' way of challenging them. The paradox of legitimate transgression has its roots in a much older paradox, the wisdom of the fool. Walter Kaiser explains the potency of this figure:

> Since he does not comprehend the conventions of society, the natural fool is invariably irreverent of those conventions, not out of any motives of iconoclasm but simply because he does not know any better. This fact, of course, poses a problem for society, because the fool is a potentially subversive element in its midst. For the most part, however, the Middle Ages tended to tolerate the fool's non-conformity . . . He was therefore not expected to obey any code, and in this respect medieval tolerance gave the idiot considerable freedom to speak and act in ways for which others would have been summarily punished. (Kaiser 1984: 87–8)

According to Kaiser, Renaissance literature 'appropriated' the licence of the natural fool, endowing the 'artificial' fool with the figure's privileged freedom of speech. The fool became a figure speaking truth through the guise of idiocy, who could give voice to the transgressive desires of society, even when such desires were beyond his comprehension.[3]

As the consensus surrounding the heroic Everyman fragmented, a comic surrogate arose in its place. The pluck, reserve and homosocial banter of the national hero was replaced by luck, sentiment and, as the 1950s gave way to the 1960s, an increasingly camp heterosexuality. The emergence of the heroic fool and the loveable rogue took place alongside a number of other comic trends in the postwar era. What Michael Balcon described as the 'mild anarchy' (1969: 159) permeating Ealing comedy was, over the course of the decade, usurped by the moderate anarchy of the *St Trinians* and *Carry On* films. These series were characterised by a notable lack of respect for English institutions, and such group identities as they manifest represent the corrupt and inverted doubles of the wartime ideal. In the world of St Trinians, for example, the community is held together by greed, self-interest and lust. In Launder and Gilliat's *The Belles of St Trinians* (1954) the girls are outrageously entrepreneurial, indulging in gambling, theft and the manufacture of gin, while the staff specialise in the seduction of inspectors from the Ministry of Education. The girls also partici- pate in gratuitous violence, torture and deception, reducing a hockey match to a battlefield and waging war against staff and each other. The film's plot, such as it is, concludes with the financial salvation of the school (thanks to a well- placed bet) and the headmistress, Miss Fritton (Alastair Sim), claiming she's too polite to tell a group of outraged parents exactly where they can send their daughters. The triumph, however, is short-lived, and is followed by a coda in which the faceless mass of the girls steal the school's silverware at a prize-giving ceremony. Not even the unscrupulous Miss Fritton constitutes the law in this environment, and in this respect the film undoubtedly puts a dent in such cher- ished English values as fair play and sportsmanship. However, St Trinians is a girls' school, and the cultural construction of women has always placed them beyond the social, needing to be tamed by the laws of patriarchy and domes- ticity. Left to their own devices, women are dangerous – and in making the demonic private school the site of women's excesses, the film cannot help but replicate a series of all too familiar assumptions. Consequently it is difficult to determine to what extent this anarchic comedy succeeds in challenging the institutional structures it abuses. Harper and Porter see the success of Launder and Gilliat and the Boulting brothers as indicative of the 'decline of deference' that characterised the 1950s, arguing that 'the contempt for traditional class structures, which was enshrined in [their films] found favour with large parts of the cinema audience' (2003: 113). Geraghty, however, is not so certain, con- tending that the comedy of the decade hovers between the 'traditional and the modern' and resists 'the challenges and risks that comedy can present' (2000: 56). It is beyond the scope of this study to resolve this debate, but it is undoubtedly the case that the box office played a key role in determining acceptable comic forms. As the 1950s progressed, British cinema depended largely upon the genres of comedy and the war film for its box-office receipts, and it seems likely that the potential of comedy to disrupt or reconfigure the class and gender norms of postwar Britain was necessarily limited by the genre's own desire to be loved. Certainly, as the evidence of Mills's own comic perfor- mances will suggest, the restorative conventions of romance comedy were a more reliable box-office guarantee than the challenges of anarchic rebellion.

Nonetheless, it would be a mistake to see the conservative dimension of comedy as necessarily its dominant force. Irrespective of the comfy and con- ventional endings that characterise so much of British comedy, the genre remains the most viable space for the expression of Spicer's 'alternative mas- culinities'. The gender-dissonant heroes of comedy open up a transgressive space within which traditional patriarchal heterosexual masculinity is exposed and ridiculed through a variety of strategies. While plots enable the little man to outwit figures of authority, championing the cause of the underdog, comic performances have the potential to expose the constructed nature of gender identities. In the disjuncture between the actor's body and the cultural ideal, the ideal itself becomes subject to scrutiny, and films that cast actors such as Norman Wisdom and Charles Hawtrey as objects of heterosexual desire make heterosexuality itself ridiculous. Within comedy, the repeated 'failure' of actors adequately to perform heteronormative masculinity – or indeed, the presentation of an obviously subordinate masculinity as dominant – creates a significant challenge to the ideological forces policing gender norms.

Comedy thus remains a prime location for the expression of queer, subversive and non-conforming masculinities, and in the context of the previous chapter it might be tempting to argue that either the fool or the object of comic derision represents the teleological end point of Mills's career and his ability to embody a representative national masculinity. Yet a survey of Mills's films reveals that his comic performances were not confined to his later career, and his comic personae can more accurately be conceived in terms of a parallel disruptive trajectory that haunts and, at times, actively disrupts, his dominant representations of English masculinity. In the terms of the psychoanalyst Julia Kristeva, Mills's full-scale comedy roles might be seen as a form of 'underlying causality'. These intermittent, less familiar performances embody 'the social contradictions that a given society can provisionally subdue in order to constitute itself as such' (Kristeva 1986: 153), and in their non-conformity they articulate the failure of heroic masculinity. This is not to suggest that Mills had an equal and opposite comic persona that mirrored his English Everyman, rather it suggests an uncomfortable dialogue between the dominant and subordinate masculinities the actor was capable of embodying, and it has significant implications for the construction and maintenance of the Mills screen persona.

The success or failure of Mills's comic performances can be related to the changes in his status as a star and national exemplar, and to the transitions of the British film economy. Although his early cinema roles as a comic stooge, a rebellious youth and a prototypical rogue had given him plenty of comic experience, his success as a wartime Everyman and heroic adventurer had largely overwritten this memory. After his final appearance with Will Hay in *The Black Sheep of Whitehall* (1942) he made no more appearances as a chancer or rogue, and indeed in the postwar period he was not obviously regarded as a comic actor.[4] Probably his most successful comic role, for example, came by chance rather than design. Kevin Brownlow records the crisis that struck David Lean's production of *Hobson's Choice* when Robert Donat, the original choice for Willie Mossop, was forced to withdraw through illness. Lean turned to Mills after remembering how the actor had entertained the cast of *Great Expectations* by pretending to be seasick, recalling that, off camera, he was a 'very funny comedian' (1996: 301). But in the immediate aftermath of the war, this perception of Mills simply did not exist: his star persona, premised upon such roles as Captain Scott, precluded the possibility of comedy. That this was the case was made abundantly clear to Mills as actor and producer when he chose to give himself a break from heroic masculinity and cast himself in *The History of Mr Polly* (1949).

GOING TOO FAR: *THE HISTORY OF MR POLLY*

'Hate Fishbourne, hate the High Street, hate the shop, hate Miriam, hate the neighbours, every blessed one of them. Hate myself, too.' ('Mr Polly', in *The History of Mr Polly*)

In their influential essay collection *The Age of Austerity* (1963) Michael Sissons and Philip French detail the collapse of British influence in the aftermath of war. Whether they are focusing on politics, culture, fashion or films, the volume's contributors recount the spiritual, moral and financial exhaustion of the nation. In this context, Mills's Mr Polly could be seen as an ideal hero for the new era: an impoverished, impotent dreamer and fantasist obsessed with past glories enshrined in literature and myth. But audiences in 1949 were unable, or unwilling, to accept this version of their hero or their nation, and the film was not a success. It was, however, critically well-received. A. E. Wilson in *The Star* described Mills as 'the ideal Polly' giving a 'warmly human and lovely performance' (11 February 1949), Campbell Dixon in the *Daily Telegraph* called his performance 'extraordinarily skilful and charming'(14 February 1949), while Dilys Powell was prompted to write a review in the malapropistic style of Polly, opening her comments with a cry of 'Rapchurious!' (*Sunday Times*, 13 February 1949).[5] It was Stephen Watts in the *Sunday Express*, however, who asked the most pertinent question for the new actor/producer: 'How will Mills fans take their hero as a shabby, pathetic-romantic, dyspeptic Victorian small shopkeeper with a nagging wife?' (13 February 1949). Watts believed Mills's performance would win them over, but the film's poor box-office performance suggests otherwise:

It has always disappointed me that *Polly* didn't succeed at the box office. I've seen it several times since at the British Film Academy: looking at it objectively, it was nothing to be ashamed of. In fact it was a professional and extremely well-made and well-acted film. The sad fact of the matter is that at that time the public were not ready for it, disliked me in the character and did not besiege the cinemas to see it. (Mills 2001: 299)

The relative failure of the film is indicative of the investment of the public in the screen persona of the man described by Rank publicity as 'Britain's most popular star'. However, it is must also be recognised that the choice of Mr Polly as a change of role undoubtedly contributed to the problem. Polly is too uncomfortable and disruptive a character to permit easy identification, and the film does not flinch from showing him at his worst. As I suggested above, comedy has traditionally been theorised as either corrective or anarchic. The first type of comedy works to bring its characters back within the social fold, usually concluding in marriage and the restoration of the status quo. The second resists such closure, inverting and disrupting cultural norms and practices, and as such cannot easily be assimilated within realist conventions. This in itself provides a useful framework for understanding the tensions within Polly's story, but a further dimension is added if the distinction is conceptualised in Freudian terms, as Andrew Horton illustrates:

> In light of developments in psychoanalytic theory, however, it seems more useful to speak of Oedipal (accommodation, compromise, social integration) comedy and pre-Oedipal (wish fulfilment, dreams) comedy. Freud speaks of the comic as a sudden adult regaining of 'the lost laughter of childhood'. (1991: 10)

This distinction is particularly appropriate for an analysis of Mr Polly. Wells's original character can be seen as a half-socialised child who, in the absence of both mother and father, exists in a constant state of crisis in relation to the rules of appropriate behaviour. This tension is embodied in particular in his failure to be appropriately masculine. In the work-place he daydreams or reads; in the company of women, in particular his voracious female cousins, he verges on hysteria, alternatively talking too much, or panicking, departing the room with such memorable outbursts of nonsense as 'Little dog! . . . Eating my bicycle tyre' (Wells 1993: 76). Not surprisingly, when he attempts to regain agency by setting fire to his shop, his destructive childish impulses have consequences far beyond those he had imagined.

This is the Mr Polly that Pélissier and Mills brought to the screen: a comic hybrid, part rogue and part fool, whose unstable transition from childhood to adult masculinity avoids nearly all the heroic virtues of honesty, self-restraint, stoicism and duty. The character, then, is resolutely anti-meritocratic, and his story is a defiantly anti-Oedipal narrative in which the demands of realism and responsibility give way to glorious wish fulfilment. Alfred Polly, draper's assistant, is unhappy and unemployed until he inherits £500 on the death of his father. A dreamer, a romantic and fundamentally lazy, he fantasises about escaping the drudgery of shop-work, but a bruising encounter with 'romance' and class prejudice leads him to make the drastic mistake of marrying his cousin

Miriam and setting up a respectable business as a shop keeper. Polly hates his life, his wife and his neighbours, and his unhappiness is only mitigated by the books he continues to read. After an attempt to burn down his shop ends in an unlikely act of heroism, Polly abandons Miriam and takes to the open road, eventually finding happiness at the Potwell Inn. The Potwell is a site of prelapsarian fantasy presided over by Polly's soul mate, the plump woman (Megs Jenkins). In marked contrast to Miriam, the plump woman is conspicuously maternal. We first see her asleep in a chair with a paper on her lap – a vision that prompts Polly to exclaim, 'My sort!'. But in spite of the two characters' evident compatibility, the plump woman is not constructed as a sexual mate for Polly. Rather in entering the maternal territory of the inn, he acquires an instant family, comprising the plump woman, her 7-year-old niece, and a terrifying, perverse father figure, Uncle Jim (Finlay Currie). Within the family drama, Polly himself is configured as a child, and if he is to guarantee his access to the 'safety of the womb' (Anderson 1988: 153), he must defeat the father and the threatening outside world he represents. The final segment of both book and film is thus constructed as a series of mock-heroic tests, in which the child Polly ultimately triumphs over Jim and ensures that the fantasy of maternal plenitude will continue. Ironically, asserting his masculinity in slapstick battle ensures that Polly never has to return to the horrors of the adult world.

The film oscillates between the quiet, more or less sympathetic musings of 'the hero' and a series of set-piece scenes which present a hostile and cacophonous adult world. Pélissier and Mills's Polly is a bewildered child-man who, on acquiring money, is thrust into a position of adult responsibility for which he is utterly unprepared. 'I suppose I must have mourning?' he asks before his father's funeral in a succinct illustration of his distance from the rituals and conventions of society, a distance that is further emphasised by Pélissier's grotesque framing of the funeral gathering itself. A montage of close-ups focuses on mouths simultaneously eating and talking. Fragments of absurd conversation complement the dizzying catalogue of fragmentary body parts as faces, mouths, teeth, noses and food spin before the overwhelmed Polly. Mills's performance here, as elsewhere in the first part of the film, is built around the body language of childhood. An expression of wide-eyed amazement that mutates easily into horror speaks of the enormity of the world he confronts, while his costumes work to reduce his stature, in particular the too-large hat that drops down over his ears when he prepares to lead the funeral procession. Childhood is also key to the opening sequence of the film. When Polly's illicit reading leads to a confrontation with authority, he plays a hopeless game of hide-and-seek, ultimately freezing on the floor in the child's mistaken belief that stillness can be equated with invisibility. This technique is repeated at intervals throughout the film, and comes to have a cartoon-like quality, freezing time, while our 'hero' regroups.[6]

These characteristic traits form part of a comic ideolect that can be both distinguished from and related to Mills's dramatic performances. This ideolect, or 'set of performing traits' (Naremore 1988: 4) has its roots in Mills's earlier roles. For example, the class comedy of *Great Expectations*, built around a sense of conflict with the physical world as manifested in suits, hats and cutlery, is similarly utilised to emphasise Polly's misfit status. The too-tight suit of Polly's marriage is a symbolic strait-jacket, but it also helps to stiffen Mills's limbs, making his movements forced and artificial, rather than fluent and naturalistic. Later in the film, he is relieved of the suit, but the pent-up frustration it encoded is present in conflicts with a range of expressive objects including bicycles and buckets. The most obvious echo of earlier work, however, is found at the funeral meal, where his repeated failure to get a tomato from fork to mouth becomes an anxious reworking of Pip's potato-eating scene with Herbert Pocket. But while *Great Expectations* subordinated comedy to more dramatic narrative devices, Polly's physical battles are central to the construction of the film. Pélissier makes extensive use of physical comedy and slapstick, with the result that Mills's actions are often exaggerated and his movements telegraphed beyond the conventions of realism. Although Polly is a passive and reactive figure, pushed and pulled by the opinions and desires of others, Mills is permitted a performance that reveals the flexibility of features that had previously been required to repress rather than express emotion.

But what makes this Polly disquieting rather than comfortable or wholly sympathetic is that he also embodies the aggression of childhood. As the film progresses, Polly becomes a figure of pent-up rage, expressed through the bodily and facial contortions of Mills. From the first signs of Polly's symbolic dyspepsia, which necessitates an energetic self-flagellation, to the uncontrollable, Tourette-like verbal tics and explosions, to the overwhelming desire to kick his neighbour for showing too much of the 'end elevation', there is an id-like quality to the character's behaviour. Trapped in his loveless marriage, he seems literally unable to police his mind and body, finally exploding into a tantrum of rage in which Mills screws his face and body into an almost unrecognisable state. His cheeks swell, his eyes pop, his body turns rigid with fury, and his clenched fists form the first manifestation of a gesture that would be characteristic of his later frustrated authority figures [Fig. 7.1]. This is a film in which Mills makes himself ugly, deconstructing his heroic persona to present the adult Polly as a petulant, cowardly, resentful, bad-tempered man with thin, greasy hair and a shaggy moustache. These uninspiring characteristics are presented wordlessly in a variety of gestures and stances. In the shop, he leans against the door like a sulky teenager; with Miriam, his head slumps forward in an attitude of defeat; alone in the house, his limp arms and rounded shoulders speak of his defeat by this 'beastly, silly, wheeze of a hole'. In its presentation of

Fig. 7.1 Alternative masculinities: Mr Polly explodes in *The History of Mr Polly* (1949). British Film Institute/London Features International

a man almost destroyed by mean-spirited domesticity and narrow-minded respectability, *Polly* was perhaps ahead of its time. Films that recognised the incompatibility of masculinity and domesticity, and turned the disaffected male into a hero, would follow in the 1950s.

Yet questions still remain as to why the film so alienated Mills's fan-base. In part it seems likely that the film was simply too transgressive for its time. The ugly Mills revealed in the excesses of Polly must, like the villainous Mills that briefly surfaced in *Cottage to Let*, remain repressed for his heroic persona to function. This 'other' Mills would not be permitted (by fans, producers and directors) to resurface until the carefully constructed heroic surface had already begun to crack, and Mills had seen the back of the national popularity polls. This decline in popularity was not long in coming. The relative failure of *Polly* and his other production project *The Rocking Horse Winner*, were followed by a number of insipid dramas and the notable failure of his wife's play *The Uninvited Guest*.[7] Yet once this intense ideological investment in his persona had begun to fade, Mills acquired new freedom to play against type. In his memoirs, the actor attributes the revitalisation of his career to two films: David Lean's *Hobson's Choice* (1954) and Guy Hamilton's *The Colditz Story* (1955) (2001: 323, 411), both of which offered Mills the opportunity to reconstruct his heroic persona in comic terms.[8] While *The Colditz Story* reinstated Mills as a reliable officer-hero, albeit in the nostalgic mode of postwar representations, the success of *Hobson's Choice*, only five years after the relative failure of *Polly* begs questions about the changing tastes of cinema audiences. Were audiences more receptive to the simple-minded, the innocent and the childish in 1954 than in 1949? This seems unlikely, and it might be more appropriate to suggest that there are fundamental differences between the 'foolishness' of Willie Mossop and that of Alfred Polly, differences that makes one acceptable and the other unpalatable to the national taste. Both films focus on class and self-improvement, but while Mossop is built upon the model of the discovered genius – an innocent who does not know his own worth – Polly is initially posited as a man who cannot be satisfied with his lot. The differences are clear: one model complies with traditional conceptions of national diffidence, the other misguidedly chaffs against the bit of educational limitations and social hypocrisy. Unable to challenge the ghastly restrictions of his world, Polly inevitably emerges as a rogue as well as a fool, rejecting the demands of a capitalist economy and a Protestant work ethic. Willie Mossop, by contrast, follows the trajectory of Oedipal comedy, embracing capitalism and the work ethic in a narrative ideally suited to the evolving 'age of affluence'. The shift in national self-perception that accompanied such mood-enhancing events as the Festival of Britain, the coronation, and the conquest of Everest was paralleled in the cinema by such frivolous, feel-good comedies as *Genevieve* (1952) and *Doctor in the House* (1954). In spite of being a period piece, *Hobson's Choice* is similarly imbued with the optimistic spirit of the early 1950s, celebrating both eccentricity and modernity in its assault on the patriarchal masculinity of an earlier generation.

MAN-MAKING REVISITED: *HOBSON'S CHOICE*

'Will Mossop – you're my man . . . You're a business idea in the shape of a man . . . My brains and your hands'll make a working partnership.' ('Maggie Hobson', in *Hobson's Choice*)

Although far removed from the *Bildungsroman* of the 1930s, *Hobson's Choice* is undoubtedly a narrative of man-making. After Maggie Hobson (Brenda de Banzie) is told by her overbearing drunken father (Charles Laughton) that she's 'tough ancient leather' and a 'proper old maid', she undertakes to turn her father's 'natural' boothand Willie Mossop into both her husband and a successful businessman. Willie is a very literal manifestation of the 'underlying causality' upon which the social order is founded. Repressed and oppressed, he inhabits the basement workroom of Hobson's Salford shoe shop, emerging from below 'like a rabbit' when summoned by his class superiors. Yet, as the film immediately makes clear, the Hobson empire is founded upon Mossop's remarkable skills as a bootmaker, and without him, the old order represented by Laughton's tyrannical patriarch will crumble. Typically, this patriarchy also depends upon the unpaid labour of daughters, and fears nothing more than the 'uppishness' of women and the working classes. But the story is a socialist rather than a Marxist fable, and it is cooperation between the classes, embodied by Maggie and Will, that enables the new generation to outstrip the old.

However, before such a triumph is possible, Maggie Hobson must first make her man, and in the figure of the timid, illiterate Willie Mossop, she faces a not inconsiderable challenge [Fig. 7.2]. For his performance as the boothand, Mills draws on familiar techniques from his comic ideolect, but the impact of these is greatly heightened by the character's make-up. When Mossop first emerges he looks like a child's drawing of Mills's familiar face. A gruesome pudding-basin haircut surrounds eyes so wide as to be almost circular, topped off by eyebrows painted on as stubby black lines. As the film progresses these eyebrows come to acquire a life of their own, moving animatedly and seemingly independently of the actor's other features. Mossop's costumes alternate between his bootmaker's apron and a series of formal suits, the first of which recalls the strait-jacket of Alfred Polly's wedding day. In the case of Willie Mossop, the too-tight Sunday suit and the too-large hat mark him out as an incongruous suitor for Maggie, who has demanded that he 'walk out' with her in Salford's Peel Park. The tightness of his clothes immediately connotes Mossop's discomfort, and his restricted limbs move like those of an automaton. In a later scene, however, when Willie and Maggie are obliged to make a hasty departure from the house of the woman to whom he had been 'token', the outfit,

Fig. 7.2 A business proposition: Mills and Brenda de Banzie in *Hobson's Choice* (1954). Canal+ Image UK Ltd

combined with his high-kneed comic run, gives him the exaggerated backside and scrawny legs of a chicken.

In its construction of Mossop and Maggie, the film undoubtedly plays with the traditional stereotypes of the henpecked husband and the shrewish wife, but it does so in a manner that undermines rather than reinforces the dichotomy, not least because both characters end up happy with the role reversal. It is also the case that, like Shaw's Pygmalion, the pupil learns more than the master intended. Mossop undergoes a marked transition after the success of his wedding night, with the result that Maggie becomes both mother and lover to the hero. Unlike Alfred Polly, then, Willie Mossop becomes a man within the boundaries of patriarchal society, a conclusion that aligns the film with the reassuring conventions of Oedipal comedy. Yet although the film conforms in outline, its performances subtly work to undermine the man-making process. Having been so conspicuously made by a woman, Mossop's performance of adult masculinity undoubtedly retains the distance of mimicry. Much of the comedy of *Hobson's Choice* emerges from the spectacle of seeing Laughton's patriarchal masculinity parodied by the performance of the timid Willie. In the final scenes of the film,

Mills replicates Laughton's characteristic gestures and stances, hooking his fingers in his watch pocket, rocking on his toes and adopting the sharp tones of command and authority. Yet although Hobson and Maggie's sisters are fooled, the spectator – who has seen Willie psyching himself up for the confrontation – remains in no doubt of the inauthenticity of the performance.

If clothes have traditionally made the man, then Willie undoubtedly benefits from improved tailoring in the second half of the film. Yet the man-making process of the sexual act demands that he shed his protective clothing, and the wedding night sequence is crucial to the construction of Mossop as a comic hero. In an extended piece of mime, a mock-epic parody is created as Mills undergoes the dis-arming of the warrior hero. The wedding suit becomes a suit of armour, protecting the anxious groom against the terror induced by middle-class female sexuality. The removal of the suit also exposes Willie's tenuous hold on his new status as an entrepreneur: the ceremonial removal of cuffs and shirt-front reveal a sleeveless vest replete with darning. The cuffs and false front, which are altogether stiffer than the hero's resolve, are placed on the mantel-piece to form a heraldic shield. The clothing provides a set of objects through which to express his anxious procrastination, and throughout this process Mills concentrates determinedly upon his materials, his face a mask of bemusement that is somewhat reminiscent of Stan Laurel. This blank face is ruptured to considerable effect when the cry of 'Willie, I'm ready' cuts through the room. The camera angle changes to frame Mills against the open bedroom door, the counterpointed musical themes give way to a drum roll, and the epic hero squares himself for battle. With a last glance at his shirt-front alter-ego, he arms himself with his ritually folded trousers and marches defiantly forward to his fate.

As this sequence suggests, the construction of Mossop as a hero is integral to the success of *Hobson's Choice*, and the film alternately draws upon and undercuts Mills's more familiar Everyman persona. Mossop is afraid of Maggie, but within both the conventions of cinema comedy and the homosocial narratives of British film drama, that is only logical: she represents the incomprehensible force of femininity. However, he is not afraid of any man, and his customary class deference towards Hobson evaporates when 'the Master' threatens to beat him:

> 'You're making a great mistake, Mr Hobson . . . I was none wanting thy Maggie. It was her that was after me. But I tell you this, Mr Hobson, if you touch me with that belt, I'll take her quick, aye, and stick to her like glue.'

This is Willie's longest speech in the film to date, and it represents a heroic act of self-assertion.[9] Hobson's bullying violence pushes Mossop into an acceptance of Maggie's plans, and Mills, breathless with effort, draws himself up to his full height before striding to the door with Maggie. But the hero is not allowed to triumph for long, and a bathetic pratfall awaits him in the street outside. Nonetheless, as the film progresses, Mossop is revealed as a quick learner. Circumstances rather than nature had made him a fool, and the traits which initially connoted stupidity are reinscribed as sense. Mills makes considerable use of stillness in the performance of Mossop. This is not the frozen movements that characterised the slapstick of Mr Polly, but rather a carefully characterised absence of extraneous movement that differentiates Mossop from the superficially dynamic men and women around him. This stillness connotes the distinction between surface and depth, but it also mobilises a variety of comic effects, making Mossop variously the paralysed animal, caught in the glare of more dazzling characters; a motionless puppet awaiting Maggie's hand on the strings; and the holy, unworldly innocent. With these paradoxical possibilities in play, the film is able to exploit the contrast between the 'natural' and the 'artificial' fool to comic effect. Recalling Kaiser's observation that, 'because the fool is not expected to *know* anything, he readily became an expression of all the mischievous and rebellious desires in man which society attempts to control' (1984: 88), the film allows Willie to use his faux-naïve voice to articulate the unspeakable, and when Hobson faces disgrace, he rubs salt into the wounds: 'Eh, bah, gum, think of that. Why it's very near worthwhile to be ruined for pleasure of reading about self in printed paper.'[10]

Willie, then, embodies many of the traits traditionally associated with heroic masculinities. He is inarticulate, dutiful, loyal and brave, and he displays a fear of women wholly appropriate to the homosociality of traditional English masculinities. But, ultimately, the modern masculinity of the film belongs not to Willie, but to Maggie. He is her disguise and her projection, functioning as a form of drag that permits her to enact a masculinity she cannot physically embody, and which society will not allow her to perform.

Willie Mossop can thus be seen as both reinvention and repetition. He revitalised Mills's career, but he did so by combining familiar heroic traits with the actor's evolving comic ideolect. In this, he represented an altogether safer figure than the disturbing Alfred Polly, and revealed the extent to which Mills's screen persona had itself become a signifier of reassurance. The security the actor had come to represent is made abundantly clear in the improbable success of the musical *It's Great To Be Young* (Cyril Frankel 1956). This story of a school rebellion and subsequent siege is an example of a potentially subversive narrative made safe, in part, through the casting of Mills. A new headmaster, Mr Frome (Cecil Parker) arrives at Angel Hill School to find the children obsessed with music and devoted to their teacher and band-leader, Mr Dingle (John Mills). To improve academic standards, music is banned, but Dingle and the pupils conspire through various means to keep the orchestra alive. The cumulative weight of Mills's screen performances undoubtedly makes him the last man in the world to lead a teenage revolution, yet that is what his eventual dismissal sets in motion. With the willing suspension of disbelief, the film succeeds because Mills once again draws upon the childlike qualities of his comic ideolect. His Mr Dingle runs in the corridors, slams doors when frustrated and rushes to be first at the tea-table. His unworldliness traverses the binary of teen/adult conflict, and this alternative state is facilitated through his love of music. Music is a force that absolutely disrupts his sense of propriety, acting as a semiotic force that makes him forget the rules he theoretically represents [Fig. 7.3]. Dingle is not specifically constructed as a subversive figure, but his innocent love of music has a subversive outcome. When he is forced to resign for breaking the rules, the children respond with an impressively well-organised campaign of civil disobedience, which escalates into a lock-in at the gymnasium.

Structurally, *It's Great To Be Young* reaches an impasse at this point. The film has worked hard to emphasise that the headmaster is a fair man with right on his side, but the children have all the audience sympathy in their campaign to save the values embodied in Dingle and his ecumenical love of both jazz and

Fig. 7.3 Subverting authority: Impaling Cecil Parker in *It's Great To Be Young* (1956). Canal+ Image UK Ltd

classical music. Ultimately, it is a very British cascade of self-sacrifice that enables the narrative crisis to be resolved. Acknowledging failure, Frome proposes his own resignation, prompting Mills's Dingle to resurrect the wartime Everyman. He rejects his pupils' adoration and asks them: 'Since when has the part been greater than the whole?', at which Frome is so impressed that he gives Dingle his job back, and everyone gets three cheers from the joyous mass of the pupils. The restored community surges out of the gym holding both Dingle and Frome aloft, and the film has just about managed to have its cake and eat it too. *It's Great To Be Young* is a subversive story performed in an utterly safe and reassuring manner, and its crises are resolved through the nostalgic display of archetypally English virtues. In comedy as well as in drama, Mills's screen persona could be relied upon to suggest that boyish enthusiasm could restore even the most dysfunctional of communities.

The 1950s can thus be seen as a period of flux for Mills's screen persona. His Everyman identity lost ground to a resurgent individualist ethos, and the Britishness he had so ably represented began to be seen as residual. Yet the decade also presented the actor with new possibilities, enabling him to rework familiar performance tropes in the guise of the fool. Although confined to the margins, this figure had a cultural appeal that drew on similar needs and values as that of the heroic Everyman. In the words of Enid Welsford: 'Every man . . . is prepared to identify himself with the fool, as he turns the tables on his chastisers, defeats the powerful, outwits the wise, and assumes the most effective of all rôles, the rôle of David against Goliath' (1968: 315). Yet not all cinema fools are equipped with this facility for survival and self-assertion, and in the 1960s Mills was offered a number of roles that enabled him to develop the fool in more complex and ambiguous ways. As the previous chapter indicated, both Barney in *Summer of the Seventeenth Doll* and Ezra Fitton in *The Family Way* can be seen as 'tragic' fools: figures who do not fully understand their own desires or the desires of those around them. The films in which they appear have comic elements, but are not straightforwardly categorisable as comedies, and in their different ways the two characters move from self-appointed positions as court jesters, to states of loneliness and grief. Barney and Ezra are late developers, finally being forced from second childhood into the adult world of loss, and in this sense their comic trajectories can be read as educational and Oedipal. In terms of the masculinity they represent, however, the trajectory is a repressive one, which sees two transgressive figures painfully recuperated by the heterosexual matrix. Barney and Ezra can neither subvert nor reassure, but while these characters suggest the limits of the fool as a disruptive figure, in 1970 Mills appeared in a role that reinstated the fool as an anti-social and potentially destabilising force. In David Lean's *Ryan's Daughter* Mills's performance as Michael refuses all the reassuring qualities traditionally associated with the actor. The

familiar body that once worked to make the subversive secure is here transformed into the uncanny, opening up a space of ambiguity and uncertainty
within the film text.[11] 'The uncanny,' writes Freud, 'is that class of the frightening which leads back to what is known and long familiar' (1955: 220), and it
depends upon a disturbing sense of repetition. It also draws upon the repressed
and the unspeakable and, quoting Schelling, Freud suggests that ' *"Unheimlich" is
the name for everything that ought to have remained . . . secret and hidden but has come
to light*' (p. 224). Nowhere is this uncanny sense of the familiar made frightening more powerfully manifest than in *Ryan's Daughter*, in which the comfortably
known features of Mills are distorted almost beyond recognition. Michael, the
village idiot, says nothing but appears everywhere, and Mills imbues the character as much with guile as with innocence. This is a fool with the power to bring
secrets to light and, removed from the 'self' of his customary screen persona,
Mills gives a performance that is unsettling, disturbing and far from comic.

'A Perfect Fool'?: *Ryan's Daughter*

'Oh, Michael, you're a perfect fool. You ask for trouble.'

He [Robert Mitchum] is much comforted by Trevor Howard who plays
the local priest and much puzzled by John Mills as the village idiot, who
keeps popping up all over the shop like some sort of Everymute. (Derek
Malcolm, *Guardian*, 10 December 1970)

It is an unmistakable irony that, after thirty-eight years on the screen, Mills
should receive an Oscar for his least characteristic or recognisable performance.
Yet win he did, picking up the award for Best Supporting Actor, one of only
two Oscars collected by Lean's epic and expensive melodrama.[12] Publicity for
the film made much of Mills's 'heroic' piece of acting, suggesting that as the
'mute, misshapen village freak [he has] only his eyes left to act with'. In fact
Mills's increasingly mobile features and pronounced crow's feet left him a few
more parts with which to play, but nonetheless, the performance demanded that
his familiar naturalistic acting style be replaced by the broader brush of mime.
Critically, his performance was better received than the film itself.[13] Margaret
Hinxman called Michael 'a genuinely fresh and touching performance' (*Sunday
Telegraph*, 13 December 1970) while Dilys Powell suggested that Mills did
'absolutely the best that can be done with no words and a make-up suggesting
that someone has run the garden roller over the Hunchback of Notre Dame'
(*Sunday Times*, 13 December 1970). Yet there was also criticism, not least of the
crude symbolism that the repulsive 'other' of Michael seemed intended to represent (*Time*, 16 November 1970), and this complaint prompts questions regarding both the role of the character and the impact of Mills's 'uncanny' casting.

Ryan's Daughter is set in 1916, in the Ireland of the Troubles, and the film tells the story of Rosy Ryan (Sarah Miles) an excessively romantic young woman who marries her former teacher, the middle-aged Charles Shaughnessy (Robert Mitchum). Swiftly and inevitably disappointed in the marriage, she is warned by the village priest, Father Collins (Trevor Howard), not to nurse her wishes, or 'sure to God you'll get what you're wishing for'. Which is exactly what happens when she is swept off her feet by an encounter with the shell-shocked British officer, Major Randolph Doryan (Christopher Jones). As they commence a somewhat luridly imagined affair, replete with trumpeting lilies, bluebell woods and an excess of pathetic fallacy, IRA commandant Tim O'Leary (Barry Foster) prepares to receive a shipment of German guns. An awe-inspiring storm, however, prevents the straightforward landing of the arms, and the entire village arrives at the beach to take part in a dramatic rescue of the weapons. O'Leary and his men leave the beach as heroes, only to be stopped in their tracks by Doryan, who had been alerted by an informer, the publican Thomas Ryan. The village, already aware of Rosy's affair, attributes the treachery to her rather than her father, and an angry mob descend upon the school house to cut off her hair. Doryan meanwhile blows himself up on the beach. Neither Rosy nor Shaughnessy can remain in the village, and they depart for Dublin at least temporarily together. By this, or any other account Mills's character, Michael, is extraneous to the plot. Yet the character was present in the earliest conceptions of the film, which at one point was entitled *Michael's Day* (Brownlow 1997: 555). Michael, then, would appear to be either symbol or commentator, and the critic Tom Milne has little sympathy with the first of these functions:

> What is really unforgivable, however, is the crashing obviousness with which the details in this story are symbolically underlined. To take only one example, there is a village idiot (played as to the manner born by John Mills) who is madly in love with Rosy but whom she shrinks from kissing even during her wedding celebrations because he is so ugly. He drags his leg, so does the English officer, and this already glaring parallel is burdened with yet another twist when the idiot conceives a doglike devotion to the war hero and begins to follow him around in mimicry. Then, just to bleed the last drop of blood out of the stone, Rosy begins to get another slant on ugliness when her hair is cut off and she plants a remorseful kiss on the idiot's cheek. (*Observer*, 13 December 1970)

While Milne reads Michael as a device to make Rosy's learning curve more explicit, Aubrey Dillon-Malone argues that the character is a 'grotesque but gentle commentator on the action' (1996: 53). There are problems with both interpretations. In the first place it is difficult to square Michael's devotion to both Rosy and Doryan with his actions, which intentionally or accidentally result in the public shaming of one and the death of the other. If he is a symbolic double of Doryan, then he is a destructive and violent alter ego rather than a 'doglike' devotee. And if he is one of cinema's few mute narrators, his commentary most certainly cannot be described as gentle. Michael, as Derek Malcolm observes, pops up everywhere, and it seems more appropriate to describe his presence as a harsh, disruptive, asocial parody of the film's much-vaunted love story.

Michael's commentary, then, is far from innocent, and his behaviour begs questions regarding the distinction between what he knows, what he under-stands, and what he does. We first see the figure clowning with Rosy's umbrella which he has rescued from the sea. Maurice Jarre's excessively perky score adds to the initial perception of the character as a circus clown whose gurning face seems to seek nothing more than the approval of the pretty lady. Yet the events that follow Rosy's somewhat forced 'Thank you' indicate the extent to which Michael is constructed as a sentient being, capable not only of desire but of agency. Seeking something else to give to Rosy, Michael swiftly returns with a live lobster:

> Father Collins: (Lightly) 'Give him a smile and you'll maybe get one of the claws for your supper.'
> *Rosy gives Michael an exasperated and very false half smile, at which he looks delighted, and promptly wrenches a claw off the lobster.*
> Father Collins: (Angrily) 'Michael! I've told you Michael, they're created creatures!'
> *Michael looks at the claw with evident disbelief and offers it to Rosy nonetheless.*
> Rosy: 'Be off. It'll make me sick.'
> *Michael limps off into the distance.*
> Father Collins: 'Poor Mike's no answer to a young maid's dreams, but do you not think he just possibly knows that?'

The exchange encodes both Michael's desire and his at least basic grasp of cause and effect. Father Collins's joke about the claw is taken literally and Michael has no compunction about maiming the lobster for the benefit of Rosy. The question of how much Michael understands is similarly mobilised by the later arrival of the illegal arms. He may not understand what the weapons can do, but he immediately grasps their value; with the result that while the British officers conduct a fruitless search of the beach, Michael floats out at sea in a boat laden with dynamite, guns and grenades. If he understands this much, how are we to read the impersonation of Rosy's lover that is probably Michael's most significant 'commentary' in the film?

Michael is, predictably, the first to know about the affair between Rosy and
Doryan, and after finding a button from the major's uniform, he decides to
reinvent himself as a suitable suitor for the object of his desire. In a sequence
filmed through the reflection of a battered mirror, Michael dresses himself in
a black jacket and white collar, makes himself a medal and attempts to hold his
body to attention. Hoisting up his shoulders he salutes and grimaces before
adding the final touch of a handful of confetti. Having thus become both
groom and lover, he limps determinedly up the street saluting the men playing
hockey there. Mills's performance here and elsewhere in the film is a fascinating combination of athleticism and abnormality, and the ill-fitting suit once
again works to give his body a curious set of inappropriate angles. The crowd
immediately read his performance as a parody of the major, and as such he
almost wins their approval – but they, and Father Collins, underestimate what
is involved in the pantomime. In an unexpectedly shocking turn of events,
Michael refuses to let Father Collins deprive him of his medal, and picks up
an iron bar to ward off the priest [Fig. 7.4]. Mills's eyes in this sequence move
between a curious knowingness and a bleary innocence, as if to suggest there
are two Michaels: the one good-natured and innocent, the other driven by
violent desires. As the priest confronts him, his face gradually collapses. Mills's
eyes droop, his facial muscles slacken and he drools discreetly, giving the
impression that the character had had a 'turn', but is now emerging from the
'madness' that had seized him [Fig 7.5]. The respite is short-lived, however, for
the arrival of Rosy reanimates Michael, and he stands before her, sprinkling
confetti over his head and raising a painful, lop-sided salute. Michael has
attempted to cover all his bases, and his costume evokes Shaughnessy's wedding
attire as much as it does the major's uniform, but the outcome of the performance is clear. Michael has exposed Rosy's secret and set in motion the train
of events that will end in her humiliation and her lover's death.

Yet such a performance also renders the actions of the principals ridiculous
and in this Michael really does enact the disturbing, disruptive role of the renaissance fool.[14] The only difference is that he must do this without speech – and
having no words, his body and his body language are of the utmost significance.
It matters, therefore, that Lean is unflinching in his depiction of Michael's
grotesque form, and it is significant that Michael doesn't just 'pop up' everywhere, he actively initiates and influences events. To return to Kristeva's
concept of 'underlying causality', he encodes not simply the return of the
repressed, but also its inescapable productive force:

> 'Underlying causality' . . . is also used to designate that 'other scene': the
> unconscious, drive-related and trans verbal scene whose eruptions deter-
> mine not only my speech or my inter-personal relationships, but even the

Fig. 7.4 Michael as lover: *Ryan's Daughter* (1970). MGM/The Kobal Collection

complex relations of production and reproduction which we so frequently
see only as dependent on, rather than shaping, the economy. (Kristeva
1986: 153)

Michael does not simply respond to or even parody the narrative, nor is his
function confined to the representation of uncanny and abject doubles; rather
he actively determines the narrative and shapes the 'economy' of the film.

The relationship between Michael and Doryan illustrates the extent of this
shaping power. It is Michael's foot repeatedly kicking the bench in the pub that
prompts Doryan's attack of shell-shock, although as the major's body begins to
lurch uncontrollably, it is Michael who is horrified by this vision of the beautiful body made grotesque. Nonetheless, it is Michael's exposing presence that

Fig. 7.5 Michael as fool: *Ryan's Daughter* (1970). MGM/The Kobal Collection

prompts Doryan's self-revelation, and which leads Rosy to his side. In the film's denouement, Michael again is linked to Doryan, giving him death in exchange for the kindness the major has shown him. The two characters meet on the beach. Doryan greets Michael gently, offering him first a cigarette and then his silver cigarette case. Michael is suitably amazed, turning the valuable object over in his hands. When he looks up, Doryan is limping off across the dunes. The major looks back at Michael, and thus encouraged, Mills follows him, giving Lean an intensely stylised shot of two stiff-legged men lurching elegantly across the sand as the sun sinks in the sky behind them. The stylised approach to the encounter continues when Michael overtakes Doryan and invites him to see his toys. In an extended mime, described in one of the film's worst reviews as 'pseudo-Fellini' (John Coleman, *New Statesman*, 11 December 1970), Mills displays his treasure to the major, who is suitably impressed. As with the opening sequence when Michael offers the claw to Rosy, it is made clear here that the character understands systems of exchange. In return for the cigarette case, he hands Doryan a grenade. The scene is in many ways absurd. In a performance for an audience of one, the idiot becomes a clown/magician, pulling explosive rabbits from the hat of his cache. Each time he opens a new box, Mills repeats a suspense-building pause over the catch, looking up to ensure he has Doryan's complete attention. An incongruous captive crab is treated to a stylised shrug, and uninteresting items are tossed over his shoulder as he reaches for the real prize. With a series of looks that say, 'Wait until you see what I've got here' and 'You'll love this one', he produces first dynamite and then detonators. Finally Doryan voices concern, which simply prompts the gleeful child Michael to refuse to hand over the goods. The encounter concludes with Doryan exploding a detonator in an attempt to illustrate how dangerous they are. As before, when Doryan's body 'exploded', the violence panics Michael, and Mills scrabbles energetically away across the dunes. Doryan is left holding the means of his own death, exclaiming in exasperation, 'For Christ's sake man, I'm not going to hurt you.'

Robert Bolt, author of the screenplay, claimed that 'there ought to be something about Randolph which makes us admire him but also makes us secretly relieved that Rosy and he are parted. He ought to have some quite forbidding darkness in him' (Brownlow 1997: 560). Yet Jones is given very little to work with in the construction of this darkness – nothing more in fact than a couple of swift flashbacks to the trenches – with the consequence that the character is almost as mute and inarticulate as Michael. With only the gift of the cigarette case to give any hint of Doryan's suicidal mindset, it seems as if Michael is meant externally to convey the deathly decision-making process of his 'double'. Yet, given the already expressed violence of his feelings for Rosy, the Michael of this sequence appears closer to a Mephistopheles than to a Fellini-esque clown. Either way Michael's otherness simply cannot carry enough explanation to resolve the mystery of why Doryan blows himself up, not least because this 'fool' has complexities beyond his function as a symbolic double. Although an obvious parallel has been constructed between the external beauty/internal torment of Christopher Jones and the abject body of John Mills, we have no evidence to suggest that the character of Michael actually is beautiful within. Rather Mills's performance once again suggests the chaotic, the anarchic and the pre-Oedipal, and his capering movements encode the selfish impulses, desires and drives of childhood. Michael's mute power and his endless returns suggest the possibility of reading him as the underlying causality of the community, the destructive pre-Oedipal child and, indeed, the embodiment of the uncanny force of the death drive, and these possibilities make him not just unfamiliar, but deeply sinister.

Michael, then, can be seen to represent the disruptive, grotesque body of the Irish mass, even while that body variously torments and punishes him. The idiot symbolises an unpredictable dissonant force that renders ridiculous the forces of order, culture and spiritual authority embodied in Doryan, Shaughnessy and Father Collins. But this is a performance with both intra- and extra-diegetic resonances. Just as the role of Michael distorts Mills's features and his familiar screen persona, so the knowledge that it is Mills incarcerated within this grotesque body destabilises our reception of the character. In spite of its atypicality, the performance of Michael nonetheless bears the imprint of Mills. Even here, in the supposedly self-dissolving space of 'character' acting, the cumulative cultural product of the actor cannot be wholly obliterated, and a residual flag of national identity remains. Everyman becomes 'Everymute', the distorted other of the nation, and a symbol of marginality. Paradoxically, this transition enabled a British actor to conquer America and win an Oscar, but – in national terms – this triumph can at best be seen as a consolation prize: an award for conspicuous acting that in no way challenges the cultural hegemony of American films and stardom. Yet the success of Mills's performance acts as a pertinent reminder that Michael is a site of multiple significations, a representation in which the demands of character are complicated by the corporeal narratives of nation, masculinity and age. Reading the film through Mills's dominant screen persona illustrates this complexity. Michael's pivotal impersonation of Doryan, the English soldier, enacts both a private and a public exposure. The major's love affair is revealed, but so is the fallibility of colonial power, and in this perverse 'performance' of a role once integral to his stardom, Mills provides the concept of national decline with perhaps its harshest embodiment. Mills-as-Michael becomes not simply a parodic lover, but equally and also the portrait in the attic of English masculinity.

Historically, the role of the fool is transgressive and non-conforming. Fools articulate the unspeakable – or enact the unrepresentable – and the films in this final chapter indicate some of the ways in which Mills embodied the 'others' of the national psyche. His fools are very much products of the postwar era, and their relative success or failure can be read as significant indicators of the national mood. But although these characters emerge in the second half of the period considered by this book, they should not simply be seen as the products of age or a declining career. Rather, Mills's capacity to embody a variety of innocent, idiotic, misguided and anarchic individuals forms an uncomfortable counter-current that shadows and at times disrupts his heroic screen persona. This counter-current, or trace of the other, that permeates Mills's performances returns us to the vulnerability that is crucial to the Everyman persona, and to the pressures of performing the ordinary masculinities of everyday life. The past twenty years have seen considerable progress in answering Steve Neale's demand that 'men and the male image' be problematised and investigated (1983: 15), but it remains the case that the male bodies most commonly subject to scrutiny are the spectacular bodies of Hollywood stardom. If the power of gender imperatives is ever to be challenged, however, it is the day-to-day compulsions of masculine performance that must be rendered visible and understood. Mills represented on screen the full range of unspectacular British masculinities – both dominant and subordinate – and he did so not only by being ordinary, but through the work of generic narrative trajectories that forced him time and again to prove his worth. As I suggested in the introduction, Everyman cannot be Superman, and as such his masculinity is always provisional, always on trial. Michael Kimmel summarises what is at stake: 'Masculinity is a *homosocial* enactment. We test ourselves, perform heroic feats, take enormous risks, all because we want other men to grant us our manhood' (2001: 275). Watching Mills in the cinema vicariously works and reworks exactly this dynamic. In film after film his Everyman persona, his easily identifiable 'heroic' ordinariness is tested, found worthy and rewarded. It is this ability to endure, and to connote the possible rather than the impossible agency of masculinity, that has made Mills exemplary for the purposes of this study.

As far as British cinema is concerned, however, this book ends where it began, with the fraught relationship between Britain and America. The postwar decline in British influence abroad was matched by the steady rise of American cultural hegemony. As Jeffrey Richards observes, from the later 1950s onwards American money made British films, a process that rapidly escalated when the new Britishness of Connery, Finney and Caine made the nation temporarily fashionable. Richards records that by 1966, '75 per cent of British first features were American financed; by 1968, 90 per cent' (1997: 166).[15] Independent filmmaking could not compete, and even those few British directors classed as 'auteurs' were underpinned by American money. The Hollywood product was everywhere, and to work for David Lean was also to work for Sam Spiegel and Columbia Pictures. In filmmaking, then, as in modes of heroism, nationality came to reside in the individual rather than the group. There were British directors and British stars, but very few British films. And yet, although new actors and stars came to be identified as English or British, it is not clear that this new generation of performers shared the same relationship to concepts of national identity as had their predecessors. Indeed, given the radical transitions that film production had undergone, how could they? Since the 1950s, Hollywood had exported films aimed at a youth market which sought to erase rather than reinforce national boundaries, and the evolving concept of the teenager had the effect of diluting the nationally specific qualities of masculinity. Teenagers were increasingly international, their interests and identities formed through reference to American as much as British culture, and even when Britain became fashionable in the 1960s, it was the cosmopolitan potential embodied by the city that appealed. London was 'swinging', not Englishness, and in this context, only older – and, by extension, defunct – masculinities could maintain any claim to a national specificity.

Thus it can be argued that Mills's career documents the rise and fall of a particular mode of heroic national masculinity. As a juvenile lead, then a leading man, and finally a 'character' actor, his performances drew on a readily recognisable set of characteristics understood to be 'national'. But, when age and cultural mores made heroic leading roles a thing of the past, there was no 'new' John Mills to take his place, nor roles for such a figure to occupy. As the changes set in motion by the Second World War finally began to effect an explicit cultural transformation, the type he represented was no longer seen as relevant to the national self-perception. Robert Colls puts the case succinctly:

> Anyone born in England between 1945 and 1955 was brought up with the myths of the Anglo-British imperial state embedded in their lives. The world was the backdrop, much of it British, while in the foreground was Great Britain, a state beyond question, a moral force undoubtedly, the main focus of how lives were lived. Most identities seemed secure . . . Then, from the mid-1950s to the mid-1970s, there was a gradual realization that the British world didn't *have* to be like this and wasn't going to be for very much longer . . . Everything stood ready to be 'restructured', and by the 1990s the British knew that they weren't what they were any more. (2002: 4–5)

In Mills's films of the 1960s it is possible to perceive a shift of polarities similar to that which Richards identifies in the career of Jack Hawkins (1997: 168). Suddenly the English Everyman had become the representative of a deadly and defunct generation. From *Tunes of Glory* (1960), to *Tiara Tahiti* (1963), to *King Rat* (1965), to *Oh! What a Lovely War* (1969) Mills came to occupy the territory of the residual, the redundant, the phoney, the ineffectual, and – in Field Marshal Haig – the actively dangerous. The once-valued qualities he represented were now the stuff of ridicule.

Yet the shift I am describing is predominantly related to nation and generation. It cannot be read as indicative of a major shift in gender norms or expectations. The 1960s marked the end of a particular mode of masculinity, but films such as *The Family Way* suggest that this transformation is superficial, and the central demands of masculine performance remain the same. At base, masculinity remains disturbingly unperturbed by the flaws and crises exposed by repetition. Consequently, although the exact disposition of hegemonic masculinities may change, masculinity itself remains hegemonic, the dominant formation of a still fundamentally patriarchal society. Such a conclusion suggests, then, that the 'death' of the English Everyman cannot be attributed to the collapse of a masculine paradigm, or to fundamental shifts in the construction of masculinity. Rather the 'problem', as Colls's analysis suggests, resides in the erosion of Englishness as it had been known and understood since the mid-Victorian period. By 1970, the concept of a specifically 'English' masculinity is simply no longer viable. The masculinity remains, but what it meant, or might mean to be English had calcified into the limited stereotypes of toffs, cockneys and gents.

Given this conclusion, a final question arises. What do people see when they encounter these films today? The films of John Mills and his contemporaries are cycled and recycled around the television schedules, enjoying a shadowy after-life as daytime viewing and schedule fillers. Who watches these now and what do they see? What impact do they have on an audience of students, home workers, the retired? Such questions could easily be the subject of another book: a study of the nostalgia that draws the nation inexorably back to its 'finest hour'. But, irrespective of who watches, it would be a mistake to believe that these texts have ceased to signify and no longer have the power to challenge, confuse and enlighten their audience. I first encountered these films as a literature student, viewing them initially by accident, and then by design, as I realised the extent to which the British war movie could help me understand the culture of the Second World War. Recognising Mills as a linchpin of these productions, I came to believe that the Ministry of Information must have decreed that the actor could not die on screen, his value to the nation as the plucky survivor beyond measure in propaganda terms. It was, thus, with absolute disbelief that I sat through my first viewing of *Morning Departure*. They had left John Mills on the bottom of the sea, and I was too shocked even to cry.

Beyond the perhaps impossible question of what impact these films might be having on audiences outside the circle of historians and critics, are further questions regarding which films get shown and why. These are questions of economics and copyright, of who owns the archives and what is released to the TV companies. But irrespective of who makes the decisions, the fact remains that only a fraction of the body of British cinema is available for viewing, and in the few films scattered about the afternoon schedules we see the formation of a canon that is as limited and limiting as canons always are. In response to this, the films in this book have been a mixture of the well-known and the obscure. I have sought to examine films that 'everybody' knows and to introduce less familiar productions which can augment our understanding of performance and context. I have also confined myself to a period that can be seen as culturally homogeneous, a space within which it has been possible to draw some provisional conclusions about the relationship between cinema, society and screen persona. Mills, the actor, lived and performed for another thirty years after *Ryan's Daughter*, slowly developing into the cultural icon with whose obituaries this study began. His legacy to cinema, however, is not an Oscar for the performance of a sinister deaf-mute, but rather the preservation on celluloid of a mode of national self-perception that will soon have passed into history. To have a record of this national masculinity is invaluable, as is the recognition of its complexity and longevity. There can be no 'national' masculinity outside representation, and Mills more than any other actor of his generation constructed and performed an Englishness with which the nation could identify. His Englishness is undoubtedly a residual formation – a thing of the past – but, as the response to Mills's death reveals, there is something about this English Everyman that still resonates to this day.

Notes

1. This is in contrast to his early career when he made regular 'roguish' appearances. Examples include the dirt-track racing son in *Britannia of Billingsgate* (1933), the adopted son who leads Will Hay astray in *Those Were the Days* (1934), and Young Bill in *Old Bill and Son* (1940), although in the last of these, the imperative of war demands the character's reformation, and he ends the film a model soldier.
2. See Chapter 5 for a more extensive discussion of the conflict between modernity and tradition that characterised generic forms in the 1950s.
3. The fool has traditionally been a masculine or asexual figure. Women, although habitually characterised as foolish, seldom appear in the guise of the fool.
4. Working with Hay involved acting as a straight man to the comic's bumbling persona, reeling off a script comprised of puns, malapropisms and misunderstandings. *The Black Sheep of Whitehall* also demanded a considerable amount of slapstick and physical comedy, and Mills obliged with an energetic and unsubtle performance.
5. The most prominent dissident voice amongst the general critical approval belonged to C. A. Lejeune whose review 'Not So Pretty Polly' began: 'Mr. John Mills is such a competent actor that it seems a shame they should put him into such dull pictures, or perhaps I should say, allow him to put himself into such dull pictures' (*Observer*, 13 February 1949).
6. Other examples include the pause before assaulting Jim with a broken bottle, and the memorable dead stop which occurs when, during Polly's final flight from Jim, his nightshirt catches on a tombstone.
7. Mary Hayley Bell's play provided a substantial leading role for Mills, whose performance was well-received, but in spite of a successful tour, the London critics gave the play a merciless reception and it closed after two and a half weeks (Mills 2001: 316–22).
8. *The Colditz Story* sets the seriousness of war alongside the institutional comedy of a school story. Although less anarchic than the 'belles' of St Trinians, the prisoners exist in a constant state of disobedience, perpetually seeking to challenge and undermine the authority of the Germans. Significantly, Mills's performance as Major Pat Reid lacks the actor's usual dutifulness, and the character frequently comes across as childish, putting the 'thrill' of escape before the responsibilities of command.
9. Indeed, in terms of Mills's screen persona, the encounter affectionately parodies the trope of plucky Everyman's stand against the great dictators.

10. One of Mills's achievements in the film is to illustrate the entire range of expressive possibilities contained in the phrase 'By gum!'. These include terror, bewilderment, assent, enthusiasm, lust and excitement.

11. Mills's performance as Field Marshal Sir Douglas Haig in Richard Attenborough's *Oh! What a Lovely War* (1969) could also be seen as an uncanny performance in its deployment of Mills's familiar body in a newly frightening manifestation. However, Mills's absolutely straight-faced performance of monumental self-deception forbids any sympathy, making it difficult to fit the role into the traditional categories of the fool.

12. The other Oscar went to Freddie Young for his breathtaking cinematography, the beauty of which was acknowledged even in the teeth of the film's poor reviews: '[*Ryan's Daughter*] represents 14 million dollars worth of bad weather magnificently photographed by Freddie Young' (Alexander Walker, *Evening Standard*, 10 December 1970).

13. The film's reception was harsh, but perhaps not as bad as legend has it. The more highbrow critics of *The Times*, the *Observer*, the *New Statesman* and, famously, the *New Yorker* were unstinting in their abuse, but redeeming features were identified by, amongst others, the *Sunday Telegraph*, the *Daily Telegraph* and the *Daily Mail*. Although Kevin Brownlow indicates that Lean did not wholly give up his filmmaking plans in the hiatus that followed *Ryan's Daughter*, he did not make another film until *A Passage to India* in 1984 (1997: 588–9).

14. The exposure and ridicule of Rosy is much to the satisfaction of the crude village mob who are hysterically delighted by this turn of events. Depicted like extras from an early Frankenstein movie, they are never happier than when lynching an outsider.

15. Richards records that the bubble soon burst: 'By 1969 almost all the Hollywood film companies were heavily in debt, the taste for Britishness had passed . . . The American companies pulled out virtually all at once, leaving the British film industry flat on its back' (1997: 167).

Filmography

This list is based on that provided by Scott Palmer in his *British Film Actors' Credits, 1895–1987* (1988). It excludes voice-overs, and has been cross-referenced against Robert Tanitch, *John Mills* (1993). There are a number of discrepancies, particularly with regard to dates, between this list and that provided by Mills in his autobiography *Up in the Clouds, Gentlemen Please* (2001). It seems likely that Mills has listed his films by the year in which he remembers making them, rather than according to the date of their cinema release.

1932	*The Midshipmaid*
1933	*The Ghost Camera*
	Britannia of Billingsgate
1934	*River Wolves*
	A Political Party
	Those Were the Days
	The Lash
	Blind Justice
	Doctor's Orders
1935	*Royal Cavalcade*
	Forever England (aka. *Brown on Resolution*)
	Charing Cross Road
	Car of Dreams
1936	*First Offence*
	Tudor Rose
1937	*OHMS*
	The Green Cockatoo

1939	*Goodbye Mr Chips*
1940	*All Hands*
	Old Bill and Son
1941	*Cottage to Let*
	The Black Sheep of Whitehall
1942	*The Big Blockade*
	The Young Mr Pitt
	In Which We Serve
1943	*We Dive At Dawn*
1944	*This Happy Breed*
	Victory Wedding
1945	*Waterloo Road*
	The Way to the Stars
	The Sky's the Limit
1946	*Great Expectations*
1947	*So Well Remembered*
	The October Man
1948	*Scott of the Antarctic*
1949	*The History of Mr Polly*
1950	*The Rocking Horse Winner*
	Morning Departure
1951	*Mr Denning Drives North*
1952	*The Gentle Gunman*
1953	*The Long Memory*
1954	*Hobson's Choice*
1955	*The Colditz Story*
	The End of the Affair
	Above Us the Waves
	Escapade
1956	*War and Peace*
	Around the World in 80 Days
	It's Great To Be Young
	The Baby and the Battleship
1957	*Town on Trial*
	Vicious Circle
1958	*Dunkirk*
	Ice Cold in Alex
	I Was Monty's Double
1959	*Tiger Bay*
1960	*Summer of the Seventeenth Doll*
	Tunes of Glory
	The Swiss Family Robinson

1961	*Flame in the Streets*
	The Singer Not the Song
1962	*The Valiant*
	The Interrogator (not listed by Tanitch)
1963	*Tiara Tahiti*
1964	*The Chalk Garden*
	The Hell Walkers (not listed by Mills)
1965	*The Truth about Spring*
	Operation Crossbow
	King Rat
1966	*The Wrong Box*
	The Family Way
1967	*Chuka*
1968	*Showdown*
	Emma Hamilton
1969	*A Black Veil for Lisa*
	Run Wild Run Free
	Oh! What A Lovely War
1970	*Ryan's Daughter*
	Adam's Woman

Bibliography

Aldgate, Anthony and Jeffrey Richards [1986] (1994), *Britain Can Take It: The British Cinema in the Second World War*, Edinburgh: Edinburgh University Press.

Anderson, Benedict (1983), *Imagined Communities*, London: Verso.

Anderson, Linda R. (1988), *Bennett, Wells and Conrad: Narrative in Transition*, London: Macmillan.

Armes, Roy (1978), *A Critical History of British Cinema*, London: Secker and Warburg.

Ashby, Justine and Andrew Higson (2000), *British Cinema, Past and Present*, London: Routledge.

Asquith, Anthony (1945), 'Realler than the Real Thing', *The Cine-Technician*, 53(11), March–April, pp. 25–7.

Babington, Bruce (ed.) (2001), *British Stars and Stardom: From Alma Taylor to Sean Connery*, Manchester: Manchester University Press.

Baker, Roy Ward (1961), 'Discovering where the Truth Lies', *Films and Filming*, May, p. 17, p. 38.

—— (2000), *The Director's Cut: A Memoir of 60 Years in Film and Television*, London: Reynolds and Hearn.

Balcon, Michael (1947), *Twenty Years of British Film*, London.

—— (1969), *Michael Balcon Presents . . . A Lifetime of Films*, London: Hutchinson.

Bamford, Kenton (1999), *Distorted Images: National Identity and Film in the 1920s*, London: I. B. Tauris.

Barker, Sir Ernest [1927] (1948), *National Character*, London: Methuen.

—— (ed.) [1947] (1976), *The Character of England*, Westport: Greenwood Press.

Barr, Charles (ed.) (1986), *All Our Yesterdays: 90 Years of British Cinema*, London: BFI.

Barrell, John (1990), 'Sir Joshua Reynolds and the Englishness of English Art', in Bhabha, pp. 154–76.

Bell, Mary Hayley (1968), *What Shall We Do Tomorrow? An Autobiography*, London: Cassell and Co.

Bhabha, Homi K. (1990), *Nation and Narration*, London: Routledge.

Billig, Michael (1995), *Banal Nationalism*, London: Sage.

Bogarde, Dirk [1978] (1979), *Snakes and Ladders*, London: Triad Granada.

Bourne, Stephen (1996), *Brief Encounters: Lesbians and Gays in British Cinema 1930–1971*, London: Cassell.

Brod, Harry and Michael Kaufman (eds) (1994), *Theorizing Masculinities*, London: Sage.

Brooke, Rupert [1918] (1932), *The Complete Poems*, London: Sidgwick and Jackson.

Brownlow, Kevin [1996] (1997), *David Lean: A Biography*, London: Richard Cohen Books.

Burton, Alan, Tim O'Sullivan and Paul Wells (eds) (2000), *The Family Way: The Boulting Brothers and Postwar British Film Culture*, Trowbridge: Flicks Books.

Butler, Judith (1990), *Gender Trouble: Feminism and the Subversion of Identity*, London: Routledge.

—— (1993), *Bodies That Matter: On the Discursive Limits of 'Sex'*, London: Routledge.

Byers, Thomas B. (1995), 'Terminating the Postmodern: Masculinity and Pomophobia', in *Modern Fiction Studies* 41 (1), pp. 5–33.

Cain, P. J. and A. G. Hopkins (1993), *British Imperialism: Crisis and Deconstruction, 1914–1990*, London: Longman.

Calder, Angus (1991), *The Myth of the Blitz*, London: Jonathan Cape.

Chapman, James (1998), *The British at War: Cinema, State and Propaganda, 1939–1945*, London: I. B. Tauris.

Chibnall, Steve (2000), *J. Lee Thompson*, Manchester: Manchester University Press.

Chibnall, Steve and Robert Murphy (eds) (1999), *British Crime Cinema*, London: Routledge.

Clay, Andrew (1999), 'Men, Women and Money: Masculinity in Crisis in the British Professional Crime Film 1946–1965', in Chibnall and Murphy, pp. 51–65.

Cohan, Steven and Ina Rae Hark (eds) (1993), *Screening the Male: Exploring Masculinities in Hollywood Cinema*, London: Routledge.

Cohan, Steven (1997), *Masked Men: Masculinity and Movies in the Fifties*, Bloomington: Indiana University Press.

Coldstream, John (2004), *Dirk Bogarde*, London: Weidenfeld and Nicolson.

Colley, Linda (1992), *Britons*, London: Yale University Press.

Colls, Robert (2002), *The Identity of England*, Oxford: Oxford University Press.

Commager, Henry Steele (ed.) (1974), *Britain through American Eyes*, New York: McGraw-Hill.

Connell, R. W. (1995), *Masculinities*, St Leonards: Allen and Unwin.

Cook, Pam (1996), *Fashioning the Nation: Costume and Identity in British Cinema*, London: BFI.

—— (ed.) (1997), *Gainsborough Pictures*, London: Cassell.

Cooper, Susan [1963] (1986), 'Snoek Piquante', in Sissons and French, pp. 21–42.

Creekmur, Corey K. and Alexander Doty (eds) (1995), *Out in Culture: Gay, Lesbian and Queer Essays on Popular Culture*, London: Cassell.

Cubitt, Geoffrey (ed.) (1998), *Imagining Nations*, Manchester: Manchester University Press.

Curran, James and Vincent Porter (eds) (1983), *British Cinema History*, London: Weidenfeld and Nicholson.

Dawson, Graham (1994), *Soldier Heroes: British Adventure, Empire and the Imagining of Masculinities*, London: Routledge.

D'Cruze, Shani (1995), 'Women and the Family' in Purvis, pp. 51–83.

De Cordova, Richard (1995), 'Genre and Performance: An Overview', in Grant, pp. 129–39.

Dillon-Malone, Aubrey (1996), *Movies Made in Ireland: Ryan's Daughter*, Dublin: GLI Ltd.

Dixon, Wheeler Winston (ed.) (1994), *Re-viewing British Cinema, 1900–1992*, Albany: State University of New York Press.

Doty, Alexander (1993), *Making Things Perfectly Queer*, Minneapolis: University of Minnesota Press.

—— (1995), 'There's Something Queer Here', in Creekmur and Doty, pp. 71–90.

Durgnat, Raymond (1970), *A Mirror for England: British Movies from Austerity to Affluence*, London: Faber and Faber.

Dyer, Richard [1979] (1998), *Stars*, London: BFI.

—— (1987), *Heavenly Bodies: Film Stars and Society*, London: BFI/Macmillan.

—— (1993), *The Matter of Images: Essays on Representations*, London: Routledge.

—— (1997), *White*, London: Routledge.

—— (2002), *The Culture of Queers*, London: Routledge.

Easthope, Anthony [1990] (1992), *What a Man's Gotta Do: The Masculine Myth in Popular Culture*, London: Routledge.

—— (1999), *Englishness and National Culture*, London: Routledge.

Edley, Nigel and Margaret Wetherell (eds) (1995), *Men in Perspective: Practice, Power and Identity*, London: Prentice Hall.

Ellis, John [1982] (1992), *Visible Fictions*, London: Routledge and Kegan Paul.

—— (1996), 'The Quality Film Adventure: British Critics and the Cinema 1942–1948', in Higson, pp. 66–93.

Evans, E. R. G. R. (1924), *South with Scott*, London: Collins.

Evans, Peter William (2001), 'James Mason: The Man Between', in Babington, pp. 108–19.

Findlater, Richard (1956), *Michael Redgrave: Actor*, London: Heinemann.

Fischer, Lucy and Marcia Landy (2004), *Stars: The Film Reader*, London: Routledge.

Forbes, Bryan (1974), *Notes for a Life*, London: Collins.

Forster, Peter [1963] (1986), 'J. Arthur Rank and the Shrinking Screen', in Sissons and French, pp. 265–82.

Freud, Sigmund [1905] (1960), *Jokes and their Relation to the Unconscious*, in James Strachey (ed.), *The Standard Edition of the Complete Psychological Works of Sigmund Freud*, vol. VIII, London: Hogarth.

Freud, Sigmund [1919] (1955), 'The "Uncanny"', in *The Standard Edition*, vol. XVII, London: Hogarth, pp. 217–56.

Frosh, Stephen (1994), *Sexual Difference: Masculinity and Psychoanalysis*, London: Routledge.

Gardiner, Judith Kegan (ed.) (2002), *Masculinity Studies and Feminist Theory: New Directions*, New York: Columbia University Press.

Gardner, Brian (ed.) [1966] (1999), *The Terrible Rain: The War Poets, 1939–1945*, London: Methuen.

Geraghty, Christine (2000), *British Cinema in the Fifties: Gender, Genre and the 'New Look'*, London: Routledge.

Giles, Judy and Tim Middleton (1995), *Writing Englishness: 1900–1950*, London: Routledge.

Glancy, H. Mark (1999), *When Hollywood Loved Britain: The Hollywood 'British' Film 1939–45*, Manchester: Manchester University Press.

Gledhill, Christine (ed.) (1991), *Stardom: Industry of Desire*, London: Routledge.

Gorer, Geoffrey (1955), *Exploring English Character*, London: The Cresset Press.

Granger, Stewart (1981), *Sparks Fly Upward*, London: Granada.

Grant, Barry Keith (ed.), *Film Genre Reader II*, Austin: University of Texas Press.

Guinness, Alec [1996] (1997), *My Name Escapes Me: The Diary of a Retiring Actor*, Harmondsworth: Penguin.

Harper, Sue (1994), *Picturing the Past: The Rise and Fall of the British Costume Film*, London: BFI.

Harper, Sue and Vincent Porter (2003), *British Cinema of the 1950s: The Decline of Deference*, Oxford: Oxford University Press.

Hennessy, Peter [1992] (1993), *Never Again: Britain 1945–1951*, London: Vintage.

Higson, Andrew [1995] (1997), *Waving the Flag: Constructing a National Cinema in Britain*, Oxford: The Clarendon Press.

—— (ed.) (1996), *Dissolving Views: Key Writings on British Cinema*, London: Cassell.

Hill, John (1986), *Sex, Class and Realism: British Cinema 1956–1963*, London: BFI.

Hill, John and Pamela Church Gibson (eds) (1998), *The Oxford Guide to Film Studies*, Oxford: Oxford University Press.

Hjort, Mette and Scott MacKenzie (eds) (2000), *Cinema and Nation*, London: Routledge.

Hoare, Philip [1995] (1996), *Noël Coward: A Biography*, London: Mandarin.

Horton, Andrew S. (ed.) (1991), *Comedy/Cinema/Theory*, Berkeley: University of California Press.

Huntford, Roland (1979), *Scott and Amundsen*, London: Hodder and Stoughton.

Hurd, Geoff (ed.) (1984), *National Fictions: World War Two in British Films and Television*, London: BFI.

Irigaray, Luce (1985), *This Sex Which Is Not One*, trans. Catherine Porter, New York: Cornell University Press.

James, David (1948), *Scott of the Antarctic: The Film and its Production*, London: Convoy Publications.

Johnson, Ian (1962), 'Mills', in *Films and Filming*, June, pp. 22–3, 49–51.

Kaiser, Walter [1963] (1984), 'The Wisdom of the Fool', in Palmer, pp. 85–94.

Kennaway, James [1956] (1988), *Tunes of Glory*, Edinburgh: Canongate.

King, Barry (1985), 'Articulating Stardom', in *Screen* 26(5), Sept.–Oct., pp. 27–50.

Kimmel, Michael (2001), 'Masculinity as Homophobia: Fear, Shame, and Silence in the Construction of Gender Identity', in Whitehead and Barrett, pp. 266–85.

Kirkham, Pat and Janet Thumin (eds) (1993), *You Tarzan: Masculinity, Movies and Men*, London: Lawrence and Wishart.

Kristeva, Julia [1974] (1986), 'About Chinese Women', in Moi, pp. 138–59.

Kumar, Krishan (2003), *The Making of English National Identity*, Cambridge: Cambridge University Press.

Landy, Marcia (1991), *British Genres: Cinema and Society, 1930–1960*, Princeton: Princeton University Press.

Leavis, Q. D. [1932] (1978), *Fiction and the Reading Public*, London: Chatto and Windus.

Light, Alison (1991), *Forever England: Femininity, Literature and Conservatism Between the Wars*, London: Routledge.

Lovell, Alan and Peter Krämer (1999), *Screen Acting*, London: Routledge.

Low, Rachel (1997), *The History of British Film, vol. VII, 1929–1939: Film Making in 1930s Britain*, London: Routledge.

McCabe, John [1998] (2002), *Cagney*, London: Aurum Press.

McCann, Graham (1997), *Cary Grant: A Class Apart*, London: Fourth Estate.

McClintock, Anne (1997), 'No Longer in a Future Heaven: Gender, Race and Nationalism' in McClintock, Mufti and Shohat, pp. 89–112.

McClintock, Anne, Aamir Mufti and Ellen Shohat (1997), *Dangerous Liaisons: Gender, Nation and Postcolonial Perspectives*, Minneapolis: University of Minnesota Press.

McFarlane, Brian (1997), *An Autobiography of British Cinema as Told by the Filmmakers and Actors who Made it*, London: Methuen.

Mackay, Robert (1999), *The Test of War: Inside Britain 1939–45*, London: UCL Press.

McKibbin, Ross (1998), *Classes and Cultures: England 1918–1951*, Oxford: Oxford University Press.

Macnab, Geoffrey (1993), *J. Arthur Rank and the British Film Industry*, London: Routledge.

—— (2000), *Searching for Stars: Stardom and Screen Acting in British Cinema*, London: Cassell.

—— (2001), 'Trevor, not Leslie, Howard', in Babington, pp. 132–42.

Manvell, Roger (1974), *Films and the Second World War*, London: J. M. Dent and Sons.

Marwick, Arthur [1982] (2003), *British Society since 1945*, 4th edn, London: Penguin.

Mason, James (1981), *Before I Forget*, London: Hamish Hamilton.

Mayer, J. P. (1946), *Sociology of Film*, London: Faber and Faber.

—— (1948), *British Cinemas and their Audiences*, London: Dennis Dobson.

Mayne, Judith (1993), *Cinema and Spectatorship*, London: Routledge.

Medhurst, Andy (1986), 'Music Hall and British Cinema', in Barr, pp. 168–88.

—— (1993), ' "It's as a man that you've failed": Masculinity and Forbidden Desire in *The Spanish Gardener*', in Kirkham and Thumin, pp. 95–105.

Miles, Peter and Malcolm Smith (1987), *Cinema, Literature and Society: Elite and Mass Culture in Interwar Britain*, London: Croom Helm.

Mills, John [1980] (2001), *Up in the Clouds, Gentlemen Please*, London: Orion.

—— (2000), *Still Memories: An Autobiography in Photography*, London: Hutchinson.

Minney, R. J. (1973), *Puffin Asquith*, London: Leslie Frewin.

Moi, Toril (1986), *The Kristeva Reader*, Oxford: Blackwell.

Monk, Clare and Amy Sargeant (2002), *British Historical Cinema*, London: Routledge.

More, Kenneth (1978), *More or Less*, London: Hodder and Stoughton.

Morgan, David and Mary Evans (1993), *The Battle for Britain: Citizenship and Ideology in the Second World War*, London: Routledge.

Morris, Pam (1994), *The Bakhtin Reader*, London: Edward Arnold.

Murphy, Robert (1989), *Realism and Tinsel: Cinema and Society in Britain, 1939–1948*, London: Routledge.

—— (1992), *Sixties British Cinema*, London: BFI Publishing.

—— (2000), *British Cinema and the Second World War*, London and New York: Continuum.

Napper, Lawrence and Michael Williams (2001), 'The Curious Appeal of Ivor Novello', in Babington, pp. 42–55.

Naremore, James [1988] (1990), *Acting in the Cinema*, Berkeley: University of California Press.

Neale, Steve (1983), 'Masculinity as Spectacle: On Men and Mainstream Cinema', in *Screen*, 24(6), pp. 2–16.

Noble, Peter (1947), 'Profile of John Mills', *Stage and Screen*, Spring.

Orwell, George, [1941] (1970), 'The Lion and the Unicorn: Socialism and the English Genius', in Sonia Orwell and Ian Angus (eds), *The Collected Essays, Journalism and Letters*, vol. 2, London: Penguin, pp. 74–134.

Palmer, D. J. (1984), *Comedy: Developments in Criticism*, London: Macmillan.

Palmer, Jerry (1988), *The Logic of the Absurd: Film and Television Comedy*, London: BFI.

Palmer, Scott (1988), *British Film Actors' Credits, 1895–1987*, Jefferson and London: McFarland and Co.

Paxman, Jeremy [1998] (1999), *The English: Portrait of a People*, London: Penguin.

Pettigrew, Terence (2001), *Trevor Howard, A Personal Biography*, London: Peter Owen.

Powell, Dilys (1947), *Films since 1939*, London: British Council.

—— (1989), *The Golden Screen: Fifty Years of Films*, ed. George Perry, London: Headline.

Powrie, Phil, Ann Davies and Bruce Babington (eds) (2004), *The Trouble with Men: Masculinities in European and Hollywood Cinema*, London: Wallflower Press.

Pratley, Gerald (1974), *The Cinema of David Lean*, London: The Tantivy Press.

Priestley, J. B. [1933] (1997), *English Journey*, London: The Folio Society.

—— (1940), *Postscripts*, London: Heinemann.

Purvis, June (ed.) (1995), *Women's History: Britain, 1850–1945*, London: UCL Press.

Read, Piers Paul (2003), *Alec Guinness*, London: Simon and Schuster.

Richards, Jeffrey (1984), *The Age of the Dream Palace: Cinema and Society in Britain, 1930–1939*, London: Routledge and Kegan Paul.

Richards, Jeffrey (1997), *Films and British National Identity: From Dickens to Dad's Army*, Manchester: Manchester University Press.

—— (ed.) (1998), *The Unknown 1930s: An Alternative History of the British Cinema, 1929–1939*, London: I. B. Tauris.

Russo, Vito [1981] (1987), *The Celluloid Closet: Homosexuality in the Movies*, revd edn, New York: Harper and Row.

Samuel, Raphael (ed.) (1987), *Patriotism: The Making and Unmaking of British National Identity*, London: Routledge.

Scott, R. F. (1913), *Scott's Last Expedition, vol. I: The Journals of Captain R. F. Scott, R. N., C. V. O.*, arranged by Leonard Huxley, London: John Murray.

Sedgwick, Eve Kosofsky (1985), *Between Men: English Literature and Male Homosocial Desire*, New York: Columbia University Press.

—— [1990] (1994), *Epistemology of the Closet*, London: Penguin.

Sedgwick, John (2000), *Popular Filmgoing in 1930s Britain – A Choice of Pleasures*, Exeter: University of Exeter Press.

Segal, Lynne (1990), *Slow Motion: Changing Masculinities, Changing Men*, London: Virago.

Shafer, Stephen C. (1997), *British Popular Films 1929–1939: The Cinema of Reassurance*, London: Routledge.

Shail, Robert (2004), 'Masculinity and Class: Michael Caine as "Working-Class Hero"', in Powrie et al., pp. 66–76.

Sheridan, Dorothy (ed.) [1990] (1991), *Wartime Women: A Mass-Observation Anthology*, London: Mandarin.

Showalter, Elaine (1987), *The Female Malady: Women, Madness and English Culture, 1830–1980*, London: Virago.

Silver, Alain and James Ursini (1974), *David Lean and his Films*, London: Leslie Frewin.

Silverman, Kaja (1992), *Male Subjectivity at the Margins*, London: Routledge.

Silverman, Stephen M. (1989), *David Lean*, London: Andre Deutsch.

Sinfield, Alan (1989), *Literature, Politics and Culture in Postwar Britain*, Oxford: Blackwell.

Sissons, Michael and Philip French (eds) [1963] (1986), *The Age of Austerity*, Oxford: Oxford University Press.

Smith, Anthony D. (1991), *National Identity*, London: Penguin.

Smith, Stevie [1949] (1979), *The Holiday*, London: Virago.

Spicer, Andrew (2000), 'Misfits and the Marginalised: Gender in the Boultings' Feature Films', in Burton et al., pp. 68–80.

—— (2001), *Typical Men: The Representation of Masculinity in Popular British Cinema*, London: I. B. Tauris.

Spufford, Francis (1996), *I May Be Some Time: Ice and the English Imagination*, London: Faber and Faber.

Street, Sarah (1997), *British National Cinema*, London: Routledge.

—— (2000), 'Stepping Westward: The Distribution of British Feature Films in America, and the Case of *The Private Life of Henry VIII*', in Ashby and Higson, pp. 51–62.

Sutton, David (2000), *A Chorus of Raspberries: British Film Comedy 1929–1939*, Exeter: University of Exeter Press.

Tanitch, Robert (1993), *John Mills*, London: Collins and Brown.

Taylor, A. J. P. [1965] (1992), *English History, 1914–1945*, Oxford: Oxford University Press.

Taylor, Philip M. (ed.) (1981), *Britain and the Cinema in the Second World War*, Basingstoke: Macmillan.

Thomson, David (1975) [2003], *The New Biographical Dictionary of Film*, 4th edn, London: Little, Brown.

Thompson, John O. (1978), 'Screen Acting and the Commutation Test', in *Screen* 19(2), pp. 55–69.

Wells, H. G. [1910] (1993), *The History of Mr Polly*, London: J. M. Dent.

Welsford, Enid [1935] (1968), *The Fool: His Social and Literary History*, London: Faber and Faber.

Whatling, Clare (1997), *Screen Dreams: Fantasising Lesbians in Film*, Manchester: Manchester University Press.

Whitehead, Stephen M. and Frank Barrett (2001), *The Masculinities Reader*, Cambridge: Polity Press.

Williams, Marjory (1943), 'We Dive at Dawn', *Picturegoer*, 24 July, 14.

Williams, Tony (2000), *Structures of Desire: British Cinema, 1939–1955*, Albany: State University of New York Press.

Wojcik, Pamela Robertson (ed.) (2004), *Movie Acting, The Film Reader*, London: Routledge.

Young, Lola (1996), *Fear of the Dark: 'Race', Gender and Sexuality in the Cinema*, London: Routledge.

Index